References for the Rest of Us!®

BESTSELLING BOOK SERIES

Do you find that traditional reference books are overloaded with technical details and advice you'll never use? Do you postpone important life decisions because you just don't want to deal with them? Then our *For Dummies*® business and general reference book series is for you.

For Dummies business and general reference books are written for those frustrated and hard-working souls who know they aren't dumb, but find that the myriad of personal and business issues and the accompanying horror stories make them feel helpless. *For Dummies* books use a lighthearted approach, a down-to-earth style, and even cartoons and humorous icons to dispel fears and build confidence. Lighthearted but not lightweight, these books are perfect survival guides to solve your everyday personal and business problems.

> *"More than a publishing phenomenon, 'Dummies' is a sign of the times."*
>
> — *The New York Times*

> *"...you won't go wrong buying them."*
>
> — *Walter Mossberg, Wall Street Journal, on For Dummies books*

> *"A world of detailed and authoritative information is packed into them..."*
>
> — *U.S. News and World Report*

Already, millions of satisfied readers agree. They have made For Dummies the #1 introductory level computer book series and a best-selling business book series. They have written asking for more. So, if you're looking for the best and easiest way to learn about business and other general reference topics, look to For Dummies to give you a helping hand.

Hungry Minds™

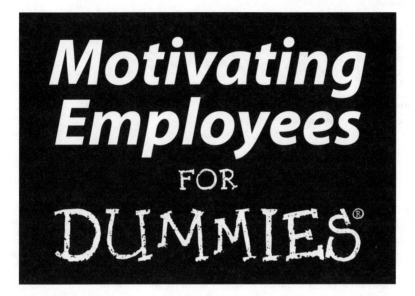

by Max Messmer

Hungry Minds™

HUNGRY MINDS, INC.

New York, NY ◆ Cleveland, OH ◆ Indianapolis, IN

Motivating Employees For Dummies®

Published by:
Hungry Minds, Inc.
909 Third Avenue
New York, NY 10022
www.hungryminds.com
www.dummies.com

Library of Congress Control Number: 2001086403

ISBN: 0-7645-5327-5

Printed in the United States of America

10 9 8 7 6 5 4 3 2 1

1B/QS/QV/QR/IN

Distributed in the United States by Hungry Minds, Inc.

Distributed by CDG Books Canada Inc. for Canada; by Transworld Publishers Limited in the United Kingdom; by IDG Norge Books for Norway; by IDG Sweden Books for Sweden; by IDG Books Australia Publishing Corporation Pty. Ltd. for Australia and New Zealand; by TransQuest Publishers Pte Ltd. for Singapore, Malaysia, Thailand, Indonesia, and Hong Kong; by Gotop Information Inc. for Taiwan; by ICG Muse, Inc. for Japan; by Intersoft for South Africa; by Eyrolles for France; by International Thomson Publishing for Germany, Austria and Switzerland; by Distribuidora Cuspide for Argentina; by LR International for Brazil; by Galileo Libros for Chile; by Ediciones ZETA S.C.R. Ltda. for Peru; by WS Computer Publishing Corporation, Inc., for the Philippines; by Contemporanea de Ediciones for Venezuela; by Express Computer Distributors for the Caribbean and West Indies; by Micronesia Media Distributor, Inc. for Micronesia; by Chips Computadoras S.A. de C.V. for Mexico; by Editorial Norma de Panama S.A. for Panama; by American Bookshops for Finland.

For general information on Hungry Minds' products and services please contact our Customer Care department; within the U.S. at 800-762-2974, outside the U.S. at 317-572-3993 or fax 317-572-4002.

For sales inquiries and resellers information, including discounts, premium and bulk quantity sales and foreign language translations please contact our Customer Care department at 800-434-3422, fax 317-572-4002 or write to Hungry Minds, Inc., Attn: Customer Care department, 10475 Crosspoint Boulevard, Indianapolis, IN 46256.

For information on licensing foreign or domestic rights, please contact our Sub-Rights Customer Care department at 212-884-5000.

For information on using Hungry Minds' products and services in the classroom or for ordering examination copies, please contact our Educational Sales department at 800-434-2086 or fax 317-572-4005.

Please contact our Public Relations department at 212-884-5163 for press review copies or 212-884-5000 for author interviews and other publicity information or fax 212-884-5400.

For authorization to photocopy items for corporate, personal, or educational use, please contact Copyright Clearance Center, 222 Rosewood Drive, Danvers, MA 01923, or fax 978-750-4470.

Library of Congress Cataloging-in-Publication Data

Hungry Minds™ is a trademark of Hungry Minds, Inc.

About the Author

Max Messmer is chairman and chief executive officer of Robert Half International, Inc., the world's largest specialized staffing firm, and a widely recognized expert on employment and management issues.

Messmer's previous titles for Hungry Minds, Inc., include *Managing Your Career For Dummies* (2000), *Human Resources Kit For Dummies* (1999), *Job Hunting For Dummies* (1995) and *Job Hunting For Dummies*, 2nd Edition (1999). He has also authored several other critically acclaimed books, such as *The Fast Forward MBA in Hiring* (John Wiley & Sons, Inc., 1998), *50 Ways to Get Hired* (William Morrow & Co., Inc., 1994) and *Staffing Europe* (Acropolis Books Ltd., 1991). Messmer has written numerous articles and columns on job seeking, employment, and management topics, and his expertise has been featured in major business publications, including *Fortune*, *Forbes*, and *The Wall Street Journal*.

Robert Half International (NYSE symbol: RHI), a Fortune 1000 firm, has appeared for three consecutive years on the *Forbes* "Platinum List" of top business services firms for investor returns and growth. In addition, *Fortune* magazine included the company on its roster of "America's Most Admired Companies," ranking it first among all staffing services firms for the past two consecutive years. And RHI recently became the first staffing firm to be added to Standard & Poor's widely tracked S&P 500 index.

Founded in 1948, the company now has seven divisions: Accountemps, Robert Half and RHI Management Resources, for temporary, full-time, and project professionals, respectively, in the fields of accounting and finance; OfficeTeam, for highly skilled temporary administrative support; RHI Consulting, for information technology professionals; The Affiliates, for temporary, project and full-time staffing of attorneys and specialized support personnel within law firms and corporate legal departments; and The Creative Group, for creative, advertising, marketing, and web design professionals on a project basis. The company serves its clients and job candidates through more than 300 offices in North America, Europe, and Australia, and through online job search services for each division, accessible at www.rhii.com.

Messmer is a member of the board of directors of several major corporations, including Airborne Freight Corporation, Health Care Property Investors, Inc., and Spieker Properties, Inc. Previously, he served on the boards of First Interstate Bancorp, NationsBank (of North Carolina), Pacific Enterprises, and Southern California Gas Company. During the administration of President Ronald Reagan, he served two years on the President's Advisory Committee on Trade. Messmer was valedictorian of his graduating class at Loyola University in New Orleans. He graduated *cum laude* from the New York University School of Law.

Dedication

To all of my colleagues at Robert Half International, who are the foundation for the company's success. And especially for Marcia, Matthew, and Michael, who are the source of my own motivation.

Author's Acknowledgments

This book was made possible by a number of highly motivated people who offered their expertise and insight throughout the process. First of all, thank you to Lynn Taylor, vice president of research, who co-developed this book and has been a noted media source for more than a decade on emerging workplace issues. I would also like to acknowledge several of my RHI colleagues for their invaluable help in this project: Lynn Glaiser, group manager of editorial services; Reesa Staten, director of corporate communications; Laurel Goddard; and Natalie Coleman. Special thanks also go to Kelly Ewing, Marinell Jochnowitz, and Dawn Guthart for their research and assistance.

I also want to acknowledge Mr. Robert Half, our company's founder and my friend, who through his own motivation and pioneering spirit launched one of the most successful and respected companies in the world.

Publisher's Acknowledgments

We're proud of this book; please send us your comments through our Online Registration Form located at www.dummies.com.

Some of the people who helped bring this book to market include the following:

Acquisitions, Editorial, and Media Development

Project Editor: Norm Crampton

Acquisitions Editor: Holly McGuire

Copy Editor: Ben Nussbaum

Acquisitions Coordinator: Jill Alexander

Technical Editor: Gwen Thomas

Editorial Manager: Pam Mourouzis

Media Development Manager: Laura Carpenter

Editorial Assistant: Carol Strickland

Cover Photos: © International Stock / Johnny Stockshooter

Production

Project Coordinator: Maridee Ennis

Layout and Graphics: Amy Adrian, Joe Bucki, Kristin Pickett, Jacque Schneider, Jeremey Unger

Proofreaders: John Bitter, Nancy Price, Marianne Santy, Charles Spencer, Rob Springer, York Production Services, Inc.

Indexer: York Production Services, Inc.

General and Administrative

Hungry Minds, Inc.: John Kilcullen, CEO; Bill Barry, President and COO; John Ball, Executive VP, Operations & Administration; John Harris, CFO

Hungry Minds Consumer Reference Group

Business: Kathleen A. Welton, Vice President and Publisher; Kevin Thornton, Acquisitions Manager

Cooking/Gardening: Jennifer Feldman, Associate Vice President and Publisher

Education/Reference: Diane Graves Steele, Vice President and Publisher; Greg Tubach, Publishing Director

Lifestyles: Kathleen Nebenhaus, Vice President and Publisher; Tracy Boggier, Managing Editor

Pets: Dominique De Vito, Associate Vice President and Publisher; Tracy Boggier, Managing Editor

Travel: Michael Spring, Vice President and Publisher; Suzanne Jannetta, Editorial Director; Brice Gosnell, Managing Editor

Hungry Minds Consumer Editorial Services: Kathleen Nebenhaus, Vice President and Publisher; Kristin A. Cocks, Editorial Director; Cindy Kitchel, Editorial Director

Hungry Minds Consumer Production: Debbie Stailey, Production Director

◆

The publisher would like to give special thanks to Patrick J. McGovern, without whom this book would not have been possible.

◆

Contents at a Glance

Cartoons at a Glance

By Rich Tennant

Cartoon Information:
Fax: 978-546-7747
E-Mail: richtennant@the5thwave.com
World Wide Web: www.the5thwave.com

Table of Contents

Introduction

• •

*E*mployee motivation goes hand in hand with productivity and success. If you want your company to succeed, you need to make sure that your employees are satisfied, sufficiently challenged, and contributing to the bottom line. Offering your staff competitive compensation isn't enough; it's a start, but there's more to motivation than monetary rewards.

Chances are, you already know how crucial motivation is to your company's performance. You already take some steps to motivate your employees, but you feel like you need to know and do more. Well, you've come to the right place. In this book, you find all the nitty-gritty details about how to motivate your employees. And trust me, there's a lot that you can do!

About This Book

This book tells you everything you need to know and more about motivating your employees. You not only find out about the many tools at your disposal — and you have a lot — but you also discover management techniques and practices to put those tools to good use.

And while this book has a lot of great information, don't think that you have to read it from cover to cover. Like all *For Dummies* books, *Motivating Employees For Dummies* is a reference book, which means that you can start anywhere in the book and understand what you're reading. You don't have to read Chapter 1 to understand Chapter 5, and you don't even have to read an entire chapter to understand its message. Read only a section — for that matter, read a paragraph — and you will still understand important points. But if you want to read this book from front to back, by all means go ahead. It works that way, too!

Maybe your company already does a bang-up job communicating with your employees, but you realize that you need to work on building teamwork. Or maybe your company has a fantastic benefits program and offers alternative work arrangements, and you want to take it a step further by working on your employees' professional growth. No problem! This book shows you how.

Assumptions

As I wrote this book, I made a few assumptions about the reader:

- ✔ You're a middle-level manager at some type of organization.
- ✔ You're experiencing some employee motivation challenges.
- ✔ You care for your employees.
- ✔ You want to produce quality work.
- ✔ You want your employees to be happy.
- ✔ You realize that employee motivation and productivity go hand in hand.

How This Book Is Organized

This book is divided into eight parts, which are each divided into two to four chapters. Each part is centered around a particular motivation tool, while the chapters themselves explore the components of that tool in more depth.

Part I: Motivating Others: The Least You Need to Know

In this part, you discover the basics of motivation. Chapter 1 tells you why motivation plays such a crucial role in the success of your organization. Chapter 2 explains why strategic vision is the first step in motivating your employees. Chapter 3 gives you a brief look at the many tools in your motivation toolbox. These tools are also detailed in other parts of this book.

Part II: Creating a Dynamic Corporate Culture

If you're not concerned about your company's atmosphere, you should be. If you walk into work and don't want to be there because you know that you'll be bombarded with unpleasantness, your employees feel the same way. Chapter 4 describes what the phrase *corporate culture* means and shows you things you can do as a manager to create a positive environment for your employees. Chapter 5 shows you how you can design a motivating workspace, and Chapter 6 talks about alternative work arrangements and work/life benefits you may want to consider for your employees.

Part III: Fostering Open Communication

Communicate, communicate, communicate. It's the word of the day in this part. If you want your employees to be open and honest with you, you need to communicate with them. Communication doesn't mean talking *at* or *to* them. It's about talking *with* them. Chapter 7 tells you how, as a manager, you can do a better job of communicating. Chapter 8 shows you how to encourage creativity. (Hint: Your employees need to know you value their ideas.) Chapter 9 talks about communication across the organization as a whole.

Part IV: Building Home-Grown Talent

Your company's employees are its biggest assets. In fact, without employees, your company would cease to function. That's why you need to nurture your employees and their talents. Chapter 10 tells you how you can encourage your employees to take charge of their careers and responsibilities. Chapter 11 talks about mapping careers through performance appraisals and training and development programs. Chapter 12 talks about the value of mentoring.

Part V: Paying Your People — and Patting Them on the Back!

If you're reading this book, you've probably realized that there's more to motivating your staff than paying them. Sure, bonuses are nice and a competitive salary is mandatory, but praise and other non-monetary rewards also go a long way. In Chapter 13, you find out how to evaluate your company's compensation program, including salaries, benefits, and financial incentives such as stock options. And Chapter 14 tells you how to go a step further and develop and maintain an employee recognition program that truly works.

Part VI: Teamwork: Motivating Others to Cooperate and Collaborate

Imagine a basketball game where two five-man teams are playing. Team A's players are working together, passing the ball and planning their moves with the sole goal of winning. Every move is in the team's best interest. Team B, on the other hand, is made up of five players who care only about themselves. Sure, they'd like to win, but — as individuals — each is more concerned about being the top scorer than anything else. The players on Team B are the ones you don't want on your team in the office! But if you find that you're stuck with individuals who refuse to work as a team, then you'll like Chapter 15 on promoting teamwork. Chapters 16 and 17 take the team concept a step further by telling you how to incorporate offsite workers into your group.

Part VII: Overcoming Challenges to Motivation

If you're concerned about a particular challenge, then this is the part for you. Chapter 18 talks about how you can manage through staffing shortages, fast growth, mergers and acquisitions, and downsizings. Chapter 19 takes a look at habitual lateness and absenteeism, while Chapter 20 deals with stress and burnout. Chapter 21 helps you discover ways to cope with — and minimize — office politics.

Part VIII: The Part of Tens

Each of the chapters in this part is made up of ten or so little items that you can read quickly before going on your way. Chapter 22 tells you about some great companies you may want to emulate. Chapter 23 covers Web sites. Chapter 24 talks about the motivating challenges presented by ten different employee personalities. And Chapter 25 suggests how you can encourage employees to motivate one another.

Icons Used in This Book

By now, you've probably noticed those funny little pictures in the margins of *For Dummies* books. Here's what these *icons* mean:

Whenever you see this icon, you'll learn a way you can do something easier or faster.

This icon marks words of wisdom that you'll want to remember.

This icon warns you that something can go wrong if you're not careful.

Whenever you see this icon, you know that the paragraph describes an action that will demoralize your staff.

This icon marks methods that have worked in the past and will continue to work in the future for building motivation.

Part I
Motivating Others: The Least You Need to Know

The 5th Wave   By Rich Tennant

In this part . . .

Motivating your employees is about more than just saying "Nice job" occasionally and then moving on. It's about leading by example, sharing your company's big picture, and getting to know your employees.

Part I contains all this information and much more. You not only find out how to provide strategic vision, but you also discover why you need to motivate your employees in the first place. And most important of all, you are introduced to the many motivational tools at your disposal.

Chapter 1

Motivating Your Employees: Everyone Wins

In This Chapter

▶ Identifying what motivation is and isn't

▶ Knowing how motivation helps your company

▶ Ranking your company's motivation quotient

▶ Checking your own motivational skills

*Y*ou probably already recognize the importance of employee motivation — after all, you're reading this book. You know that a lack of employee motivation can significantly affect your company's productivity. At best, morale problems keep your business from reaching its full potential. At worst, they put your firm's future in jeopardy. As a manager, you're held accountable for at least part of your company's performance, and that's why you can't afford unmotivated workers — who are certain to be less productive than motivated workers. In this chapter, you find out why motivating today's workforce is a common concern for managers. You also identify the aspects of motivation where you and your company have room to improve.

What Is Motivation?

Motivation is a curious thing. Managers sometimes have a difficult time defining it, but they have no trouble figuring out when it's absent — productivity drops, creativity takes a nosedive, workers become bored with their jobs, careless mistakes increase, and the quality of products and services is compromised.

But what exactly is motivation? Some hallmarks of a motivated workplace include:

- **Commitment to results and responsibility for actions.** Every employee is committed to the overall success of the enterprise and strives to do his or her best. Because employees understand how their particular functions fit into the bigger picture, they are able to make decisions and be responsible for their actions.

- **Open communication.** In a workplace with high motivation, no secrets or hidden agendas lie under the surface. People know what's going on. Employees aren't blindsided with unexpected information. In turn, they don't conceal information or mislead their managers. Both sides provide feedback and listen to one another. Another benefit open communication is that the office grapevine tends to wither — there are better, more reliable sources of information.

- **Low employee turnover.** Motivated employees are exceptionally loyal to their employers. They feel good about their jobs and their company. They are less inclined to experience grass-is-greener syndrome or jump ship if the company goes through a difficult period.

- **Creativity and ingenuity, especially in solving problems.** Employees feel motivated when they know that they can be part of a solution or when they're encouraged to experiment with approaches they themselves develop. This sense of ownership fosters a dynamic, creative environment in which employees take initiative in clever, original ways.

- **Collaboration.** Lively, productive interaction among employees is another sign of motivation in action. Rather than toiling away in isolation or trying to outdo their coworkers, motivated employees enjoy working in teams and cooperating with one another.

- **Excellent customer service, both internally and externally.** Motivated employees provide the best service they can, helping internal customers (their coworkers) as well as external ones. Even if they never interact directly with the public, employees with high motivation realize that they can impact customer satisfaction by doing their jobs well.

Of course, motivation can also be defined by what it is not. The following are a few myths about motivation:

- **Everyone is in agreement.** Motivation does not require a uniform point of view. In fact, employees will feel unmotivated if they're required to think and act the same way.

- **Motivated employees work plenty of overtime.** Ten- or 12-hour days are not necessarily a sign of employees who are crazy about their jobs. Often, excessive overtime is an indicator of problems with staffing or operations. It can also be a sign of poor time-management skills.

- **Employees who are motivated don't need much input from management.** On the contrary, input and feedback from managers is what motivates employees to do their jobs effectively and confidently. And when their stellar performance is recognized and rewarded, employees' motivation increases even more.

✔ **A formal plan for motivating employees is unnecessary.** If the approach to motivation is haphazard, sporadic, or inconsistent, the results will be as well. A few employees may be motivated, but not for long.

✔ **Money motivates best.** Although it's true that compensation is an important factor in motivating workers, money is not the be-all and end-all. Nonmonetary benefits and perks, as well as intangibles such as praise, motivate in ways money cannot.

Why You Need to Motivate Your Employees

In the modern workplace, your employees are likely to be *knowledge workers* — individuals who possess specialized skills, extensive industry-specific expertise, or a unique depth of experience that's impossible to duplicate. Rather than punching in, performing their duties, and punching out, employees today are looking to make a contribution. As a result, they are a major source of your company's ideas and the bearers of your company's reputation. You rely on your staff to design and build the best possible product or deliver outstanding service. The profitability and success of your business depends on having employees who are motivated (read: *care enough*) to be efficient, thorough, and competent.

Counting the cost of turnover

Consider this scenario, which plays out in more companies than you may think. John manages a department of 20 employees. One of the staff members, Karl, feels unappreciated and complains to his friends in the department that John is a poor manager. Others begin to notice that they aren't adequately recognized and the grumbling slowly spreads. Morale drops, the negative attitude increases, and productivity declines. John doesn't say anything to his team because he doesn't want to draw attention to the problem or make things worse.

One employee becomes fed up with the work environment and takes a job at another company. While John searches for a replacement — paying for the cost of online advertising as well as a recruiting firm — the team members pick up the extra work. John pays even less attention to staff needs. The group is working long, hard hours, and morale begins to sink more quickly;

commitment wanes and mistakes are made. The department's overall productivity is now unmistakably affected.

After months of interviewing prospective candidates, John hires a new staff member. She needs several weeks to get up to speed on all the projects. Meanwhile, the remaining teammates — including Karl — continue to complain and carry increased workloads. Now, John's attention is focused on training the new hire, whom he hopes will help alleviate the stress and strain in the department once she's able to fully contribute. But he neglects to remedy the existing negativity. Another person quits and the cycle spirals downward.

If your employees aren't happy, they will eventually leave — or cause others to leave. The subsequent high turnover will, in turn, play a role in poor productivity, because you're constantly in training mode. And, of course, you're losing money each time you need to find a new employee. It can become a costly cycle — both financially and in terms of the toll it takes on employee morale.

For a ballpark estimate of the cost of hiring an employee, consider the steps outlined by John Sumser of interbiznet (www.interbiznet.com):

1. **Take the annual sales of your company (or division) and divide it by the number of employees. This is the annual revenue per employee.**

2. **Divide that number by 250 to get the daily revenue per employee.**

3. **Multiply daily revenue per employee by the number of days it takes to hire an employee.**

4. **If you want, add the dollars spent by the recruiting department (it's a minor fraction).**

The number you end up with is the real cost per hire; generally, it's five to ten times the administrative costs.

Dulling your competitive edge

If your workers aren't happy, don't think for a moment that it's their problem — it's yours. Discontented workers can cause you to lose your competitive advantage.

If your employees are unhappy, it will show. They may not tell you, but their performance on the job will speak louder than words. Red flags include increased absenteeism, tardiness, missed deadlines, more errors than usual, and a general slump in enthusiasm. Ever come across someone in a bad mood and notice that it's contagious? You certainly don't want an unenthusiastic attitude spreading throughout the company and spilling over the phone lines or front lines to your customers.

Remember that each of your employees is in the business of serving your customers, directly or indirectly. Here's an example of how one unmotivated employee can derail the service process:

Roger, a clerk in the shipping department of a software manufacturer, has not been recognized in three years for the time and effort he has put into his job. His manager, who supervises 50 people, doesn't remember Roger's name but complains about how Roger lacks motivation. Coworkers from other departments rarely speak to him beyond barking instructions about how to handle outgoing shipments.

Eventually, Roger's morale declines and he cares less and less about the overall quality of his work. He puts the wrong zip code on one package, forgets to send out another one on time, and doesn't take the initiative to follow up on yet another shipment. One irate client calls the company to complain. Others simply take their business elsewhere, without a word. Before you know it, Roger's lack of motivation has cost you thousands of dollars in lost revenue — if not more than that — and you have a considerable amount of damage control lying ahead of you.

U.S. companies lose about half their customers every five years, according to many experts. Much of this client turnover can be attributed to poor customer service. Don't give your competitors the chance to win over your clients. Keep your workers happy, they'll keep your customers happy, and your firm will reap the benefits.

The Changing World of Work

Economic ups and downs should not determine whether or not you put effort into motivating your employees. Some managers ramp up the motivation when the employment market is tight and key performers are leaving. These same managers can become complacent about motivation when the economy is slow and vacant positions are easy to fill.

Whether the economy is weak or strong, motivation must be a high priority for you and your company. In a tight labor market, unmotivated employees simply quit. During a downturn, these same employees may not leave — they'll simply go through the motions, biding their time until conditions change.

To make things worse, the layoffs, downsizings, and restructurings of recent years have weakened employee loyalty. Whether your company is experiencing good times or bad, now is the time to motivate your staff — and keep them motivated.

So what's today's workforce really like?

In today's business environment, employees are not told what to do and how to do it, as much as they're given general responsibilities and long-term objectives. They're the ones responsible for figuring out the what and the how. The important thing is that the job gets done.

Companies today also stress the value of teamwork, in particular *self-managed work teams* — groups of individuals who work collectively on a specific project. In a study commissioned by Robert Half International, 79 percent of executives polled said that self-managed teams increase productivity. But remember — your employees that make up those teams need to be motivated! (For more on teamwork, see Part VI.)

In addition, today's workforce, unlike the one of 30 years ago, isn't signing up with a company and staying with it for life. Workers are looking for opportunities to grow and develop in their careers, wherever that may be. Job hopping isn't taboo anymore.

To lure employees with hard-to-find skills, some companies may offer huge sign-on bonuses, pay referral fees to in-house employees, or even help move a new employee's pets across the country!

Even if you're winning the hiring battles, don't think that you've won the war. Retention is what matters most. And if you want to keep your employees, you need to demonstrate that you truly value them. Competitive salaries and benefits, recognition programs, and strong communication and training programs are a start. In addition, flextime, telecommuting, and job sharing, which were once offered only by the most progressive companies, are becoming more common in some industries and professions. So be sure that your firm offers its employees incentive programs that are competitive with those offered by other companies in your industry and the local market.

What about the office of the future?

In the office of the future, employees will have greater autonomy, more mobility in where and how they work, and will be more technologically proficient than ever before, according to an OfficeTeam poll of 700 working men and women. Employees' main concern will be balancing work and family demands, according to the research. Staff members will expect — and will be given — more authority to make decisions and take action. Self-managed work teams will become the norm in most offices, and employees won't be tied to a traditional job title. They'll continue to take greater ownership of projects, as more employees become the knowledge workers mentioned earlier in this chapter.

Why employees leave

If your company isn't focused on its people, you may see your employees walking out the door. A lack of respect, late performance reviews, and poor communication between management and staff have caused many employees to look for greener pastures. Even life changes, such as having a child and wanting to scale back hours, have prompted employees to go elsewhere. So what can you do?

As a manager, knowing why your employees are leaving lets you prevent future turnover. You can schedule exit interviews to find out exactly why employees decided to leave. In fact, you may be surprised by their reasons for moving on: In a poll by Robert Half International, 25 percent of HR executives said that a lack of recognition is the most likely reason a good employee would leave a job.

And don't forget that, even though your employee is leaving, you should treat him or her with respect. If a staff member leaves on good terms, you won't have to overcome a poor reputation when recruiting new employees. On the other hand, if you treat a departing employee unfairly, everyone will know it — coworkers, job seekers, and possibly even customers.

The face of the workforce is rapidly changing — an important factor when discussing motivation. Aging baby boomers make up a significant portion of the work force. And in some industries — high-tech, for example — Generation Xers are in senior management roles.

So how do you motivate workers who may range in age from 21 to 65? Will the same motivational tools work on a first-wave baby boomer, a thirty-something mother-to-be, and someone fresh out of college? Each of these individuals is in a dramatically different stage in his or her career, and what motivates them varies widely. To illustrate, take a look at some hypothetical worker profiles.

Employee #1: Thomas is 52 and hopes to retire within the next 10 years. In the course of his career, he has been downsized and laid off more times than he cares to remember. He doesn't want to ever go on another job hunt.

Employee #2: Jill, 34, is seven months pregnant. She'd like to take a three-month maternity leave, then return to work full-time. She has been with the company for six years, and by now has an almost instinctive understanding of the business.

Employee #3: Bill graduated from college last year. At 23, he doesn't remember a time when personal computers didn't exist. He has been surfing the Internet almost half his life. He wants to make a lot of money quickly, so that he can pay off $100,000 in student loans. But he also expects work to be a setting where he can make friends and have fun.

How would you motivate these three employees? Obviously, the standard compensation and benefits package with two weeks' vacation isn't going to make them turn cartwheels. The currently popular extras, like dependent care spending accounts, may not have relevance to Thomas or Bill. Jill will probably be unable to attend after-hours parties for the staff after the baby is born.

You've probably guessed that the key is to try and offer something different for each one of the employees in the example. In Thomas's case, IRAs, a 401(k) plan, and retirement planning assistance could encourage him to spend the balance of his career with your firm. Jill would be motivated by a paid maternity leave and childcare referrals. For Bill, incentives such as profit sharing or bonuses would address his desire to earn more income, while staff lunches and a team-based approach to work would satisfy his need for social interaction.

But beyond these tangible benefits, what else could you do to motivate each person? Think about other ways in which they're different. Thomas has experienced periods of involuntary unemployment. Jill has tenure with the company — and likely has the knowledge and efficiency that often accompanies that. Bill grew up during the technological revolution of the 1990s and is completely at home online.

If you were the manager, you'd factor these considerations into your motivation plan for each employee. You may let Thomas know that you staff in a way that protects the firm's full-time employees from fluctuations in business. This knowledge would give him a much-needed sense of stability. Asking Jill to serve as a mentor to a junior employee (like Bill) would be a good (and motivating) way for you to recognize her seniority and expertise. By asking Bill to help coworkers with technical matters, you acknowledge his special skills and give him another opportunity to build relationships.

No one-size-fits-all approach exists to motivate everyone, especially with the rapidly changing demographics of the workforce. As a manager, you need to evaluate the needs of each staff member and tailor your approach to suit the each individual you supervise.

How Does Your Firm Measure Up?

Not all companies are created equal. That's why some organizations are made up of happy, motivated, satisfied workers, and some organizations are made up of workers who occupy the other side of the spectrum. How does your company stack up? Find out by reading the following sections. If you decide that you need to know more about any area, just check out the chapter or part listed for more information.

Do you offer a positive work environment?

One of the main factors in your employees' motivation level is your company's culture. Your company is not a good fit for every person, nor should it try to be. But your company should be a place where people *want* to work. The staff should build each other up, not tear one another down. Employees should feel as if they're trusted and valued and that they make a difference to the company. They should not be criticized unfairly, ridiculed, or made to feel inadequate.

Think about how you've felt working at your company — and how you've treated your staff. How has your manager treated you? If you think your company's work environment needs improvement, check out Part II.

Having a great corporate culture is about more than demonstrating trust and designing a user-friendly office setting. It's also about showing you care about your employees as individuals. Staff members aren't just employees; they have distinct personalities and lives of their own. Don't overlook policies that promote work/life balance, such as flextime or company-subsidized concierge services, depending on what works in your particular line of business.

If employees aren't able to pursue the things they love away from the office — spending time with family or outside interests — then they won't be happy on the job. That's why promoting a work/life balance is important.

Are the lines of communication open?

Communication, communication, communication. Even if you're doing everything else right as a manager, if you're not communicating effectively, you're not doing a good job. And communication is more than just telling employees what you want them to know. It's about fostering a two-way conversation. It's about finding out employees' career goals, offering information before they hear it from someone else, and encouraging risks. As a manager, you can't afford to sit back and observe. You need to build consensus, get a pulse on your employees, and help them learn from their successes and failures. If you need help in this area, check out Part III.

When you think about how well you communicate, don't forget to include off-site employees, such as independent contractors, telecommuters, and those who work in remote offices. To be effective in this environment, you have to be clear and precise in your objectives, expectations, and deadlines.

Do you provide opportunities for advancement?

Have you ever been bored with a job? It's not fun or interesting to do the same task day in and day out. And bored workers soon become unmotivated workers, who soon become employees working for someone else! So take steps early to keep your staff members interested in their jobs. Don't micromanage your team; empower them instead. Offer training programs. Provide feedback on a regular basis. Encourage in-house training, online courses, and seminars. And don't forget the gigantic impact that being a mentor can have on how a person perceives his or her job. If you'd like more ideas on how to implement some of these programs, see Part IV.

Are your compensation packages fair?

Money alone doesn't keep an overworked, unmotivated employee at your company. But it does play a large role in keeping employees happy. Think of fair compensation as a type of preventive maintenance. Make sure that you're paying your employees fairly, while at the same time offering other important benefits, such as insurance, and opportunities for career advancement. For more on developing a strong compensation plan with a good mix of both money and benefits, see Chapter 13.

Do you recognize and reward your employees?

As a manager, you need to appreciate your employees and know what motivates them as individuals and as a group. A good manager makes his or her employees feel valued and encourages strong performance. To find out more about recognizing your employees, see Chapter 14.

Do you encourage teamwork?

A great company is made up of several unified teams working toward common goals. As a manager, it's your responsibility to promote and encourage teamwork. Your team should use words such as *our* and *we* and work together, rather than independently. If you think your department needs to improve its collaboration, then see Part VI.

Are You a Motivational Manager?

Just as not all companies are equally inspiring, not all managers make the grade when it comes to motivating members of their staff. Some managers possess a seemingly innate ability to encourage their employees to reach new heights of excellence and productivity. Others seem unable even to motivate themselves, let alone those around them. And then there are those who try hard to motivate, but with uneven results.

As a manager, where do you fit in along the motivation spectrum? The following self-test helps you assess your abilities. The "correct" answer is normally obvious, so be sure to be as honest as possible. If you need improvement in any area, the answer key refers you to specific chapters for additional guidance and suggestions.

1. Which of the following best describes your management style?

    a. I like to leave my employees to their own devices and see what ideas and solutions they come up with by themselves.

    b. Managers should be actively engaged in their employees' professional lives. That's why I'm always talking to my staff — whether it's giving advice about career development or reminding them to file all reports.

    c. I see myself as a coach who enables people to play to their strengths and make meaningful contributions to the team. I'm lavish with praise and sparing with criticism. I reward extra effort and helpful ideas. If a project ever changes direction or has problems, I make sure that people know what's happening and what's expected of them.

2. When providing feedback to your employees, what do you do?

    a. Comment only if someone has made a mistake. Why should I recognize people for doing what they're paid to do?

    b. Get very specific about how to improve the product or their performance; I tell them what to do and how to do it, because that's clear communication.

    c. I always give encouragement first ("I can tell you worked hard on this"). Then, if any changes or modifications need to be made, I'm careful to critique the work, not the individual. In addition to informal, day-to-day feedback, I hold annual performance appraisals for each employee.

3. What do you do to create a positive, pleasant workplace?

   a. I make it a point not to yell at anyone.

   b. I always ask my employees what I can do to make their work experience better. I usually don't follow up on their requests or complaints, but at least I ask.

   c. I try always to be pleasant and positive myself, even if I don't feel that way on a particular day. I foster camaraderie by holding monthly recognition days and periodic staff lunches. I talk to people about their families, children, pets, and hobbies, as well as their jobs. I encourage people to be creative and take new approaches to doing their work.

4. How do you help employees with work/life balance issues?

   a. I figure they can run their private lives without my interference. But I do make sure that every employee knows the number of their nearest crisis intervention center.

   b. If they're having a problem, I tell them what I think they should do and where to find useful resources. Then, to show that I care, I always check back with them later to see if they took my advice.

   c. I try to determine what they need from me to help ease the pressure or stress they're experiencing (for instance, I may offer to reassign part of their workload).

5. To help employee work teams be more efficient and productive, I:

   a. Stay out of their way!

   b. Require daily status reports from all team members so that I can nip problems in the bud. I also attend every meeting of every team.

   c. Give them the tools and resources they need, as well as appropriate decision-making authority (so that I don't end up micromanaging). I also try to let them know how their project fits into the bigger picture, so that they have a sense of purpose. And, once or twice a year, I hold team- and consensus-building exercises to sharpen their skills.

6. If two of your employees have problems working together, what do you do?

   a. Sit back and wait — they'll either work it out themselves or one of them will quit.

   b. Get them both in a room together with me, and tell them that I expect professionalism at all times and that their behavior has to change immediately, or they'll face serious consequences.

   c. Speak to each one separately and privately as a first step. The nature of the problem determines the next steps. My ultimate goal is to defuse the situation without losing a valuable employee or disrupting the work of other staff members.

7. Your company was just acquired by a larger firm, and duplicate positions will be eliminated. No one knows what to expect and your staff is extremely anxious. What do you do to help them through this time?

   a. Nothing — my own head may be on the chopping block!

   b. I promise that I will do everything I can to protect their positions — even though I don't have any real "power."

   c. At a general staff meeting, I acknowledge that this is a high anxiety time for everyone, myself included. I assure them that I will provide updates as I learn about them and I encourage them to talk to me about their concerns throughout the coming weeks. I thank them for their dedication and hard work over the years, and I tell them we'll get through this time.

8. One of your employees comes in 45 minutes late every day and leaves half an hour early on Fridays. She calls her husband at least twice a day and speaks loudly enough for workers in neighboring cubicles to hear. Sometimes she fails to meet deadlines, which places a burden on other members of her work team. Her coworkers are grumbling. How do you handle this problem?

   a. Copy the sections of the employee manual that discuss work hours and phone use and leave them on her desk. As for missing deadlines, suggest to her teammates that they automatically build an extra week into the timetable when assigning projects to this individual.

   b. Confront her publicly about her tardiness. Then, make her move to a cubicle right outside my office so that I can monitor her phone calls. Threaten to suspend her the next time she misses a deadline.

   c. Have a private meeting with this employee and explain that I want to discuss certain habits of hers that are problematic. Start with the missed deadlines, since this directly impacts the performance of others. Find out why she didn't turn work in on time and help her plan for the future to avoid this problem. Finally, review company policy about work hours and personal phone calls and ask her to comply, because I know she wants to be fair to her coworkers.

9. Two of your staff members are on vacation and one's on extended sick leave. The rest of your employees have been desperately trying to pick up the slack, but they're starting to show signs of strain and even burnout. Now, a big project that will tax everyone to the limit has just landed on your desk. You respond by:

   a. Taking a few personal days to collect your wits.

   b. Giving your staff your best pep talk and promising them all a special treat once they finish the project.

   c. Asking each employee about current workload and impending deadlines. If it looks like everyone is already stretched too thin to handle one more thing, you bring in consultants and temporary employees to ease the pressure.

10. Employees are motivated by a manager who:

   a. Isn't bossy and overbearing.

   b. Is involved in every aspect of operations and has control of all the details.

   c. Is sincerely enthusiastic and takes pride in his or her employees' work.

The answer key

If the majority of your answers were "c," then you are generally a motivating manager. You are effective and flexible in your use of a variety of motivational tools. If you chose "a" or "b" for some of the questions, see the section "Motivation Rx" — it directs you to specific chapters of this book that help you be an even better motivator.

If you chose "b" for most of your answers, you are generally an overactive manager. You try hard to motivate, but your methods often backfire. You frequently mistake micromanaging for motivation, and you tend to go overboard with motivational tools like praise or rewards, promising more than you can possibly deliver. This may be because you misunderstand what motivation is or how it works. Check the "Motivation Rx" section for the chapters or sections to focus on.

If "a" was your answer to most of the questions, you are generally a passive manager. Your laid-back style causes you to err on the side of being too hands-off when it comes to motivation. Perhaps you feel that nothing you do can possibly motivate others. This may be because you believe that motivation can only come from within — a common misperception. Check "Motivation Rx" for fix-it strategies.

Motivation Rx

If you answered "a" or "b" to:

   #1: Take a look at Chapters 2 and 10.

   #2: Check the suggestions in Chapters 7 and 11.

   #3: Chapters 4 and 5 provide helpful ideas.

   #4: See Chapter 6 for new approaches.

   #5: Refer to Chapters 10 and 11 for fresh ideas.

   #6: Turn to Chapter 19 for help.

   #7: Chapter 18 has effective strategies.

   #8: See Chapter 19 for proven remedies.

   #9: The suggestions in Chapters 18 and 20 will help you cope.

   #10: See Chapters 2 and 7.

Chapter 2

Do You See What I See?
Providing Strategic Vision

· ·

In This Chapter

▶ Being an example

▶ Motivating yourself

▶ Leading the way with actions

▶ Communicating your vision

· ·

Motivating someone is *never* easy, especially when that person doesn't have a particular desire to be motivated. But consider this: How can you motivate someone if you yourself aren't motivated?

In this chapter, I show you not only how to keep yourself motivated, but also how to lead others by being a role model. You also gain insight on how to share your company's vision — the big picture — with your employees.

To Motivate Others, You Need to Be Motivated

Motivating others requires energizing them to take action. Empowerment, communication, training, and compensation — all issues you can read about in Part II — help you motivate, encourage, and inspire others. But as a leader, remember that you set the tone. Others follow your lead. For example, if you're having a bad day and snap at an employee, that employee won't be in such a good mood and will probably take out his frustration on someone else. It's a vicious cycle.

Anyone can be a leader. But a *good* leader makes positive things happen by creating a positive tone.

When you're asking people to be more productive with fewer resources and less staff — and most companies are doing just that these days — you need to give your employees all the inspiration you can. If you're not inspirational, then you can't expect your employees to be inspired. (Bear in mind that being inspirational doesn't mean you have to act like a football coach at half-time, requiring everyone to huddle while you give a pep talk!)

In fact, in a recent Accountemps survey of executives, more than a third of the respondents cited a positive attitude as the interpersonal skill that they most value in employees. Executives are looking for enthusiastic managers who can motivate and retain their staff members — particularly important in a tight employment market. Another reason that enthusiasm is so important — both the enthusiasm that you have and the enthusiasm that you generate in others — is that more employees are having to take on responsibilities that fall outside of their traditional roles.

Choosing your attitude

You may not have control over what happens to you, but you do have complete control over how you respond and react to what happens to you. The fact that you can choose to be upbeat while your important project goes down the drain may not seem like much of a consolation, but, in the long run, a positive attitude is your most precious commodity.

In other words, if you're not feeling motivated, you're *choosing* not to feel that way. Sure, a lot of factors come into play that make it difficult to be motivated. Maybe you're struggling with physical health or maybe your boss won't give you a raise. Ultimately, however, you're the one responsible for what you do and do not do — and the way you feel. You can choose to be motivated.

Enthusiasm and optimism are contagious. Choose to be upbeat and positive, and others will soon be that way too.

Say that you're facing a big deadline and your company's network is down. Being positive is even *more* important now than when things are going well. Not only will you reduce your stress level, but you'll also be able to focus on the task at hand instead of worrying or panicking. Others will emulate your behavior as well.

Of course, being positive is easier said than done, but here are a few tips to help you stay upbeat:

> ✔ **Laugh it up.** Humor not only relieves tension, it also encourages a light-hearted atmosphere. The Creative Group asked advertising executives: "How important is a sense of humor in reaching senior management levels?" Fifty-one percent rated humor as a very important factor, while another 46 percent rated it as being at least somewhat important. (For more on why humor works, see the sidebar.)

✔ **Be cooperative and approachable.** Be a team player by honoring deadlines, delivering top-quality work, and providing your expertise to help others succeed. Even offer to pitch in on big projects when necessary. Your cooperative attitude will be noted by others and reciprocated. And isn't it more fun to work in a place where people treat each other well?

✔ **Practice open communication.** Regular communication prevents many problems from occurring in the first place. Good communication also helps solve the problems that do pop up. Instead of making statements, ask questions — you avoid making assumptions and can check that everyone is on the same page.

✔ **Stay calm.** When you're faced with a difficult situation, don't allow emotions and pressure to affect how you communicate. Instead, give yourself a moment to take a deep breath, and think before you speak.

✔ **Be part of the solution.** Don't just identify a problem — propose solutions. Encourage your employees to do the same.

✔ **Choose your friends.** Just as enthusiasm is contagious, so is a bleak attitude. If you're around negative associates and coworkers, they will eventually drag your morale down, too.

✔ **Keep it to yourself.** If you're having a particularly bad day or a crisis, consider spending some time alone. That way, you won't do or say something you'll regret later.

✔ **Spread good news.** When something good happens, share the news with others and praise those who made it happen. If a new company policy helped you better balance your workload, for example, let your supervisor know about it. When a colleague gives an outstanding presentation, say so. Recognizing achievements will make both you and those around you feel good.

Why humor works

No one wants to be around a spoilsport — the person who is always down and complaining. No matter how upbeat you try to be, you always leave conversations with her in a bad mood yourself.

That's one reason humor can be a career catalyst. When you're upbeat and good-natured, you're able to laugh at things that may otherwise bring you down. You more easily build rapport with your coworkers, which in turn facilitates open communication and a positive work environment.

So when things aren't going your way, look for a silver lining. Remaining in good spirits can relieve high-pressure situations caused by looming deadlines and competition. (For more on combating stress, see Chapter 20.)

One caveat though — you should never laugh at an inappropriate occasion, and you should never make another person the object of your jokes. Clearly, jokes about race, gender, sex, age, national origin, religion, and disabilities are never appropriate at work.

Finding personal motivation

A key element in personal motivation is passion about your work. Have you ever noticed how people who love what they do seem to excel? If you can be passionate, success is likely to follow.

If you're not passionate about your work, you're probably not going to give your all. But you can find ways to inspire yourself, become passionate, and give your all to your work.

Whatever you do, don't just *wish* that things were different. *Make* them different.

Take pride in your work

Pride is a funny thing. It can make or break your day. Have you ever rushed through a project just to meet a deadline? Maybe if you would have had more time you would've reread that section of the proposal that just didn't seem to click. Or you would have run a spellcheck. Or followed up with a coworker on a point that you didn't quite understand. But you didn't do these things, and — inevitably — something didn't work out so well. And that probably didn't make you feel very proud at all.

And just imagine how the bigger issues factor in — you know, the things that go beyond the everyday details. For example, say that your company entrusts you and your team with a high-profile special project that can earn millions for your company. But — unfortunately — it doesn't go well. Not only have you lost potential revenue for your company, but your pride, self-worth, and dignity are harmed as well.

But when things go well — you catch all the little details or your team nails the project — doesn't that feel great? You're in a fantastic mood, your boss loves the project, and your coworkers notice your upbeat attitude. Isn't that the kind of behavior you want your staff to emulate?

If you're not going to take pride in how you handled a particular project when you're finished, then you need to do something about it early on to change the direction of the project. If you do a lackluster job, not only will you not have pride in your work, but you may spend more time fixing it, in the long run, than you would have spent doing the job right the first time.

And if you did your best job and you still failed, you need to put things in perspective. You did your best, and that's what's important. The next step is to learn from your mistake. Why didn't the project succeed? What can you do differently next time? Then move on. Dwelling on a mistake doesn't help anything.

No matter what job you're doing, do it well. Others will notice and follow suit.

Practice good time-management skills

Time limitations almost always play a factor in how well you can do a job. If you're constantly overwhelmed, focusing and doing your best work is difficult.

Effective time management is critical. Take Elizabeth and Herb as examples. Both have the same job title and are responsible for the same number of projects and the same amount of work. Elizabeth works a 40-hour week, produces stellar work, and is positive, energetic, and upbeat. Herb, on the other hand, puts in 60 hours a week, delivers projects that lack focus, and is stressed and on the verge of burnout. If workload isn't a factor, then what's the problem? Time management skills! Elizabeth has them and Herb needs them!

Your time management skills can make you or break you. Organize yourself and prioritize your daily tasks. (See the sidebar on getting organized for tips to get you started.)

Pat yourself on the back

When you're faced with an uphill battle, getting discouraged is easy. The same is true for the people you manage. During the rough times, keeping your chin up is especially important. That's when you need to pull out your *feel-good folder*.

A feel-good folder lists all of your accomplishments and kudos — you know, the stuff that makes you feel great whenever you look at it. Got an e-mail congratulating you on a job well done? Print it and file it in your feel-good folder. Have a photo of your team goofing around at your last department offsite? File that in your folder, too.

When things aren't going well — your team isn't particularly clicking or a new obstacle has surfaced — pull out your feel-good folder and remind yourself of your past successes.

Indulge your passion — wherever it may be

You've probably heard it countless times — do what you love, and the money will follow. Although that works for some people, it doesn't work for everyone. In fact, I know one professional who is doing something he likes — not loves — so that he can enjoy the things he is passionate about in his free time.

If you're not passionate about your work, find a hobby that you love — sky diving, cooking, bicycling, whatever. The key is to be connected regularly with your passion, whether at work or after hours.

Getting organized

Are you in charge of your day or is your day in charge of you? Do you spend 15 minutes looking for a piece of paper? Arrive to meetings late? Forget to tackle important projects? Then you need to get organized, fast!

You say that you don't have time to get organized. Actually, you don't have time *not* to get organized! Try these tips to turn your work life around:

✔ **Invest in a good planner.** First things first: You need a good planner. If you use your planner correctly, you'll be lost without it. Record everything in it — meetings, to-do lists, contact information, and even your personal engagements. (You don't want to agree to work late on your wedding anniversary, for example.) And that brings me to planner point No. 2: Use only one planner!

✔ **Make a to-do list.** Think about each project you're working on. What do you have to do to ensure success? If you have to make a phone call, write that down. If you have to order supplies, write that down, too. Need to research some dates? That's right — write it down.

✔ **Prioritize.** After you've compiled a list of things to do, you need to start prioritizing. When does each item need to be completed? Is one task contingent on another being done first? Things that must be done right away or that need to be done before something else are your A priorities. (For example, you need information from a coworker to compile a report due May 1, but she'll be gone the last week of April, and it's April 18. You need to take action soon!) Those are the things you should plan to tackle that day. Your B priorities are items that would be nice to get done but aren't

crucial. Your C priorities are to-do items that need to be done but are low on your list.

After you assign each item a letter, examine all your A priorities. Which is the No. 1 task that day? That's your A1 item. What's the second thing you need to get done? That's A2. You get the idea.

✔ **Write it down and then forget about it.** Well, you don't actually forget about it — you just don't think about it. Say that you need to meet with Mike in accounting as soon as possible, but he's on vacation this week. Instead of writing it down every day, go to the day he's due back from vacation and write "Schedule meeting with Mike." Then don't think about it again until you flip to that day in your planner.

This idea works with other tasks as well. For example, say that you've asked Sheila for some important information and she says that she'll get back with you in two weeks. Flip to two weeks later and write yourself a note, "Follow up with Sheila about the Ryan project." Then you don't have to worry about remembering.

✔ **Touch each paper only once.** When you get your office mail (and your personal mail for that matter), you should only touch it once. It shouldn't linger on your desk until you decide what to do with it. Either toss it, file it, forward it, or place it in a To-Read folder. That's that.

✔ **Leave detailed phone messages.** Phone tag is a big time waster. Don't you hate it when someone calls you and just says, "Hi, it's Phyllis. Call me." Then you call her back and she's not there, and she calls you back and you're not there, and . . . well, you get the picture. Think of all the time you're wasting! Leave a detailed message on her voicemail to alleviate the problem of phone tag. Want information on the market research survey? Say so. That way, you're getting the ball rolling even though you're just leaving a message. (And you won't waste six calls only to find out that Phyllis isn't the person you needed to contact!)

✔ **Plan for the unexpected.** Don't plan eight hours of work for an eight-hour workday. What if an employee needs to bounce some ideas off you? What if you have to attend a last-minute meeting? Plan for the unexpected. Only schedule about six hours of your day. And when the day finally arrives during which you have nothing unexpected come up (it could happen!), then go home happy because you're now two hours ahead on your to-do list.

✔ **Clean up before you go home.** No one likes to come into a disorganized, cluttered office. Straighten your desk before you go home, so that when you come in the next day, you won't immediately be in the panicked state you were in at 5 p.m. the day before. (But if you follow these time-management tips, your frenzied days should be a thing of the past.)

For more organizational tips, see *Time Management For Dummies,* 2nd Edition (Hungry Minds, Inc.) by Jeffrey J. Mayer.

Take some classes

If you're an accountant who loves to decorate, indulge your creative side and sign up for some interior decorating courses. Likewise, if you secretly want to be a chef, whip up some culinary delights in a cooking class. The mental stimulation of doing something you love causes you to be more positive. And a positive person carries that positive energy over to others, including his or her coworkers.

Try these resources when you're looking for a class:

✔ Surf the Internet.

✔ Check out the community resource section of your local newspaper.

✔ Call your town's community center and inquire about courses.

✔ Look into continuing education courses offered at local universities.

✔ Contact related stores or service providers listed in the phone book to see whether they offer any classes.

✔ Ask your friends.

Make time for friends

Feeling down? Overworked? Unmotivated? Then make a lunch date. There's nothing like getting together with a friend to make you forget about your woes. And just when you stop thinking about what has been bothering you at work, you'll probably come up with a great solution!

Not only do friends relieve stress, but they also help you see that there's more to life than work. If you get together with friends from work, make sure that you don't let your jobs enter into the conversation.

Do something totally different from your work

Do you ever feel like you need a change? Sure, you can try driving a different route to work, but sometimes you need something more to get motivated. That's when you need to do something totally different from your daily routine. Don't just drive a different route to work — take a vacation day!

Spend a day off reading a novel alone or try something outrageous (think hang gliding!). And if you're a chef? Why not go out to dinner and let someone serve you for a change?

Relax over the weekends

Weekends are made for relaxing. Unfortunately, more and more people think they're made for catching up on all the things they didn't do during the week.

When you're working day in and day out with no end in sight, keeping your momentum going is tough. Don't plan to work on the weekend unless it's truly a desperate situation (which should be the exception, not the rule).

Relaxing on the weekend applies to your home life as well — you know, laundry, dishes, ironing, grocery shopping. Instead of trying to get everything done on the homefront in just two days, take a weekend off from everything. Do your grocery shopping and laundry during the week. Then relax on Saturday and Sunday!

Take a vacation

Don't be someone who skips your vacation every year because you have too much work. You need the time away from work to rejuvenate.

You don't need to travel to have a good time — sometimes the most relaxing vacations are those spent at home! But don't tell anyone you're vacationing at home. Otherwise, you'll be bombarded with phone calls from work — and you're supposed to be taking a break from work, remember?

If you do decide to leave home, remember to *plan* your trip, no matter how busy you are. Careful preparation ultimately allows you more time to enjoy the actual vacation. After all, how relaxing can it be to arrive at your destination only to find that a convention is going on and you have nowhere to stay?

Change your routine

Sometimes, renewing your motivation is as simple as changing your routine. The break in monotony may be just what you need to start seeing things in a new light.

Try going to a different coffee shop in the morning or redoing your filing system. The change of pace may get you going again.

Pay attention to your health

Your physical condition plays a big role in your mental well-being. In fact, exercise releases endorphins that make you feel better mentally. And when you feel good, how can you not be motivated?

So if you're not doing so already, start an exercise program. Watch your diet. (Heavy lunches can leave you ready for a nap.) And start alleviating stress in your life. (Stress actually affects short-term memory.) Not only will you feel better physically, but you'll have more energy and think more clearly as well. You may even find that you have a new outlook on long-term challenges.

Check out Chapter 20 for more information on stress management.

Leading by Example: Establishing Ethics

If you're in a position of authority, you're a role model — whether you want to be or not. As a manager or senior person in your department, your actions and demeanor set the stage for others. Always remember that people will look to you as the example of what's expected.

Think about it — aren't bad moods contagious? If your boss is having a bad day, it probably isn't too long until you're having one yourself. And then your employees may be in a bad mood before long (although you need to make sure that doesn't happen!).

Of course, leading by example is about more than having the type of attitude that you wish your employees had. It's about demonstrating the behavior you want others to model. If you'd like everyone to be ready to work at 8 a.m., then you shouldn't saunter in at that time and spend the next ten minutes by the coffee machine. If you want everyone to be on time at meetings and for the meeting leaders to have an agenda, then *you* need to be on time and have an agenda.

Watch your language!

What you say means a lot, especially if your actions prove you're practicing what you preach. But here's something you may not have thought of: The words you choose affect how your message is perceived.

Say that you have a new member on your team who is straight out of college. You certainly wouldn't want to call him the "new kid" — even if you don't mean anything by it. Likewise, describing someone as an "average Joe" can have a demoralizing effect, especially if that person is working long and hard to produce the best work he can.

The same is true in how you provide feedback. If you only point out what someone does wrong, you make the person wonder if he's capable of ever doing anything right in your opinion. But if you mention the things he or she does well, then the occasional constructive criticism should not cause harsh feelings.

For example, if Holly has shown up on time every day for the last year and then is late twice in one week, don't say, "Your tardiness is unacceptable. If it happens again, you're gone."

Instead, take a step back and choose your words carefully: "Holly, your promptness has never before been a concern. However, I've noticed that you've been late twice in the past week, which is very unlike you. Is there a problem?" Give Holly a chance to respond. She may be suffering from the flu, experiencing car trouble, or have another reason. Your ultimate goal is to get Holly to work on time — not to get rid of her.

Make sure that your words and actions are in sync

One of the most important things to remember in business is an old adage: "Actions speak louder than words." Employees want a leader who does what she says she will do. Sure, they'll listen to what you're saying, but if your actions are contradicting your words, then your message is lost.

Employees will watch your behavior as a guide to what is acceptable office conduct. You are the rule, not the exception. That means you need to establish the behavior that you expect or want others to adopt. You can't just pay lip service to a policy and then disregard it with your actions. If what you say and what you do contradict each other, your employees will become cynical and distrustful — quite the opposite of motivated.

Here are just a few ways you can lead by example:

- ✔ If you want people to come back on time from lunch, then you should set the example by doing the same.

- ✔ If you want them to honor deadlines and commitments, you need to do so as well.

- ✔ If something comes up and you can't attend a meeting, arrange for someone else to take your place.

✔ If attendance is important, then make sure that you show up for work each day.

✔ If you want your employees to help each other, offer to assist when you can.

✔ If you say you care about your employees, then show them that you do by remembering their birthdays, taking them to lunch on occasion, and regularly thanking them for a job well done.

✔ If you want your employees to help out new team members, take them under your wing as well.

Keeping your words and actions consistent shouldn't be difficult if you're basing all your decisions on your company's values and mission.

Base your decisions on values

Every strategic decision you make should be based on the company's values or mission statement. Your employees should be able to determine your firm's values just by watching the decisions you make. By using the mission statement as a guide, the actions that you and your employees make will be consonant with the company's overall direction.

Values are your first step toward employee empowerment and teamwork. When all employees in a company share similar values, then you're well on your way to attaining a higher level of performance. Shared values make your employees feel like a team; they inspire trust, loyalty, pride, optimism, and caring. They also can alleviate feelings of stress.

Don't be the type of leader who makes decisions randomly. If you're not basing your decision on something you believe in, then you'll be easily swayed . . . and there goes your credibility. If you base your decisions on your company's mission statement, then you'll always have the same purpose in mind and decisions will be easier to make (and stick to). Your employees will also discover how to make similar decisions on their own if they can see a definite pattern to your choices.

Be ethical

Here's a quick way to test whether you're making an ethical decision: Ask yourself if you would be able to tell friends, family, and coworkers what you had done and be proud of it. For example, if one of your employees comes up with a fabulous idea and you take credit for it, you probably wouldn't be proud of your actions.

If you said you'd do it, do it

Telling people that you'll do something and then not honoring your commitment is an easy way to quickly get out of a situation. But it's certainly not the right way. Maybe it's not giving Alicia the data she needed by Friday like you promised. Or maybe it's something more serious, like skipping out on a meeting (because you didn't take the time to prepare) in which you were supposed to play a crucial role.

If you find yourself using the "say it, don't do it" technique to ease your way out of situations, expect the consequences to come back around to you. First of all, your credibility will be damaged — and it may take a long while to rebuild the trust you've lost. Don't think that you can get away with this behavior for very long. People

will talk, and your reputation for honesty and reliability will be affected. What's more, your staff may begin to mirror your behavior. Maybe your employees will start to be late with important projects or not show up for meetings.

Think about your commitments before you take them on, and then follow through on them — that's why they're called commitments. Your word should mean something — something good. And remember: Inconvenience is not an acceptable excuse for not following through. Your staff will remember your lack of follow-through long after the fact. When you're faced with some annoying and unavoidable inconveniences, just plow ahead and do what you said you'd do.

As an example of how the mission statement should be used, say that your company's goal is to produce the highest-quality product possible. You need to decide between manufacturing Product A, which is of extremely high quality, and Product B, which is of lesser quality, but can be produced sooner. Because you're aware of the company's mission, you choose Product A.

Don't obsess entirely about results; instead, focus on values. If you act according to your company's values, the results will follow.

You need to be able to tell employees what the company stands for and what it's trying to achieve. Then you need to practice what you preach.

The Big Picture: Sharing Your Vision

People don't want to feel that their work is irrelevant or unimportant. Instead, they like to know how the task they're doing fits into the big picture. That's where effective leaders come in. They offer a compelling vision (the company's mission) and then encourage and inspire others to fulfill it.

One example of sharing the big picture is Anaheim, California-based Odetics, a manufacturer of data management products, that lost nearly 40 percent of one division's sales when its major customer bought one of its competitors. Although layoffs were necessary, the company managed to maintain morale by holding employee meetings to discuss and ask for input about the problem. The company then based all decisions on the plan developed at this meeting and let employees in on all progress made. Not only were the employees invested in the big picture, but they could celebrate the achievements along the way as well.

Odetics could have kept silent about its predicament and then sprung the layoffs on employees. But the company realized that fear of the unknown impacts morale.

Odetics also realized that its employees were a valuable asset who could help it reach its goals. But your employees need to know the goals to reach them. They need to know what they can do to help.

Your company's mission statement is a crucial component of motivating your employees. It tells your employees why the company exists, what it wants to accomplish, and how its goals should be reached. Without a mission statement, your company is a ship sailing without a destination or even a charted course.

Writing a Mission Statement

Although this book isn't about writing a mission statement, I give you the basic facts of writing one in this section. Hopefully, though, your company already has a mission statement. After all, how can your firm have leaders if the leaders don't know where the firm is going?

The mission can't be something you simply develop on your own and start touting for your individual team or department; it needs to be created by senior-level management.

Whatever your mission, it shouldn't focus solely on profit. You need a business that's built on values — values that can inspire employees when the profits can't. The statement should cover your company's core business activities, such as the areas and clients it serves and its products and services. It should also point out the things that make your company different from all the other companies in the same industry. Try to work your company's strategic goals over the next several years into the mission statement as well.

No matter what your mission statement says, it needs to be clear and concise — ideally 50 words or less.

Chapter 3

Stocking Your Motivation Toolbox

· ·

In This Chapter

▶ Identifying what motivates your employees

▶ Knowing what's in your motivation toolbox

▶ Getting acquainted with the basic strategies

· ·

*T*he same things don't motivate everyone. Some people want a higher salary. Others want a company car. And still others want a great insurance plan. Then you have those employees who care about less tangible things than compensation and benefits. They want to work for a company that really cares about them, and that shows it cares by offering great training opportunities, a positive corporate culture, and open communication.

If your employees are having a motivation problem, you need to think about each individual employee's wants and desires. Then you need to take a peek inside your motivation toolbox. Just as you wouldn't want to put together a bookcase with a wrench or tighten a bolt with a chisel, you need to find the right motivational tool for the particular workplace job. Develop a toolbox that contains lots of ways to motivate your employees and you'll be on the path to creating a workplace that is filled with enthusiasm.

This chapter describes your basic strategies; if you see one you particularly like, check out Parts II and III of this book, in which I give you more details.

What's Their Motivation? Getting to Know Your Employees

Claire woke up one Monday morning and couldn't drag herself out of bed for work. (Well, she finally did, but she sulked all the way to the office and arrived ten minutes late.) This reluctance wasn't just the result of an overexuberant weekend. Claire was losing her motivation.

Lack of motivation doesn't happen overnight, though; it's the result of a downward spiral into apathy. Sure, everyone has days when they feel less than enthusiastic about their jobs. But that's normal. Low motivation becomes a problem when it's a pattern of behavior, not an occasional bad day at the office. For some people, that slide downhill may happen fairly quickly. For most, it's a gradual process. The key to turning around the situation is in identifying the cause, which can vary from person to person. But before you can know what causes demotivation, you have to know what causes motivation.

Most often, motivation comes from doing something rewarding, something intrinsically valuable. People want to use their talents, skills, and knowledge in the best way possible. Applying that concept to the workplace means employees need to be contributors to the organization — and then they need be recognized for their contributions. But exactly how they need to contribute and be recognized varies according to the individual. For example, some staff members prefer to work as part of a team and may be quite content to receive praise as a team. But others may like to work independently. And if you recognize their efforts only as part of a team, you may eventually notice a very unmotivated employee.

 Different things motivate different people. Money, of course, is important. Most people can't afford to work for free. (You do need to eat, right?) But money isn't the only component of a motivated workforce. How your employees feel when they're at work plays a crucial role in their happiness — and the success of the company.

This list contains a brief overview of some of the tools that you can use to keep your workforce upbeat and enthusiastic. For the full details, refer to the specific chapters.

- ✔ **Balance:** All work and no play makes Jack a grumpy employee. Even if some of your employees are workaholics, there will come a time when they need a break. You need to show your employees that you realize they have a life outside of work. (Chapter 6.)

- ✔ **Benefits:** Even if the money is great, some employees won't be satisfied — and understandably so. Your compensation package can't compete if you leave out insurance, retirement plans, and other financial incentives. (Chapter 13.)

- ✔ **Communication:** Foster an open communication environment. Employees want to know that they can talk with you about what's going on at work, and they want honest feedback from you. (Chapter 7.)

- ✔ **Compensation:** Monetary compensation — as long as people feel like their remuneration is fair — isn't the most important motivating factor for many people. But it *is* important, of course. (Chapter 13.)

- ✔ **Corporate culture:** What's it like to work for your company? When employees describe their organization's environment — managers' attitudes, hours, and the other elements that create a work life — they're talking about the *corporate culture*. A company that discourages smart risks, stifles creativity, and berates employees doesn't have a positive corporate culture. (Chapter 4.)

✔ **Recognition and rewards:** Some people are really excited by public recognition and rewards. They want some recognition for their hard work, other than a paycheck, and they want someone to know that their performance is outstanding. Celebrate your above-and-beyond performers. (Chapter 14.)

✔ **Responsibility:** Employees want to be able to contribute. Empower your employees so that they feel responsible, and they'll reward you for your trust. (Chapter 10.)

✔ **Teamwork:** Many people enjoy collaborating when they build something great — flying solo isn't for everyone. Being part of a successful team doesn't even feel like work for some of your employees. If your company is going to succeed, teams should play a big part in your work style — so promote teamwork. (Chapter 15.)

✔ **Training and promotions:** Without opportunities for professional growth, work becomes routine and unfulfilling. Help your employees contribute more and more to your firm's success while developing their careers. (Chapter 11.)

What motivates you doesn't always motivate your staff.

Motivating others takes time, and it's certainly not something you can do overnight — or order someone else to do. Like most improvement projects, transforming an unmotivated staff into a motivated, synergistic team requires plenty of consistent, hard work.

What other companies do

If you're noticing that your employees are starting to just go through the motions — they show up barely on time, take long lunches, and turn in shabby work — then you may need to do something about their motivation. If you know that you need to do something to motivate your employees, but you're not sure what exactly to do, try taking your cue from these companies, and see Chapter 22 for more ideas.

✔ Tom's of Maine (the natural toothpaste maker) encourages employees to devote 5 percent of their paid time — about two hours a week — to volunteerism. The results? Better performance and employees who are in touch with what they care about.

✔ Netscape and Autodesk, two firms in northern California, realize that although child-care benefits are important for working parents, employees without children need a perk too. These companies allow people to bring their pets to work.

Nip demotivation in the bud!

Pandora was a talented employee who could do her job well. The problem was that she liked to complain. A lot. She complained about the weather. She complained about the management. She complained about meetings. In fact, you couldn't talk to Pandora without hearing her complaints. She'd pop into offices uninvited, spreading her tales of woe. Coworkers began to close their doors so that they could avoid her. Pandora walked in anyway.

Well, it wasn't long before — you guessed it — Pandora's misery spread. Soon everyone was viewing the company through Pandora's eyes. No one wanted to do his or her job. No one wanted to come to work. People began to leave the company. And all because management failed to deal with Pandora's motivation problem when it first became apparent.

Pandora was what you might call a "challenging" employee. (See Chapter 19 to find out ways to deal with these problems, er, challenges.)

You are an important element in your team's motivation. In order for your employees to be motivated, you need to be motivated. (If you're not, see Chapter 2.) You also need to be a leader and be able to identify your staff's needs. Your daily communication, attention to detail, and pride in your work influence others — hopefully in positive ways.

Mission statement

Do you remember the old TV program *Mission Impossible*? The hero always knew what his mission was and had the tools at his disposal to accomplish his mission.

Just like the hero of *Mission Impossible,* every employee should know your company's mission statement and make decisions in line with that statement. (Every company has a mission statement — or at least every company should. If yours doesn't have one, see Chapter 2 for the full scoop on mission statements.)

A mission statement is important because your employees need to know where the company is going if they're helping to drive the company to its destination. And they need to know what steps are acceptable in reaching that destination. For example, if they know that excellent customer service is valued, they will recognize the need to go the extra mile for a client as necessary. But if they don't know that customer service is integral to the mission of your organization, they may occasionally see those "extra" requests from clients as a waste of time and nonessential to their responsibilities.

Don't just hand out assignments and assign projects. Tell employees how their part in the project will help the company's overall mission — not just the bottom line. Instead of saying, "You're helping support a project that will grow revenue by 20 percent," say, "You're working on a project that will change the way people think about learning."

Teamwork

Teamwork occurs when a group of people share a common goal and understanding and work together to accomplish a specific project. When a team is in sync, the individuals working together on that team produce more, collectively, than they would each working alone. The team's success is more important than the success of the individuals who make up the team. Not only does effective teamwork help the company achieve its objectives, but working as a team also makes your employees feel good about themselves and their contributions.

When you're doing a good job fostering teamwork, you won't see a lot of finger-pointing, destructive competition, or excessive personality clashes. Sure, situations may occur every so often; that's typical whenever a group of people works together closely. But it won't be the norm. A team that works well together doesn't have individuals who continually blame one another, fight over personal turf, or disagree over anything and everything.

Compensation

Money talks — at least for some people. You can't expect people to do a job for free. If money motivates them, and Company A is equal to Company B in all respects, but Company B pays more, then Company B will win out with most employees. And why not?

Hey, John is behind schedule!

A team needs deadlines and standards. According to a Robert Half International survey, 37 percent of executives define team players as those who meet deadlines. Managers seek reliable employees who deliver projects on time. If one person doesn't, the success of the whole team is undermined.

Setting fair, but challenging, deadlines helps employees budget their time and meet their goals. Break large projects into smaller parts and make sure that you maintain regular communication to determine when a deadline needs to be extended. That way, you'll help your team avoid a crisis, burnout, or stress. See Part VI for more on teamwork.

You can't underpay your employees and expect them to stay. You must pay them competitively, even if you're offering fantastic benefits and an ideal corporate culture. If you're underpaying your employees, you're sending the message that they are not that valuable to your success. (For more on compensation, see Chapter 13.)

Corporate culture

Corporate culture plays a bigger motivating role than even compensation for some people. In a nutshell, corporate culture is your business environment, the unwritten rules of the road that govern how work gets done. Hewlett-Packard is often recognized as the pioneer of corporate culture with their now-famous HP Way, which outlines the company's values and vision. (For more on HP, see Chapter 22.)

Each year, *Fortune* magazine publishes a list of the 100 best companies to work for in America. In its December 2000 issue, it noted that while offering attractive perks and benefits help recruiting efforts, having a culture where employees are treated with respect and feel like they are cared about goes a long way toward helping retention.

Communication

Never underestimate the power of communication. It's the key to success in almost everything you do. For example, if your employees are comfortable talking with you, they're more likely to be loyal to the company. They are also more likely to let you know if they're thinking of leaving. How you communicate is so important that it can determine whether an initiative succeeds or fails.

Here are a few general communication tips. (See Chapter 7 for more.)

- ✔ **Foster an open-door policy.** You want your employees to be able to come to you whenever they have concerns or questions — work related and otherwise. Not only do you care about their productivity, but you want your employees to know that you value them as people. If they feel valued as individuals, they will also value the work they do. If your office door is constantly shut and you're not spending time actually talking to your employees, then you're not practicing an open-door policy.

- ✔ **Interact with your employees.** Get to know their work. Know them personally. It's harder to let someone down when you know them as a friend — so be your employees' friend!

- ✔ **Give credit to your outstanding performers.** One way is to start an Employee of the Month program. (See Chapter 14 for other ideas.)

✔ **Start a company newsletter.** People love to know what's going on. Having a newsletter is one way to keep everyone informed. Plus, you can let people know who the Employee of the Month is!

✔ **Keep employees informed about the business.** Nothing is more discouraging than hearing a big announcement about the company from someone outside the company.

✔ **If you must turn down an employee's request (a day off, a raise, or a deadline extension), explain why.** Determine whether you can offer something else instead, or set a specific time in the future to reconsider the request.

✔ **Give feedback, even if it isn't positive.** When you have to deliver constructive criticism, do it in private and use the kind of words you would want to hear if you were on the receiving end. You don't want to embarrass anyone or point fingers. And certainly provide feedback if your employee is doing a great job!

Recognition

If your employees are doing a great job, let them know it. You want your employees to know you care about their performance. If you never tell staff members how they're doing, how will they know that their work even matters? A recent OfficeTeam survey revealed that a lack of recognition was a major reason employees quit their jobs.

Recognizing your employees is a huge part of their motivation. No one likes to do a job well and then feel unnoticed. This book has a whole chapter (Chapter 14) on how to recognize your employees in the most effective way.

You should praise your employees liberally and publicly whenever praise is merited. Not only does praise make a person feel good, but it also highlights the type of behavior you'd like others to emulate.

Mentoring

Mentoring occurs when one person, usually a long-term or top-performing employee, takes a newcomer under her wing and provides the newcomer with professional support. But mentees don't have to be limited to recently hired employees; a mentoring relationship can be beneficial for people at any stage in their careers.

Mentoring is a great motivational tool. Here are some of the reasons it pays off:

- ✔ New employees learn the ropes more quickly.
- ✔ They are able to understand and adjust to the corporate culture.
- ✔ They feel like they belong and are able to adapt more quickly.

As a result, their productivity increases at a faster rate. They're happy and you're happy.

Mentors themselves can get great satisfaction in sharing knowledge and experience with someone. Not only are they assisting coworkers and fostering staff camaraderie, but they strengthen their interpersonal and leadership skills as well.

To find out more about mentoring, see Chapter 12.

Training

Everyone benefits from training. Not only does the employer get people who know their jobs and can do them well, but the employees who have gone through training are more motivated and challenged. Remember that the more trained your employees are, the better they perform. The better they perform, the more you're seen as a star leader.

You may not be able to have your own university (see the sidebar), but you still have training options if your budget is tight:

- ✔ Select key employees to attend outside training or a workshop and then give them the responsibility of training others in the department when they return.
- ✔ Ask your Human Resources department to offer general in-house training. Good ideas for topics include stress management, time management, and e-mail etiquette.
- ✔ Identify key training topics that would benefit your staff — for example, improving customer service, negotiating costs with vendors, or enhancing software skills — and then approach people in your firm who are experts on these topics and invite them to speak at a brownbag lunch.

For more on training, see Chapter 11.

Back to school

You've heard of schools specializing in certain areas: hairstyling, business, photography. Now a large, Midwest-based electronics firm is taking that concept a step further, and has developed a university that specializes in the company! All employees are required to attend training at the university, where they devote nearly one week per year to courses on a variety of subjects related to technical and business skills as well as team building and quality. The company estimates that for every dollar spent on training, it gets back $30 in productivity gains. Over about a 14-year period, the company estimates it has cut costs by $3.3 billion — not by eliminating workers, but by training them to simplify processes and reduce waste. Most of the trainers are not professional instructors, but are employees who have a talent for teaching.

Other companies — such as Robert Half International and Oracle — offer their own "universities," tailored to their business needs and the professional development of their staff. It's all part of being a learning organization — a company that's committed to the professional development of its people.

Management practices

Actions speak louder than words. You can't say that you trust your staff to do a good job and then micromanage them. You need to demonstrate your confidence by allowing them to make decisions about assignments. Make sure that they keep you informed, but don't demand to be involved in every single step of the process.

How you communicate as you delegate plays a large role in employee motivation. Use language that shows your confidence in their ability. Don't just say, "Here's your next project — I'm trusting you on this, so don't let me down." Whom would that inspire? Say something like, "Most people with twice your experience would have a tough time tackling this project, but you've proven that your abilities far exceed your years in the field, so I know you can do it." This approach not only makes your employees feel good, but it shows them that you believe in them.

Show that you have good faith that staff members are using their time wisely and efficiently. If it's crunch time, you can bet that — to a reasonable extent — your employees also feel the pressure. Give them credit for understanding the importance of their projects without having to be told repeatedly how urgent it is that they finish that report on time or follow-up with a few more phone calls.

Trust requires open communication. You need employee briefings where you share information about activities, organizational goals, and financial issues. This information helps give employees the big picture and presents them with the opportunity to offer their own input.

Companies that show their trust

At Nordstrom, the popular Seattle-based retailer that brought new meaning to the term *customer service,* employees are given a one-page employee handbook that states the company's rules in a way in which trust is implicit: "Rule #1: Use your good judgment in all situations. There will be no additional rules."

For employees to grow professionally, they need to take risks. Sometimes they will make a mistake or fail. But that's okay. Don't point fingers. Instead, find out how the mistake happened so that you can implement a process to make sure that it doesn't happen again. Developing a few safeguards not only helps ensure that the employee who made that mistake won't ever make it again, but also helps ensure that the mistake won't be made by some other employee down the line.

Strategic staffing

Strategic staffing refers to the practice of bringing in extra staff whenever your workload is heavy — because of a special project or anticipated and unanticipated workload peaks, for example. By using strategic staffing, your existing team doesn't have to work overtime. Their efficiency increases significantly. (You've heard of the theory of diminishing returns, right?) You also help prevent burnout and improve retention, because employees see that you care about them and are willing to bring in extra help when needed. (For more on strategic staffing, see Chapter 18.)

The next time your department approaches a busy period (at the end of a fiscal year or annual sales meeting, for example), consider hiring temporary staff to handle the added workload.

Things That Don't Motivate Employees

Everyone seems to have an idea on how to motivate people. But some things never work to motivate and almost always, in fact, demotivate. The following is a list of motivation don'ts.

> ✔ **Never personally attack someone.** By all means, you should give constructive criticism. Feedback is important. But you should criticize only the behavior, not the person. If you find yourself saying, "You never do anything right," stop in your tracks. (See Chapter 7 for more on feedback.)

✔ **Never embarrass an employee.** Self-esteem is critical to motivation. When you do have to provide criticism, do so in private. It doesn't help for others to overhear your words; it only makes the situation worse.

✔ **Don't govern by fear.** Hear this: Fear of repercussion never causes good performance — at least not for long. If you run your department in a finger-pointing way, your best employees won't stay for long. And you're certainly not fostering open communication and teamwork, which are key motivating elements.

✔ **Don't shoulder all the responsibility.** As a manager, you're paid to delegate and lead your team. If you're doing all the "work" but neglecting those duties, you need to reexamine your priorities. Give others opportunities to learn. Not only are you making your life easier and leading by example, but you're also helping your employees feel valued and respected. (See Chapter 10.)

✔ **Don't overwork your employees.** Plan for peak work periods and take advantage of temporary staffing opportunities. Hire top performing temporary professionals. Whatever you do, don't overload your employees for long stretches of time. You're giving them an invitation to find an employer who can provide a bit of balance. (See Chapter 20.)

Hopefully, you were patting yourself on the back as you read this list because you're already avoiding these demotivation techniques!

What's All This Talk about Myers-Briggs?

I'm assuming that you're at least slightly interested in motivation — you are reading this book, after all — so you've probably heard about Myers-Briggs. You may not know exactly what it is or who Myers and Briggs are, but you have a vague idea that it's some kind of test that helps you determine something or other about personality. Well, here's the scoop.

Management by walking around

Improving relations with your employees doesn't have to be a formal process. Decades ago, Hewlett-Packard pioneered the concept of "management by walking around." Management theorist Tom Peters popularized the idea. Despite its proven success, the practice is often neglected by today's managers.

Management by walking around simply means that you're in touch with your staff through everyday interactions. Instead of being nestled all day in your office or hidden away in meetings, you spend time walking the hallways of your company, taking time to speak with employees.

What it is

Officially called *Myers-Briggs Type Indicator* (MBTI), MBTI assesses your personality type by asking you a series of questions. You choose the answer that best describes how you usually feel or act. Based on your answers, you're then placed into one of 16 personality categories.

Developed by Isabel Briggs Myers and Katherine Cook Briggs and based on Carl Jung's Theory of Type, MBTI is published by the Consulting Psychologists Press and should be completed under the guidance of a qualified test administrator.

How it's supposed to help

By being aware of your personality type, you discover your strengths and weaknesses and can develop to your full potential. In addition, you can find out how best to motivate each of your employees, depending upon their personality type. In other words, the test should help you figure out how your personality meshes with others.

The 16 types

The 16 personality types are listed in terms of letters — for example, ESFP or INTJ. Each of the four letters stands for a different trait:

- **Extroversion (E) or introversion (I):** This is more about how you process information and not about how bubbly or reserved you are. If you earned an E, you're an extrovert, which means that you tend to prefer action more than reflection. If you're an I, you're an introvert, which means that you prefer to think things through thoroughly before acting.

- **Sensation (S) or intuition (N):** If you're an S, you rely on your senses to take in information, focusing on the present. If you're an N, you rely on your intuition, with more emphasis given to the future.

- **Feeling (F) or thinking (T):** If you make decisions based on your values, you're an F. If you make decisions based on objective, logical thought processes, then you're a T.

- **Perceiving (P) or judging (J):** If you're a P, your answers indicate that you like to be spontaneous and free. If you're a J, your answers indicate that you prefer more structure and predictability.

See the sidebar for suggestions on additional information about MBTI.

Additional reading

Intrigued by the Myers-Briggs Type Indicator test? Then you may find the following titles interesting:

✔ *Please Understand Me: Character and Temperament Types,* David Keirsey and Marilyn Bates (Prometheus Nemesis Book Company).

✔ *Using the Myers-Briggs Type Indicator in Organizations: A Resource Book,* Sandra K. Hirsh (Consulting Psychological Press).

✔ *Working Together,* Olaf Isachsen and Linda Berens (New World Management Press).

✔ *Type Talk at Work,* Otto Kroeger and Janet M. Thuesen (Bantam Doubleday Dell Publishing).

✔ *Portraits of Temperament,* David Keirsey (Prometheus Nemesis Book Company).

✔ *MBTI Manual (A guide to the development and use of the Myers-Briggs Type Indicator),* Isabel Briggs Myers and Mary H. McCaulley (Consulting Psychologists Press).

✔ *Facing Your Type,* George J. Schemel and James A. Borbely (Typofile Press).

✔ *Gifts Differing,* Isabel Briggs Myers with Peter Myers (Consulting Psychologists Press).

Part II

Creating a Dynamic Corporate Culture

The 5th Wave   By Rich Tennant

Dorsey Family SPITBALL Co.

"A large part of our success is based on our ability to resolve conflicts before we get to work."

In this part . . .

Have you ever walked into a workplace and felt the energy? Everyone seemed upbeat, positive — in short, happy to be there? In this part, you discover ways you can create a dynamic corporate culture of your own. You find out how to make your office a place where people *want* to work. In addition, you learn how to design your employees' workspace to maximize productivity and motivation and how to select alternative work arrangements and benefits to best fit your employees' needs.

Chapter 4

Creating a Place Where People Want to Work

Do you ever wake up in the morning and dread a particular task that faces you that day? Perhaps you have to deliver a presentation to the company vice president — and you hate to speak in public. Maybe you have to catch up on paperwork that has been stacking up for weeks.

Whatever the case, if you like the environment where you work — even if you don't like the work that you have to do on a given day — then you look forward to going into the office. This example shows just one way in which a positive corporate culture can help you and your staff. In this chapter, you find out just what a corporate culture is and how you can help create one that makes your employees look forward to coming to work each day.

Understanding the Term "Corporate Culture"

So what does *corporate culture* mean? It means the environment in which your employees spend their time. Your company has certain goals and objectives that affect the policies and procedures you develop. And these, in turn, affect the unwritten rules of the road and the work atmosphere — which, in turn, impact your employees' morale.

To put it another way, a company's culture is defined by the company's values and the type of behavior that's accepted at the firm. In essence, a corporate culture is the business's personality. Is yelling in a meeting okay? Are pointing fingers and laying blame the norm? Or does laughter routinely resonate in the hallways? These day-to-day occurrences determine your corporate culture and say to employees, "Hey, this is how we do things around here."

Obviously, actions speak louder than words, and actions reveal the true culture of your organization. This fact means that if you allow behavior that conflicts with your values to exist — and eventually spread — you'll end up with a corporate culture that's not the one you had as your original goal.

Corporate culture isn't something that just happens. As a company, you can decide the kind of culture you'd like to have and ensure that your day-to-day actions reflect that culture. Although a corporate culture that develops without planning can nonetheless be a positive one — especially when your organization's leaders are dynamic and empathetic — cultivating a positive work environment is a good idea. If you have no concept of what your culture should be, you may be more likely to let slide behaviors that can negatively impact employee morale.

As a manager, you are the standard bearer for your company's culture. You need to examine your actions and those of your employees and determine whether they reflect corporate values. If your firm values open communication and smart risk taking, you don't want to yell at your employees when they speak freely or make an honest mistake, even though you may disagree with their approach or actions. Your behavior should be consistent with your firm's values and objectives.

Corporate culture affects such things as your firm's work style, decision-making process, modes of communication, and employees' interactions. Following are more detailed descriptions of each of these areas and how they're impacted by the work environment:

> ✔ **Work style:** Every company wants employees to work hard, but do employees come in early and stay late, only to leave with a bundle of papers in their arms? Does everyone work Saturdays? If this is the case at your office, check out Chapter 20. Your organization's demanding requirements may be burning out your staff.

> There's a big difference between working hard and working too much. Working hard is when you do your best and produce super results. Working too much is when you're routinely clocking 50-, 60-, and 70-hour weeks and you're still just getting by. A culture in which you and your employees are working around the clock, leaving no time for life outside of work, will eventually work against your company's success.

✔ **Decision making:** Does your firm offer an approach to decision making in which employees are involved in the process? Employees shouldn't be coming to you so that you can double-check everything or sign off on every step of a project.

Or does your company have a more top-down management style, in which the decisions are made by only a few individuals? If you find yourself having to check with *your* manager before you can make a decision, then the top-down approach is probably the norm at your company.

✔ **Communication:** How you communicate with others can be either a reflection of your company's overall style or reflect how you, as a manager, choose to converse. Some managers prefer to communicate via e-mail, while others want to speak face to face.

But communication involves more than the medium you choose. Do you encourage your employees to be open and honest in team meetings? Or do you prefer them to be silent? Remember: Silent employees can't contribute innovative ideas to help your company's performance.

✔ **Employee interaction:** Are people kind to each other? Or do they talk behind one another's back? Is there a spirit of camaraderie and collaboration? How employees are allowed, or even encouraged, to interact plays an important role in defining your corporate culture. Don't tolerate unkindness and don't encourage separation based on titles or job descriptions.

Be a leader: Talk to your supervisor about the potential benefits of revising workplace policies (if necessary) to breathe new life into your corporate culture.

Employees who like your corporate culture are usually involved with the company for the long haul. Employees are more motivated by their work than their compensation, provided you're paying them fairly.

Knowing Why Your Corporate Culture Matters

A positive corporate culture plays a huge role in staff recruitment and retention. In a competitive hiring environment, corporate culture can even determine whether a candidate accepts an employment offer. More and more companies are recognizing the importance of their work environment. In a survey developed by Accountemps, 33 percent of the executives polled placed a positive work atmosphere at the top of the list of considerations for keeping employees happy.

It's a match! Or is it?

Finding good employees is no easy task. After you've weeded out all the nonqualified candidates, you have to find out if the remaining applicants can truly do the job. But even if they pass that test, don't extend the offer automatically.

During the interview process, try to discover whether the person is the right fit with your corporate culture. Does your potential employee require a lot of direction? If your office is one where employees are self-directed, she may not be happy there. Does she understand your company's values? How does she handle deadlines? If she works better under pressure and yours is a deadline-driven environment, great — it's a match. Otherwise, keep looking. Find out what the candidate loves to do and then think about whether your workplace will help inspire those passions.

And once the person is onboard, continue to evaluate the match. You know you're seeing signs of a good fit when employees understand their role in the company's mission, are able to use their strengths, and are interested in their job.

When you hire someone who doesn't fit in with your company's culture, your decision can be costly — whether the person leaves or stays. If she leaves, you'll have to recruit, hire, and train someone else. If she stays, she may negatively affect the attitudes and workflow of her coworkers; morale could suffer in a short period of time. Whether she stays or leaves, she costs your organization time, energy, and productivity, not to mention morale.

Chances are, if your employees are staying around, then you're doing something right. When you treat your employees with respect and when they treat each other with courtesy and professionalism, then you'll not only foster pride and hard work, but loyalty as well.

And here's even more good news: A positive corporate culture is its own recruitment tool. Word-of-mouth works just as effectively as want ads.

If you want to retain your employees, you need to make sure that they're a good match with your corporate culture. Hire for the attitudes that complement your work environment.

Unlocking the Mysteries of Positive Corporate Culture

Certain companies have box-office appeal — that certain something about them that makes newcomers flock to them and keeps current employees working hard. But unlike Hollywood hype, corporate culture is something that stays around a long time. A culture is hard to change for the better after it has gone terribly awry, but it's easy to destroy with poor leadership.

So why do some companies have great corporate cultures and some don't? Because of their underlying values. Nontraditional, forward-thinking companies that boast great corporate cultures

- ✔ Listen to their employees and genuinely care about them. The companies realize that all people have the capacity to contribute valuable ideas.

- ✔ Make sure that employees see how they fit into the big picture and know that they matter. Employees treated this way tend to believe in the company and its products or services.

- ✔ Trust employees to do their jobs to the best of their abilities. As a result, staff members regularly go the extra mile to exceed expectations.

- ✔ Know that honesty and integrity play a huge role in a positive corporate culture. Employees don't have to compromise their beliefs to do their work well.

- ✔ Give employees the real picture, not corporate-speak from managers.

- ✔ Don't compromise quality for quantity.

- ✔ Have a participatory management style that empowers employees, rather than a dictatorial management style.

- ✔ Help their employees balance work and personal demands. Working long hours isn't rewarded unquestionably; companies with motivated employees are more concerned about results than the number of hours logged at the office.

- ✔ Offer opportunities for lifelong learning.

Discovering Your Company's Culture

Before you can live and breathe your company's values, you need to be aware of what they are. What are your firm's guiding principles? Do they include treating employees with respect? Putting the customer first? Chances are that the guiding principles encourage a combination of many of these things.

If you can't put your finger on a clear definition of your company's culture, ask fellow managers to give you their perception of it. Then run their descriptions by your employees and see whether your employees agree.

If you think you have a serious gap between management and employee perceptions, then consider hiring an outside consultant who can analyze the corporate culture and report his or her findings. Based on this analysis, managers can then work together to figure out how to close the gap. Remember, though, that change takes time.

Does your culture match your description of it?

You can describe your company's culture as friendly, relaxed, and upbeat, but how your employees act means a lot more than anything you say. (After all, as a manager, you're supposed to say good things, right?)

In reality, if your new employee arrives for his first day on the job and no one acknowledges him, he will think that your company is impersonal and uncaring. But if the receptionist or coworkers take the time to converse with the new employee (or even a prospective employee), then he will have the impression that your company is indeed just as friendly as you say it is.

Although you can't make your employees behave a certain way, you can control your own behavior. As a manager, you need to model the behavior you want your employees to adopt and also let them know just what is — and what isn't — acceptable. Take that new employee to lunch. Chat with the job candidate in the waiting area, even if you're not interviewing him. Everything you do is a reflection of your company's culture. In this case, one person truly can make a difference.

Also keep in mind that corporate culture usually is a reflection of the company's founder's actions. Senior managers can reinforce or contradict the culture, or play a role in changing it. If the company founder places the utmost importance on service, but senior managers are emphasizing a quick sale over consistent good service, the culture will move away from its original values.

Creating a Positive Environment

So you want to build a place where people like coming to work. Who wouldn't? But establishing a positive corporate culture doesn't happen overnight. You have to cultivate it just like you would anything else.

There's no one recipe for creating a positive corporate culture. Two work environments may be wildly different, but equally popular among employees. Some companies may offer flextime and sabbaticals; others may offer onsite amenities such as a cafeteria or gym. But no matter what the specific programs or fringe benefits are, a positive corporate culture values the individual and his or her contributions to success.

The following sections outline important things that you can do as a manager. These items, taken collectively, can make your company's environment warm, friendly, and motivating.

You also find advice about what *not* to do. Many managers, in an effort to improve corporate culture, end up introducing programs or ideas that are simply not effective or appropriate. And, after a program becomes entrenched in the culture, it can be very difficult to change or eliminate — even if introducing the program was a bad idea.

Start at the top

A positive corporate culture can't develop without the leadership of managers. As a manager, you help set the tone of the organization. You need to lead the way. If you want your employees to show up at a certain time, you need to do the same. If you want your employees to treat each other with kindness, you should be the first to do so. And if you want your employees to have fun at work, then — you guessed it — you need to lighten up! For more on leading by example, see Chapter 2.

Don't forget the little things: stopping by your employees' desks just to say hi, passing on articles that you think someone may be interested in, and diving into the trenches with your staff members during crunch times. These simple actions let your team know you're in it together, and it's not "us" versus "them." It also lets them know that you expect them to help others on the team — just as you do.

Keep in mind that, as a manager, you are *always* a leader. Your responses to the demands of your professional — as well as personal — life will be observed closely and imitated by your staff. If you are a workaholic, your employees will feel pressure to follow suit. On the other hand, if you take long lunches and leave early on Fridays, your staff will expect the same privileges.

A good rule is to avoid extremes. Be friendly, but not overly familiar, with your colleagues. Be enthusiastic, but don't overdo it to the point where it loses meaning ("Isn't it great that we have to work till midnight to get this done!" is probably overkill). Encourage your employees to have fun, but don't trivialize the work they do. Promote open communication, but don't tolerate rumors, gossip, or inside jokes at others' expense.

Start off on the right foot

Whether your orientation program consists of a lengthy, structured program or a quick tour and round of introductions, you need to make sure that your employees feel comfortable and welcome. If they are shown to their new work area and left alone to figure out how to turn on their computers and get to work, you're not giving them very much direction — or a welcome.

Orientation programs familiarize employees not only with benefits, but with the company's values and culture as well. When employees understand the organization, they acclimate more quickly. It's also more likely that they will feel like they belong and feel more committed to the results.

Sure, orientation programs still cover the basics, such as the company's history, office locations, work hours, compensation policies, and benefits. But the most effective employee orientation programs focus on corporate culture as much as they do policies and procedures.

To make sure that newcomers absorb as much as possible about your company's culture, don't rely on osmosis. The following tips help you introduce your company to a new employee in a motivating way:

- **Think like a tour guide.** When you visit a foreign country, isn't having a guide who can explain the nuances and unique aspects of the culture helpful? New hires need such a guide. They'll appreciate it if you take them on a guided tour of the company's culture.

  Subtle features to point out include: how coworkers prefer to communicate (whether through scheduled meetings, voicemail, e-mail, formal memos, while passing in the hallways, and so on); how the staff has fun together (for example, monthly birthday celebrations, group lunches); and how employees respond to one another's problems and crises (perhaps it's typical for a team to drop everything to pitch in when someone needs help). By sharing this type of information, you speak volumes about shared values.

- **Let the new hire be a shadow.** During the first week, focus less on having the new employee do his or her job and more on letting the individual learn about what others do. The most effective approach is to have the new hire *shadow* several coworkers for a few hours or a day. They meet a lot of people, learn about work flows, and gain an understanding of each person or department's function.

- **Involve long-time employees as mentors.** If you're unable to escort the newcomer through the first week or two on the job, ask one or two veteran employees to be mentors. Their role will be to help the new arrival settle in and become acquainted with your company's people and processes. In addition, the mentor will be the designated go-to person when the new employee has questions or problems. (See Chapter 12 for more on mentoring.)

- **Do a daily download.** For the first few days, meet with the employee for half an hour before going home. Encourage him or her to share impressions and ask questions. By allowing the person to "download" what they've learned or observed that day, you'll enhance his or her ability to process an overwhelming amount of information.

And now, here's some advice on what *not* to do when you're introducing a new employee to your company's culture:

- ✔ **Don't try to do it all in one day.** After reviewing company policy and doing employment paperwork, take a break before moving on to an overview of your firm's culture. Give the newcomer a chance to absorb information in manageable amounts. Don't try to cover everything in one meeting or even in a single day.

- ✔ **Don't take the kitchen sink approach.** As in, "everything but . . ." Avoid presenting the employee with an encyclopedic narrative about the company's history, mission, work style, and special features. Select a few employee programs or benefits as examples, and explain how they've made work more enjoyable for your staff.

- ✔ **Don't be a gossip.** Avoid using personal anecdotes as a means to make the new hire feel like an insider. Comments like "Al's fine to work with, as long as you do it his way" or "Never give Susan your only copy of something" will only lead to prejudices and mistrust.

Demonstrate trust

Many companies today strive to create an empowered staff as part of their culture. The results are often mixed, however, because a base of trust hasn't always been established. Or, if it has been, that trust is brittle and breaks the first time someone makes a mistake or does not meet standards.

What about dress codes?

One of the most visible elements of a company's culture is its dress code — what is acceptable attire for people on a day-to-day basis while performing their jobs. It's important that what you allow individuals to wear matches the culture you're promoting throughout the company.

For example, if you're working in a creative field, such as for an advertising agency, jeans or T-shirts may be commonplace. On the other hand, a more conservative industry such as financial services may require projecting a more traditional image.

In a survey developed by Accountemps, 55 percent of executives polled feel employees dress appropriately on casual dress day, while 39 percent believe workers dress too casually.

Keep in mind that if you're going to implement a casual dress policy, you should not penalize employees who follow that policy, even if you prefer a more conservative look. If dressing casually is too much of a concern, perhaps relaxed attire is not the best option for your firm.

The following are some of the do's and don'ts of demonstrating trust in the workplace.

Do

- ✔ **Encourage reasonable risk.** Let your employees know they will not be penalized for taking calculated chances, even if the gamble fails.

- ✔ **Foster autonomy.** Make recommendations instead of issuing commands. For example, don't give instructions when an employee asks, "How should I do this report?" Say, "Based on the information you've gathered, what do you think is the best approach?"

- ✔ **Analyze mistakes.** Simply pointing out a mistake is not very helpful. Instead, sit down with the employee and discuss together how the mistake occurred. Brainstorm with the employee how he or she can avoid a similar error in the future.

- ✔ **Ask employees to create solutions.** Some managers impose their own correctives. It's more effective to let employees solve problems on their own, when appropriate. Obviously, this approach applies to issues of time- or workload-management rather than personnel conflicts in which management must step in to enforce established rules.

- ✔ **Praise winning ways.** When employees meet or exceed expectations, public recognition and praise are in order. Praising builds goodwill and sends the message that your workers are doing something right.

Don't

- ✔ **Criticize in public.** Avoid humiliating an employee in front of his or her coworkers.

- ✔ **Use a "do as you're told" approach.** The days of the command-and-control, drill sergeant–style manager are long gone. You won't be encouraging creativity, originality, spontaneity, or learning.

- ✔ **Sabotage or ambush your employees.** You destroy innovative thinking, as well as morale, when you second-guess your staff or play "gotcha!" whenever someone makes even a minor mistake.

If you don't trust your employees to take risks or grab the ball and run with it, then you won't have a truly motivating corporate culture. If you want your employees to trust you, then you need to demonstrate that you trust them.

Some ways to demonstrate trust include

- ✔ Involving several employees whenever you interview a potential hire. Doing so shows that you trust and value their input.

- ✔ Use words like *we* and *us* when discussing activities and events at the company. Listen closely to determine if your employees do the same. If you hear mostly "they" and "them" in reference to management or the firm, it's a sure warning sign of a problem.

- ✔ Consider abolishing sick days and offering combined sick leave and vacation time. Then, let your workers determine when and how to use their time off. If you demand a doctor's note every time an employee is sick, you're demonstrating a lack of trust.

Promote two-way communication

Fostering open communication takes work, as Part III shows you. In this section, I give you some of the basics.

One of the best things you can do to encourage open communication is to leave your door open, even when you're talking to fellow managers. That way, your employees know that you're a team and that you're not keeping secrets.

If you want an attractive corporate culture, then make communication an area of focus. Encourage your employees to come to you with suggestions. Offer encouragement and feedback. And most of all, listen. As their manager, you should be their biggest advocate within the company.

Always assume that your employees know the real scoop behind any important announcement. When you officially deliver the news, don't try to sugarcoat it or deviate from the truth. You'll only lose your employees' trust.

Reward and praise

Ever spend a lot of hours on a project only to turn it in and hear *nothing?* So then you start asking yourself, "Is no news good news? Or is no news bad news?"

If you've ever been in that position, you know firsthand why you shouldn't put your employees in it. If you like their work or work habits, *tell them.* If you want others to emulate a certain person's behavior, reward and recognize the employee publicly. And if you think they need to improve, let them know that, too, by using the techniques described in Chapter 19.

Nothing makes an employee feel better than being recognized for a job well done. No one wants their efforts overlooked, although they may all want to be rewarded differently. Praise your employees whenever you can. And if praise doesn't come naturally to you, make sure that you see Chapter 14 to find out how you can recognize your employees for their great work.

Try to promote from within your company. Doing so shows your employees that you recognize and reward hard work. It also shows them they don't have to look elsewhere for career growth opportunities.

Promote teamwork

Even though you may be incredibly talented, you can't get a project done by doing it alone. Don't forget to tap into the creative energy of your team. Do more than just delegate; give your employees ownership. Make them aware of the results and how their jobs affect the big picture. Praise them for what they do well. And when you get kudos from your boss for a job well done, don't forget to recognize your team.

A few things are best avoided as you build team spirit:

- ✔ Don't create an atmosphere of competition in which team members feel pressure to outperform one another at the expense of the project.

- ✔ Be careful about constantly recognizing the same people and overlooking the work of others.

- ✔ Avoid promising lavish rewards if the team succeeds. For example, don't spur the team on with the prospect of a day off if you don't have the power to authorize one.

Make time for fun

Work and fun? Can they really be synonymous? Of course they can! Implementing any of a number of inexpensive ideas can infuse the workplace with a playful spirit. Having a good time encourages creativity — a real payoff for your firm's productivity!

Chapter 8 gives you the full scoop on having fun at work. Here are some of the ideas for lightening up the workplace that companies have found beneficial. They're cheap, convenient, and effective:

- ✔ Hold a monthly celebration.

- ✔ Bring doughnuts or bagels into the office once a week.

- ✔ Hold a weekly meeting every Friday afternoon in which you mix business with pleasure. Have an agenda, but take turns bringing in treats to lighten up the mood.

- ✔ Meet outside the office. Why not hold your next team meeting on the lawn?

- ✔ Celebrate met deadlines. Distribute movie passes or take the gang miniature golfing.

✔ Get to know your employees. Doesn't everyone enjoy talking about themselves?

✔ Have an office decor contest. Make sure that employees know the company guidelines, but encourage them to personalize their workspace. Then offer a small prize to the person with the most appealing workspace — voted on by the team, of course!

Your employees spend most of their waking hours at work. Why not make that time as enjoyable as possible?

Look for opportunities

Companies that have employees flocking to them aren't afraid to think beyond the traditional boundaries. As you review the following list, keep in mind that your company needs to have a unique approach to fostering positive corporate culture, based on the specific circumstances and priorities of the organization. Think of these suggestions as ticklers that may spark your own innovative ideas:

✔ Give awards to employees who find creative ways to recruit qualified candidates. For example, the employee with the most referrals during the year can win cash or a prize.

✔ Invite high school students interested in careers in your industry to work in your offices at specific times during the school year.

✔ Offer free lunches for a week when employees meet or exceed goals.

✔ In addition to conducting performance appraisals once a year, be sure to provide continual feedback. Employees should always know how they're doing and where they need to improve so that there are no surprises when review time comes around.

✔ Go beyond having just a coffeemaker in the break room. If budgets permit, provide vending machines, free bottled water, and ample supplies for meal preparation (paper products, plasticware, cups, tea bags, condiments, and so on).

✔ If feasible, offer corporate health club memberships to employees, or discounts on your company's products or services.

Chapter 5

Using the Workspace as a Motivator

*I*magine if you weren't allowed to decorate the walls of your office. Then imagine that there are no walls at all — you can see what your neighbors are doing just by turning your head. Now imagine that you don't have an office, or even a desk. Instead, you have a laptop computer that you carry with you as you travel from couch to couch in a wide-open workspace. Obviously, you'd feel differently working in each of these environments. You'd work differently, too.

Although you may not have paid much attention to it before, the physical space you and your employees work in has a huge effect on the corporate culture and on employees' motivation and productivity.

If your company strives for a relaxed, creative culture, your building and office style should reflect that. On the other hand, if you decide that you want the ultra-conservative feel, then your workspace should reflect that image and be conservative.

But the workplace should do more than just reflect — and help mold — the corporate culture. It should also encourage teamwork and interaction.

In this chapter, you discover what you need to know to create a workplace design that fits your company and your employees' work habits. I show you some advantages and disadvantages of cubicles, offices, and wide-open spaces so that you can determine what may work best for your company. In addition, I show you how important lighting is to employee morale.

If you're starting a company, moving to a new building, or simply contemplating how to reorganize your current office space, then this chapter is for you. Even if you're not making any of these changes, you can still find out ways to help your employees personalize their own workspace.

Why Design Matters

Studies show that workplace design makes a difference in your company's success. Your firm's physical environment even affects your ability to keep your current employees and attract new ones, according to a recent survey by the American Society of Interior Designers (ASID).

Not surprisingly, the survey found that employees want to work in a well-lit environment that has modern furniture and equipment. They want privacy, but they also want to be able to easily access their coworkers.

Granted, these things are easier to wish for than to create. Your company has financial constraints, after all. But the money you save by compromising comfort and creating an impersonal workspace may cost you in the long run. Are you really saving money if you hinder your employees' creativity, hamper their productivity, and diminish their happiness?

An effective workplace environment promotes collaborative learning and employee interaction on an everyday basis — not just during weekly brainstorming sessions or team meetings. Employees should feel comfortable popping over to a coworker's desk to get some input or advice. They should feel like they can access senior management easily when they need to. They can discuss projects when they pass each other in the hall or are in the printer area to pick up a report. And they know coworkers who are sitting ten feet away from them — something not all companies can boast.

In other words, the key component of a well-designed workspace is that employees are constantly able to gain knowledge from each other. If your company wants to encourage teamwork — and what successful company doesn't? — then your workplace design should encourage casual, everyday interaction whenever possible. One easy way to do so, for example, is to develop central work areas for shared printers and photocopiers and employee mailboxes.

In many large cities, businesses are converting homes that are in commercial zones into workspaces. The resulting office, unsurprisingly, has a homey feel. Firms in the creative fields have embraced the hip atmosphere of a converted warehouse or loft.

No matter what kind of building you choose for your workspace, it should have a simple, flexible, and functional design. It should also be accessible to disabled persons. If you're moving to new offices or starting a new company, consider getting input from key employees or work group leaders on the design. That way, you'll have their buy-in as you move into the new quarters.

Reflections on Cube Life

Depending on the type of work involved, cubicles have their pros and cons. If your employees have jobs that require intense concentration, individual offices make it easier to shut out distractions. If you have employees who are on the phone a lot because of their work, it's inevitable that their coworkers may at times be bothered by their conversations.

On the other hand, if your employees can tolerate the noise and distractions, cubicles give you a great opportunity to encourage teamwork. Employees can celebrate each other's successes and pop over for brainstorming sessions easier than if they're all squared away in separate offices. This type of collaboration is particularly valuable in a sales environment.

Even if you provide only cubicles for all of your employees, your workspace may inevitably convey some sort of hierarchy. Some people may have larger cubes than others; one person may be more centrally located or be in a more desirable location. Don't think that all office-envy will disappear with a doorless environment. The important thing is that your workspaces allow people to work productively, however that may translate for your company or department. If people feel as if they can do their best work — whether in an office or in a cube — they won't be as focused on what the person down the hall has that they don't have.

Let your employees — whether they work in a cubicle or in an office — individualize their surroundings. Within reason, allow pictures and other personal items. Not only will your workers feel more comfortable and more like they belong, but you'll be able to get to know them better — as will their coworkers. Having cubicles and offices that declare the personality of the inhabitants can increase camaraderie and, consequently, lead to more effective teamwork.

Before you let your employees go wild with the decor, lay down the ground rules for what is inappropriate. Obviously, anything that may result in sexual harassment concerns, such as inappropriate posters and calendars, doesn't belong in a workplace. Think about the overall image you want your company to convey. For example, if you're in financial services or the legal field, you may want your employees to project a highly professional image. On the other hand, if you're in a creative field, you'll probably want that creativity to shine through. Just be careful not to place more restrictions on individuals than you have to, as doing so can stifle creativity and even create resentment.

Full spectrum lighting — the closest thing to sunlight

Some companies have opted for full spectrum lighting, which simulates natural, outdoor light, and offers several benefits.

Full spectrum lighting can reduce fatigue and headaches and increase alertness. It also boosts crispness and clarity of colors and is thought to be easier on the eyes.

And Then There Was Light!

Lighting can play a part in your employees' productivity as well as in their mood. Several options exist that offer sufficient illumination for particular areas, tasks, and individual needs. Consulting a workplace designer or a lighting specialist to determine what's best for your firm is a good idea. Even if you're not moving to a new workspace, you may want to take the time to reevaluate your current lighting system to ensure that it meets your needs. In most states, fluorescent lighting is the norm for commercial workspaces, but other options are available. Not only does a well-thought-out lighting system provide ergonomic benefits because your employees aren't craning their necks to avoid glare, it also offers energy efficiency that can lead to bottom-line savings. In addition, lighting is known to have an affect on Seasonal Affective Disorder (SAD), a temporarily depressed condition related to the shorter periods of daylight during the winter months.

Obviously, pleasing all employees with a single lighting source can be difficult. Nonetheless, you have to make a prudent business decision that best serves your company's needs. To give employees more freedom in their choices, allow each employee a lighting source he can control, such as a small desktop lamp.

Place computer monitors perpendicular to the light source to avoid glare.

Offices versus Openness

Ever wonder why office buildings are called office buildings? Probably because they're made up of offices, right? But the phrase may be a misnomer today, because more and more companies are choosing to eliminate offices and opt for wide-open spaces complemented by employee lounges. If you're not sure which one works for your company, take a look at the following two sections.

Accommodating night workers

If you have employees who work night shifts, pay special attention to their lighting for improved productivity, safety, and morale.

There is actually computer software available to calculate optimal lighting — to improve alertness and performance while on the job — for each employee's work area. (Remember, it's dark outside, so your night employees are fighting their natural body rhythms, which makes optimal lighting even more important.) Amazing! According to research by Dr. Charles Czeisler, Associate Professor, Harvard Medical School and Director of the Laboratory for Sleep Disorders and Circadian Medicine at The Brigham and Women's Hospital in Boston, precisely timed exposure to certain intensities of light can rewire the body's signals for sleep and wakefulness. That way, employees can have daytime performance during the night! For more information on this type of lighting, see the Web site of ShiftWork Systems, Inc., at members.tripod.com/Shiftwork/index.html.

Where's my rolling cart?

To encourage teamwork and a creative environment, while at the same time limiting real estate costs, some companies are doing away with traditional offices and are opting instead for one large work area. In this setup, there are no walls.

Even more radically, employees in some of these companies no longer have desks. Instead, they have rolling carts that they move to a different work area every day to inspire creativity and innovation. In fact, many managers insist that creative types do their best work in nontraditional settings — such as an office comprised of rolling carts.

These wide-open workspaces are complemented by staff lounges and sofas to encourage employees to talk with one another. The goal is to encourage individuals to interact more frequently and become more involved in joint projects.

Although you may be concerned about noise, proponents of this layout insist that it isn't a problem. And although you don't have a desk to call your own, you gain the flexibility of rolling your chair over to a coworker and instantly working together.

Another benefit is that top managers are in the trenches working with employees. Most of the time, they don't have their own offices. They are completely accessible to their coworkers.

Check out these sites

If you're planning to redesign your workspace, you may want to check out the Web sites of a couple of industry leaders:

✔ Steelcase (www.steelcase.com). Founded in Grand Rapids, Michigan, in 1912, Steelcase aims to create high-performance work environments through a product portfolio encompassing seating and storage products, furniture systems, interior architectural products, technology products, and related products and services.

✔ Herman Miller (hermanmiller.com). The company has won awards for its innovative interior furnishings that are popular in the business world. When you visit the site, make sure that you sign up for the free biweekly newsletter, *DesignLink*.

✔ Haworth, Inc. (haworth.com). Founded in 1948 and based in Michigan, this leading designer of office furniture boasts more than 150 patents worldwide and focuses on research and development. This company has also won multiple awards.

✔ Knoll, Inc. (www.knoll.com). The company makes creative products for office and residential use, and has received numerous design awards since its founding in 1938. In fact, some of its products can be found on display in major art museums around the world.

Where's my office?

Not everyone is comfortable tearing down the walls. And a traditional office setting is appropriate to many businesses. You can modify and maximize a traditional office setting by creating small, private offices that open onto shared areas where meetings occur.

Obviously, individual offices have their perks, or they wouldn't be so common today. Employees can close the door when they need privacy to concentrate or have to make a phone call.

Where do we meet?

Whether you have an open floor plan or a layout made up of cubicles, you need conference rooms as well as informal meeting areas — sometimes referred to as *flop, touch down, chill out,* or *decompression* spaces. Informal meeting spaces encourage your employees to get involved in impromptu discussions, and not just scheduled meetings.

Chapter 6

Showing You Care: Balancing Work/Life Issues

*Y*our employees spend about eight hours a day at work — but what about the remaining 16 hours? They have families. They're involved with community groups and enjoy getting together with friends. And, of course, everyone needs time for eating and sleeping. The point is that there's more to your employees than what they do during their office hours: They have personal goals, hobbies and interests, commitments, and long-range plans. And they're probably looking for better ways to balance their home and office priorities.

As their manager, you can offer your staff members the flexibility they need without necessarily sacrificing productivity — in fact, the result may be just the opposite. In this chapter, I explore how you can help employees achieve a better work/life balance and how your company can benefit. You also discover ways to put together a work/life benefits package.

Exploring the Trend

In the past, work was work and your personal life was your personal life. Companies didn't take much notice of what employees were doing outside the office as long as they were getting the job done.

But all this has changed — and for the better. Companies today realize that balancing family and work responsibilities is difficult for a lot of people. Some managers offer flextime, so that staff members can attend their child's soccer games and school plays. Other employers may offer *telecommuting,* allowing employees to work from home.

The numbers behind the work/life balance trend

If you're a numbers person, you're in luck! The following statistics can help clue you in to why so many companies today are paying special attention to the personal needs of their employees:

✔ Almost 65 percent of today's workforce consists of two-paycheck families.

✔ In 1999, nearly 28 percent of American children lived in single-parent households (U.S. Census Bureau).

✔ More than 90 percent of major U.S. employers offer some form of childcare assistance (Hewitt Associates LLC).

✔ More than 70 percent of women with children under age 18 work (U.S. Department of Labor).

In a nationwide survey of 1,400 chief financial officers by RHI Management Resources, nearly two-thirds of the respondents said that the number of companies instituting work/life benefits has increased compared to five years ago.

Work/life benefits can attract — and retain — top talent. Arrangements that enable employees to more easily meet work and personal obligations have become a strong selling point and powerful recruiting tool for businesses today. According to a major OfficeTeam research study, Office of the Future 2005, balancing family and work demands is one of an employee's chief concerns.

Recognizing Work/Life Issues

Work/life balance isn't something that just happens. It's something that you have to work at and, as a manager, encourage your staff to pursue. But first, you need to be able to identify the signs of work/life *imbalance* within your company or department:

✔ Your company (or you, as a manager) conducts business as if work takes precedence over everything else in your employees' lives.

✔ Working long hours is a badge of honor.

✔ Employees routinely miss family commitments because of work.

✔ Staff members are reprimanded for responding to circumstances outside their control — for example, a sick child.

✔ People feel guilty if they leave the office without a briefcase full of work.

As a manager, you set the tone for your department; you lead by example. If you act as if you have no life outside of work, your employees will think that's how they need to act to get ahead. But if you show them you respect their personal lives — by respecting your own and accommodating them when they have a family emergency — then you're fostering work/life balance.

Occasional overtime is okay as long as that's what it is: occasional. But when it becomes routine, you risk losing good employees to burnout and job stress.

Considering Alternative Work Arrangements

You're probably familiar with the phrase "working nine to five." That phrase is losing currency in today's world because some companies no longer require employees to be in the office during traditional hours.

Instead, these employers are offering staff members hours that best fit their responsibilities. Employees may be required to be in the office only during core hours, such as 10 a.m. to 2 p.m. Or they may be able to work from home, work flexible hours, such as a 5 a.m. to 2 p.m. or 10 a.m. to 7 p.m., or even participate in *job sharing,* where two part-time employees share one full-time position within the company.

Why the change? Several trends are responsible for this shift:

- ✔ More and more families have both parents working or are single-parent families.
- ✔ Traffic congestion in major metro areas is lengthening commute times.
- ✔ Employees are realizing that they're missing out on family time.
- ✔ Technological advances, such as voicemail and e-mail, allow employees to be reached around the clock — and they can reach others as well.

Alternative work arrangements are not only a good recruitment tool, but they help you retain employees as well.

Alternative work arrangements describes any working schedule that deviates from the 9-to-5, 40-hour-a-week pattern. For the purposes of this book, it doesn't include independent working options, such as consulting or project-based work.

The following sections provide insight into how, when appropriate, you can benefit from considering common alternative work arrangements, such as part-time regular employment, job sharing, flextime, and telecommuting. If your company isn't offering these choices, find out which ones could meet the needs of your business and your employees.

More alternative work arrangement options

The four alternative work arrangements outlined in this chapter aren't your only choices. Although the following programs are less common, some firms are experimenting with them:

✔ **Phased retirement** programs gradually reduce work hours and responsibilities. This option may complement your firm's mentoring program because you're able to keep long-term employees who can serve as mentors to less-experienced staff.

✔ **Part-time retirement** allows full-time workers nearing retirement to become part-time.

They may possibly receive partial retirement income. If you're having trouble hiring good workers, this option can help ease the struggle of losing seasoned workers while you find and train replacements.

✔ **Voluntary reduced work or work-sharing programs:** In this arrangement, full-time employees of any age cut back on hours and compensation for a set period of time. With this program, you avoid layoffs, yet keep all of your staff, when you're experiencing a short-term diminished workload.

The benefits of alternative arrangements

Even in the best of hiring environments (from an employer's perspective), companies have difficulty finding top-notch employees to perform the jobs they need done. And when they do find those individuals, retention is always an issue. Unhappy employees don't hesitate to search for greener pastures — and it's usually your best employees who leave first.

Attracting and retaining workers is the motivation behind creating scheduling policies that accommodate the employee without inconveniencing the employer. Your company can benefit from increased loyalty, and your employees are motivated to do their best work for a firm that hears their concerns.

Part-time regular employment

Part-time employees work reduced hours, typically about 20 to 30 hours a week. They may or may not receive benefits, depending on the company's policy and the number of hours they work. Schedules vary according to the needs of the staff member and employer. A part-time employee in an information services department may work three eight-hour days, while a colleague in the human resources department may work five mornings per week.

Incorporating part-time employees into your staff allows you to accommodate good workers who may not be able to — or want to — work full-time. Part-time work is a popular option among employees who are

- Pursuing advanced degrees
- Looking to supplement their income
- Starting a family
- Caring for a parent
- Balancing two careers, such as a person who is both an artist and software engineer

Part-time employees value their work just as much as full-time employees. But they may have other priorities and may not need a full-time salary. And, after all, isn't a reliable, productive part-time employee better than a full-time staff member who's unproductive and unmotivated?

Job sharing

Job sharing is an interesting trend that has developed in recent years. With this arrangement, two part-time employees share the same full-time position's duties and responsibilities. Instead of having one manager who works 40 hours a week, you may have two managers who each work 20 hours. Each person is responsible for 50 percent of the responsibilities; how they divide up the assignments is up to them and their supervisor. One person may have stronger people skills and enjoy making calls and leading teams, while the other person has a gift for developing long-term strategies and writing reports.

Obviously, communication is key when you manage a position that's shared. Your employees must update each other on their progress and any potential snafus for job-sharing to be a successful arrangement. (You may want to schedule a half-hour of overlap everyday just for this discussion.) In addition, you need to be in the loop more often to ensure nothing falls through the cracks. You also should meet occasionally with each employee to make sure that no issues have come up, such as one person feeling like he or she is being left to do all the work. If necessary, you can then schedule a meeting with both employees at the same time to come up with solutions.

Flextime

Flextime sounds like just what it is — flexible scheduling of employees' work hours. In this arrangement, staff members work predetermined shifts that don't correspond with the typical workday. For example, if your office hours are 8:30 a.m. to 5:30 p.m., employees on flextime may work 7 a.m. to 4 p.m. or perhaps 9 a.m. to 6 p.m.

Another variation of flextime is the so-called *compressed workweek*. Instead of five eight-hour days, designated employees work four ten-hour days, resulting in one less day in the office per week.

Telecommuting

Believe it or not, some employees can have a work life outside of the office. Yes, a *work* life. Staff members who *telecommute* work offsite for a given period of time, typically a few days a week. Full-time workers still work full-time hours and perform the same job; they just spend part of the time working out of their home or from another location. Telecommuting may be an option you offer staff members on an as-needed basis.

If you're working in an environment that thrives on last-minute meetings and impromptu brainstorming sessions, telecommuting probably won't be able to replace the benefits of day-to-day interaction.

For more on telecommuting, see Chapter 17.

Weighing the Options

If you've decided that alternative work arrangements are just what your employees need to help balance their work/life priorities, great. But slow down: You've got to carefully weigh the pros and cons of the situation and then prepare your entire staff for the transition.

The following exercise lets you evaluate the impact of alternative work arrangements on each employee who may be affected:

1. **Get a sheet of paper and divide it into three columns.**

2. **In the left column, list the various functions and tasks your employee now performs in his or her job.**

3. **In the middle column, describe how each task is handled currently.**

   Think about what equipment is necessary — a high-speed copier, for example — and how many people need to be consulted on a regular basis.

4. **In the last column, describe how things would be handled under the new arrangement.**

If you uncover potential problems, consider brainstorming solutions with the employee who would be affected. If you can't come up with creative ways to overcome the hurdles, you may want to consider other arrangements.

Looking for management buy-in

You may have concluded that alternative work arrangements make good sense for some of your staff, but what does senior-level management think? Do you have sole authority to make these decisions or do you need their buy-in? Most likely, the latter.

The first thing you need to do is build a solid business case. Focus on how your department will benefit from such a change. Be sure to research the situation. Do competitors offer similar work arrangements to their employees? Are you losing employees because they can't cope with the commute? Will your proposal measurably reduce turnover or increase productivity? How?

Make sure that you tie in all benefits to the company's strategic goals.

Presenting your proposal in writing helps. That way, you show them that you've taken the time to think about the impact alternative arrangements will have on your department and its productivity. And, when a proposal is written down, it always seems to be more serious and thus garners more serious consideration.

Consider implementing a trial period to see how the transition goes. But make sure that you give yourself enough time during the trial period, so that you have a fair chance to work out any kinks.

How will it affect the employee's work performance?

Any change to basic working patterns is likely to affect an employee's job performance — especially at first. So the key question is not *whether* your staff member's job performance will be influenced by the new arrangement, but *how*. After you answer that question, you need to figure out how to prepare for and prevent any difficulties that may arise.

Don't embrace change for change's sake; be sure you're aware of any potential pitfalls and be prepared to deal with them.

How will this change affect the team's productivity?

To what extent the new work arrangement will affect the team's performance depends largely on the responsibilities of the position under consideration.

Jobs that are more independent present less issues, of course, than jobs that are more people-oriented, such as management or customer service roles. For example, if a position requires regular interaction with staff, then the employee filling that position may need to be in the office several days a week for meetings and face to face communication. If these office-days are not something the employee can arrange, the proposed working arrangement may not be a fit with the position.

How will it affect you as a manager?

Even if your hours or work situation aren't affected by any new work arrangements, don't think that you don't need to be prepared. In fact, as a manager, you need to be the most prepared of anyone for any new work arrangements. You need to be more aware of deadlines and communicate more than you would with a traditional employee.

You also need to make sure that you keep your employees in the loop, especially those who work outside the office. You may need to write longer e-mails or make more phone calls.

Ready, set, transition!

Few initiatives are an overnight success, and alternative work arrangements are no exception. Make sure that you give your new plan time to succeed — at least two to three months. Be ready to invest time upfront the first month to ensure success.

During those first few weeks, be on the lookout for potential challenges and address them right away. Some problems may not be obvious, such as slightly reduced quality of work or somewhat-reduced productivity. Get to the root of those problems. Perhaps the employee just needs time to adapt to a new schedule — or perhaps the new arrangement isn't suited to the position or the individual.

Of course, even if the trial period goes well, you still need to periodically check in with your staff to make sure that the arrangement is working over the long term.

Work/Life Benefits: Selecting the Right Options

If you're a manager of a small company or the owner of a small business, you can play an integral role in deciding which work/life benefits meet the needs of your employees and business. And if you're a middle manager in a large company with no direct decision-making power when it comes to these benefits, you can still play a role by discussing these options with your manager or human resources department.

If your firm isn't able to implement alternative work arrangements, you still have other options that can help your employees attain work/life balance. Many companies provide work/life benefits that are in addition to health and life policies. You may choose family-friendly options, such as onsite childcare facilities, dependent care reimbursement accounts, or adoption assistance programs. Or you may consider other benefits that appeal to all employees.

Health and life benefits are standard items. If you want your benefit package to be enticing, consider offering additional benefits.

Choosing the right work/life benefits for your company is a lot like creating a recipe. You have to make sure that the elements work well together and enhance each other. And you have a lot of options to choose from! The following sections outline some of the more popular work/life benefits, other than alternative work arrangements.

Some companies now refer to work/life balance as *integration,* in order to show that work and personal lives are one.

Adoption assistance

Companies realize that many of their employees are starting or expanding their families, sometimes through adoption. Whether adopting a newborn, toddler, or teenager, parents may incur significant expenses and need to devote a lot of time to the process.

In addition to helping pay the costs of adopting, some companies offer time off. According to benefits consultant Hewitt Associations, 31 percent of major U.S. companies offered adoption benefits in 1999. It cites the average financial assistance as $3,000 per adoption.

After-school and holiday care

You may already know about 3-o'clock syndrome: That's the time parents start calling home to check on their children who may be home alone. To help employees feel more secure about their children's welfare, some firms provide after-school and holiday-care assistance for school-age children.

Bring Your Child to Work day

Some companies schedule annual Bring Your Child to Work days. Kids get to see where their parents spend so much time, and coworkers get to put a face with a name.

Catered meals

Whether they're par for the course or few and far between, catered meals can be a way to say thank-you. Perhaps you can arrange catered lunches whenever you schedule a lunchtime meeting. Or maybe you spring for free pizza every Friday for a month to thank employees for a particularly successful quarter.

Celebrations

Don't overlook opportunities to celebrate. They're a great chance to spontaneously pump up your staff after a major success or deadline. And they're a huge selling point when you're recruiting. For more on rewarding and recognizing your staff, see Chapter 14.

Childcare centers and family daycare

Some companies offer onsite daycare for their employees' children. Not only are staff members able to spend more time with their children, but they spend less time commuting to and from an outside daycare provider.

Employers benefit as well, through improved retention, higher morale, increased productivity, and reduced absenteeism and tardiness. They also have a valuable recruitment tool.

Numerous legal complications come with this option. Before proposing this arrangement, be sure to check with an attorney familiar with daycare regulations and requirements.

Company events for families

When you think of company events that include significant others, probably the first thing that comes to mind is the annual holiday party. But if you want to try something less formal, consider a company picnic on office grounds or at a local park. Employees can get to know each other's families and get a new view of coworkers outside of the office.

Concierge service

Sometimes the little things make a huge difference. That's one reason offering a concierge service to help your employees conduct their day-to-day lives can be a morale booster. Here are some options for concierge services that can help relieve some of life's little stressors:

- Dry cleaning pick-up or delivery
- Banking services
- Travel services
- Gift shop
- Laundry service

Eldercare

More and more employees today are finding themselves responsible for the care of aging relatives. To be more sensitive to employees' needs, some firms offer such programs as dependent-care reimbursement accounts, which can be used by employees to set aside money for either childcare or eldercare needs.

Employee assistance programs (EAPs)

There's no question that what's going on in employees' personal lives affects their on-the-job performance, and vice-versa. Perhaps that's why nearly a third of all employers offer *employee assistance programs* (EAP) staffed by psychologists, social workers, counselors, and support staff.

These programs help employees deal with a variety of personal issues:

- Stress management and conflict resolution
- Social, psychological, and family counseling
- Alcohol and substance abuse problems
- Mental health screening and referral
- Gambling addiction and other compulsive behaviors
- Marriage counseling
- Financial issues and credit counseling
- Referral to legal services
- Pre-retirement planning

Financial planning education

Finances are one of your employees' biggest stressors. One way to improve morale is to help them manage this stress. A number of companies are rising to the occasion by offering access to education (not advice) about financial products and retirement plans. Consider sponsoring onsite workshops and seminars.

Fitness facilities or health club memberships

Here's an easy way to save money: Offer fitness facilities or health club memberships to employees. According to Dr. Roy J. Shephard in the online medical journal *The Physician and Sportsmedicine Online*, employers that invest in worksite wellness programs can see reduced absenteeism and employee turnover, and a projected savings of $100 to $400 per worker per year in medical expenditures. That money adds up when you think about the big health problems that may be prevented down the road.

Leave time

Leave time authorizes an employee to take a specified amount of time off work. Leave time is often granted due to family reasons — such as the birth of a child or the care of a parent — but you can also use leave time to grant your employees sabbaticals (paid or unpaid).

Sabbaticals are no longer a perk enjoyed only by college professors. The corporate world has gotten involved because it realizes that the benefits can far outweigh the costs.

Of course, giving employees time off does cost companies money. But sabbaticals can prevent burnout, alleviate stress, and pump up your employees so that they stay motivated.

Nap rooms

Snoozing on the job isn't always a bad thing — as long as you're in the right place at the right time.

People aren't getting enough sleep, and it's taking its toll on corporate America. According to a 1997 survey by the National Sleep Foundation, lack of sleep costs employers about $18 billion a year in lost productivity.

Brief — 15 to 20 minutes — naps can energize employees, leaving them more alert and productive. That's why some companies are creating nap rooms, where employees can catch a few z's to reenergize.

Onsite cafeterias and coffee bars

Don't have time for lunch? Sure you do. Thanks to onsite cafeterias and coffee bars, employees are able to take breaks to grab something to eat, even if it's only to take back to their desks. Again, it's the little things that make a difference.

Tuition reimbursement

Tuition reimbursements are a popular training option and a great recruitment and retention tool. Providing your employees with educational choices that make their work more satisfying enhances job performance. In addition, tuition assistance programs demonstrate your commitment to your employees' professional growth. Some companies offer employees up to $5,000 annually.

Part III

Fostering Open Communication

The 5th Wave   By Rich Tennant

"Okay — tha Interoffice Creative Expression Seminar is ready for the next group."

In this part . . .

Communication is about more than talking to your employees. It's about listening to them. In this part, you examine the different aspects of communication and find out how you can maximize their effectiveness. You learn how, as a manager, you can be a better listener and encourage creativity. And you also discover how the company's overall communication strategy can make or break your team.

Chapter 7

Communicating: It's More Than Mere Words

*E*ffective communication is a key to success in almost everything you do — personally and professionally. You need to be able to say what you mean and say it in such a way that others see your point and aren't offended. Whether you're meeting one-on-one, providing feedback, or conducting a brainstorming session, your message needs to be clear, concise, and convincing.

But communication is a two-way street. It's not just one person saying this is how it works, this is what is going to happen, and so on. Your employees need to feel that they can communicate with you and that they can give you feedback and suggestions that you'll really listen to. Of course, you don't want them to complain constantly, but you do want them to feel that they can come to you with their concerns and ideas and not face ramifications or be ignored.

This chapter examines ways to maximize your communication skills. You find out about a secret weapon that most people overlook — your *listening* skills. You also discover how to deliver your intended message successfully and, most importantly, how to inspire your employees to communicate actively with you.

Listen First

You may be the most eloquent person on Earth, but if you're not listening to those around you, you aren't a great communicator. Instead, you're simply delivering an ongoing monologue. And people will listen to you for only so long if you're not listening to them.

You know what it feels like when people aren't listening. They yawn and look around the room for something interesting. They fidget in their seats. They cross their arms. They lean away from you. And you may even hear an occasional sigh, as if they're saying, "Get on with it now."

 Don't treat your employees that way. If they feel you're not listening, they won't come to you with feedback, suggestions, or even status reports. Employees are a company's most valuable asset. They're in the trenches every day, and you need their input to best serve your customers or clients.

After all, when you know someone is really listening to you and is interested in what you're saying, don't you feel important? Someone cares about you — your thoughts, your experiences, your opinions. You want your employees to feel good every time they leave your office — even if you're delivering not-so-positive feedback. (See the section "Criticizing with Care," later in this chapter.)

A good listener:

- ✔ **Focuses on you, and you alone.** He or she doesn't check e-mail while you're talking, answer a phone call, encourage unexpected visitors, or fumble through paperwork while you talk. You are the center of his or her attention.

- ✔ **Doesn't interrupt you.** He or she doesn't finish your sentences for you, even if you're having trouble finding the right words. He or she also doesn't change the subject during the conversation.

- ✔ **Has a good rapport and trusts you.** Even if you don't see eye to eye, a good listener encourages you to share your thoughts. You know that he or she won't judge what you're saying; the person will listen and then offer advice only if asked.

- ✔ **Doesn't prejudge what the person is saying.** Good listeners think about where the other person is coming from and try to understand that person's perspective — even if it's different from their own opinion.

Good listening skills help you identify with your employees. You can find out a lot about people if you just listen to them — their career goals, what they think needs to be improved with the company, or stressors in their lives that are affecting their job performances. As a result, listening is often a prerequisite to keeping your employees happy.

Listen to me, please!

Listening is a lost art. With the invention of television — and especially talk shows — people are used to fast-paced conversations full of interruptions. Think about it. Don't you do multiple tasks if someone is dragging out a conversation that you're not particularly interested in? And how often have you received an incorrect order at a restaurant or had to repeat instructions several times?

If you listen well and pay attention to your employees, you may be able to head off departures of valuable employees.

Even if you're not naturally a good listener, you can become one. Listening isn't a talent that you're born with, it's one that you develop.

If you know you want to be a good listener, you're already halfway to improving your listening skills. Here's how to go the rest of the way:

- **Don't be distracted.** No matter where you are, focus on the person you're talking to. Even if you have half a dozen things on your mind — including a report that you have to prepare within an hour — don't think about them. If you allow yourself to be distracted, you may miss an important point and end up spending more time solving a resulting problem than if you'd simply listened carefully from the start.

  Perhaps you half-listened to a coworker bounce an idea off of you for the direction of a project. And when the project was completed, you realized that you never wanted it to go in that direction at all — only it's too late to revise the choice before the project is due to *your* boss! If you had given your employee your full attention, you could have avoided the problem.

  Most people know when you've stopped listening to them.

- **Don't interrupt.** This is a hard one, especially if you're impatient. Don't complete someone else's sentences, and don't jump in the minute he or she takes a first breath. The speaker should feel like she can pause without losing the floor.

- **Give feedback.** I'm talking about nonverbal feedback that shows the person you're listening. Nod your head at appropriate times. Say something here and there. Have an animated expression. Make eye contact. There's nothing more exasperating than talking to a brick wall or baring your soul and not getting a response.

✓ **Don't assume.** You may think that you know what someone is about to say — but there's a good chance you don't. Keep an open mind and don't try to second-guess. If you don't understand what the person is saying, ask questions or paraphrase what you heard and ask for clarification.

✓ **Think before you respond.** Don't jump in the minute the person stops talking. Really think about what she said (no, you shouldn't have been preparing your answer while she was talking!) and choose your words carefully.

Even if you're listening to someone over the phone — and they can't see you — don't check your e-mail or clean out your drawers in your desk.

Nonverbal clues to an upcoming goodbye

Obviously, if someone tells you they're unhappy, they're unhappy. That's why complaining is one clue that someone may leave the company! But you should be alert to other signs as well. If your employees used to complain and have suddenly stopped, don't fall into the comforting belief that they've acquired a new perspective. Instead, these former squeaky wheels have probably given up on the company and are planning their departure.

But not all clues to unhappiness in the workplace come verbally. In fact, almost 90 percent of the communication that takes place today is nonverbal. And if you're attuned to your employees and their needs, then you probably won't be taken by surprise when they give notice to move on to greener pastures.

Say, for example, that one of your employees, John, starts taking on projects outside of his main job duties — without first discussing these with you. That may be a sign that he's bored and is preparing himself for a new job.

Or say that Anne-Marie loved her job and was always seeking exciting projects. Suddenly, she has stopped volunteering. You may have a problem here as well.

Here are some other nonverbal signs that may indicate an impending departure:

✓ An employee suddenly stops participating in team meetings and doesn't interact with other employees any more. He may also stop participating in work-related social activities.

✓ An employee's productivity suddenly decreases.

✓ An employee changes his or her usual work hours, starts to dress up more, and takes long lunches. (Job interviews!)

✓ A staff member mentions salaries at other companies. She has probably been doing a little research.

Actions Speak Louder Than Words

Not communicating with your employees because you think you don't have the time will cost you time in the long run — not to mention money and stress. If you're not meeting with your employees on a regular basis to find out what's happening, then you'll not only have errors and missed deadlines, but poor morale and job performance as well.

On the positive side, communicating well with your employees helps relieve stress — both yours and theirs. For example, say that your employee has heard rumors of a possible merger and you know the idea has been discussed and discarded. Your employee could sit and stew about something that's not going to happen. But if he feels comfortable with you, he'll come to you to discuss his concerns.

You have to let your employees know you're available and that you want to talk to them — and you should *want* to talk to them.

Take the time upfront to find out what's going on in your employees' work lives. You save time in the long run, and you don't have to react to crises after the fact. Being proactive is always better than being reactive.

If you communicate well, you should be able to fire up your employees about your common goal. (Don't have a common goal? You need one — see Chapter 2.) Everyone wants to know why they're doing something and how their tasks affect the big picture. And it's exciting to see things come together around an agreed-upon objective. If things are going well, say so and cheer on your staff.

Communication doesn't have to be formal, either. In fact, day-to-day communication on an informal basis works best. You want your employees to feel they can contact you any time or at least schedule a meeting (see the next section) to discuss their concerns.

You may be surprised, but how well you organize your time plays a part in effective communication. When you're organized, you tend to think through things by defining your goal and planning what you want to say.

Poor communication wastes time

Executives believe that 14 percent of each 40-hour work week — a stunning seven weeks a year — is wasted due to poor communication between staff and managers, according to a nationwide survey developed by OfficeTeam. The survey included responses from 150 executives with the nation's 1,000 largest companies.

What about e-mail?

E-mail is great. It's quick, eliminates phone tag, and gives you a document trail. But the problem is that it replaces personal contact. Whenever you can, meet face to face to avoid miscommunication.

Phone calls, e-mail, and the company newsletter shouldn't be a substitute for lunches or company-wide meetings. Remember, alternative means of communication should enhance face to face communication, not replace it.

When you do rely on e-mail, remember that your recipients cannot see your face or hear your voice, so they have no idea whether you're joking or not. You'll want to make sure that you avoid sarcasm. Here are some other tips to keep in mind:

✔ Use the subject line. The subject line can help recipients prioritize their e-mails and keep track of important messages. Type a short summary of your message in the subject line. For example, if you're sending your employee some important data for the report he's working on, you might try typing "Important report data" on the subject line.

✔ Watch the Caps Lock. Whatever you do, don't use all caps in an e-mail. It implies that you're shouting at the person.

✔ Write as if the whole world is reading your message. Don't put anything in an e-mail message that you wouldn't want anyone else to see. Your message may be forwarded to many people without your knowledge.

✔ Think before you write. The nice thing about e-mail is that it's quick. The bad thing? You can send a fiery retort before you have time to cool off. Make sure that you stay away from a *flame war* (an exchange of angry messages).

✔ Don't forward chain letters. Nothing is more annoying than getting a series of chain letters via e-mail.

If you've been using e-mail for any length of time at all, you've probably seen an emoticon, which is a picture of a face made by using punctuation. (Tilt your head to the left — see the face now?) Here's what some of those funny little faces mean:

:-)	Happy face
:-(	Sad face
:-o	Shocked face
;-)	Winking face

Here are some more e-mail abbreviations (remember not to use them unless you're sure the recipient will understand):

<g>	Grin
BTW	By the way
IMO	In my opinion
IMHO	In my humble opinion
TIA	Thanks in advance

Be flexible and available

As a manager, you need to be accessible to your employees. If your staff members can't contact you, you have a problem. If you don't think so, then just remember how you felt the last time you needed a quick question answered, but you couldn't reach the person, your repeated phone calls were ignored, or you waited forever for an e-mail response.

How hard is it to contact you?

You may think that your employees have no trouble reaching you. But is that really the case? How long did it take you to respond (or even receive) your last emergency phone call? How often are you in meetings? Do your voicemail and e-mail go unchecked for more than a few hours? Do you encourage your employees to stop by? Do you play phone tag a lot?

You'll help your staff members feel comfortable speaking with you if you have an *open-door policy,* which simply means that they are welcome to stop by your office anytime. And don't just say that you have this policy — mean it. When your staff comes by, help them as much as you can. If it's really not a good time, set up an appointment after you listen to what they need so that you can determine the urgency of the situation.

You're not the only person who's busy. Communicating with your staff helps ensure that things are done right the first time, that they learn from any mistakes, and that inappropriate behavior doesn't become a lingering crisis.

One way to ensure that you have the time to meet with your employees is to leave time for the unexpected. You need unscheduled time so that you're available for sudden meetings or putting out fires. If you're a manager, allot at least 20 percent of your day to deal with unscheduled needs.

After you schedule a meeting with an employee, make sure that you keep the appointment. Rescheduling tells your employees that something else is more important than they are. And no-shows destroy morale. If you encounter an emergency, that's okay, but it should be the exception, not the rule. And you should always call, at the very least, to explain why you can't make it. People need to be able to count on you.

Know how you're coming across

Saying what you mean and knowing how you come across when you say it play crucial roles in effective communication.

I know of one person who knew exactly what she wanted to say to an employee, but didn't think about the words she'd used to introduce her ideas. The employee left offended, and the person was left wondering what went wrong. Don't make that mistake.

Here are some tips for presenting what you want to say — whether it's good, bad, or ugly:

✔ **Choose your words carefully.** Select words that say what you really mean. If you mean that the employee must shape up immediately or he's gone, don't say, "We have a small problem I'd like you to correct." Instead, say, "Some lingering concerns are still affecting your performance, and we need to rectify them immediately." (Of course, this shouldn't be the first time your employee is hearing these concerns, if he's at risk of being terminated.)

✔ **Know how you sound.** Are you talking too fast? Too high? Don't let emotions override your message. You want to sound authoritative. If you appear overly emotional, your employee will pay attention to that instead of your message.

✔ **Be specific.** If you want something done, such as a weekly status report, don't try to ask without asking. Tell your employee what you want, what you'd like to see, and how you think it will help. If you're not clear in your expectations, it's not your employee's fault if he misunderstands.

Effective communicators, in addition to listening, recognize other people's viewpoints and respect their opinions, even when they disagree. They clarify anything they're unsure of and also pick up on nonverbal cues. They're assertive — without being aggressive — and offer feedback.

Demonstrate personal conviction

You need to care about your people, and you need to care that a job is done well. (If you don't, ask yourself why and check out Chapter 2 to find out how to motivate yourself.) But it takes more than caring to be able to communicate effectively; you need to *show* you care.

No one likes to be around moody people — their responses are unpredictable. If people are wary of you, you need to ask yourself why. Throwing a temper tantrum, yelling, overreacting, panicking, and grousing don't exactly inspire faith in your professionalism or motivate people. Caring about a situation is great, but you gain more respect when you operate on an even keel.

Meet one-on-one and in groups

One manager I know schedules weekly one-on-one meetings with her employees, as well as a weekly team meeting. At the one-on-one meetings, employees have the opportunity to talk about anything work-related — concerns about a project, ideas they have, or training and development issues. Staff members know they have guaranteed face time with the boss in case they have a question about performance appraisals, a new procedure, or time management. The manager also encourages employees to stop by on an informal basis.

Deciphering body language

Have you ever walked away from a situation and said to yourself, "I just don't trust him," but you can't put your finger on why? It's usually because you've picked up on some body language that made you uncomfortable.

What you do is sometimes more meaningful than what you say. Your body language — your eyes, posture, gestures, and overall demeanor — and that of your employees can be quite revealing. Someone may say one thing, but a look in his eyes, a certain smile, or crossed arms may clue you in that what's being said isn't what's meant. For example, many people have a hard time lying when they look you in the eye. That's why eye contact builds trust; you come across as honest and confident.

You'll also want to watch out for signs of nervousness — lip biting, playing with hair, or other fidgeting, for example. Crossed arms may signify discomfort.

You should control your own body language by making sure you speak in an even tone, relax your body, and stand tall. When you look comfortable, your employee can focus on your message and not your emotional state. (For example, if you sound nervous, your employee may be thinking, "Why is she asking this way? Does she have bad news? What have I done?" instead of listening to what you're about to say.)

And in the team meetings, the team discusses only issues that affect everyone — a new procedure being implemented, or questions about an upcoming company event, for example.

If you want your staff to do well, these kinds of interactions are not only nice, but are necessary. (Of course, how often you meet depends on the type of work that's being done.) One-on-one meetings let your employees know that you care about them, and they can also brainstorm with you when faced with a challenge. And with team meetings, everyone gets the same information at once, so no miscommunication is engendered by hearing news secondhand.

Whether you're meeting one on one or as a group, you should keep an eye on the clock and plan your meeting. No one enjoys meetings that last forever, yet accomplish little — especially when they feel they already have too much on their plate.

When you schedule a group meeting, schedule an ending time and pass out an agenda.

Making Meetings Work for You

Ever been to a meeting where you just sit and wonder "Why are we having a meeting? I could've solved this in a 10-minute phone call instead of a 2 hour meeting!" Or maybe you're thinking "Why am I even here? I know nothing about this topic, and my input isn't necessary to implement the final project."

Don't have meetings just for the sake of meeting. Each gathering should have a specific purpose. You first need to establish that it's necessary to meet and that each attendee is really needed. So before you gather everyone together, make sure that you have a reason to meet — a goal — and decide who really needs to be present.

After your meeting begins, make sure that everyone has an opportunity to speak and that others listen and pay attention. (If you're a good role model, you're listening as well!)

You should leave a meeting feeling that something was actually accomplished and that the time spent was worthwhile.

Here are some tips for maximizing the effectiveness of your meetings:

- ✔ **Hold your meeting in a suitable place.** You want the room to be well lit and spacious, and you don't want your attendees to be crowded. An off-site meeting works well for brainstorming sessions.

- ✔ **Invite the smallest number of people possible.** You only want those in attendance who will be affected by the topics of discussion or who have insight, experience, or expertise on the subject. If you're afraid someone will be offended by not receiving an invitation, then let that person know the purpose of the meeting and let him or her decide whether or not to attend.

- ✔ **Prepare an agenda — and put it in writing.** Your agenda should outline what you'd like to cover at the meeting. Don't try to present too much information, though, or your attendees won't get as much out of the meeting. Also make sure that you cover the most important agenda items first so that you don't run out of time.

- ✔ **Be timely.** If the meeting is scheduled to start at 3 p.m., don't wait until 3:15. Otherwise, people will start arriving late to all of your meetings. (But if they're late to one meeting, they're less likely to be late to the next one if they missed the most important topic because of tardiness!) Likewise, end the meeting when you say you will. If you're not finished, schedule another meeting.

- ✔ **Make sure that everyone has his or her say.** Don't let one person dominate the meeting. Solicit input from quieter staffers, if necessary.

✔ **Stay focused.** If you come across a great, unrelated idea during the meeting, schedule another meeting to discuss it and then continue to stay on track with the agenda. But be sure to do this tactfully, especially if someone else proposed the new idea. Acknowledge the value of the topic and say that the issue is important enough to be put on the agenda for the next meeting, to give it adequate time for discussion.

✔ **Write it down.** You don't want all your important decisions to be forgotten. Someone needs to be responsible for writing things down and noting any action items. Then you can prepare minutes for those who weren't able to make the meeting, if necessary.

Criticizing with Care

Inevitably, no matter how stellar an employee's performance, you need to deliver less-than-favorable feedback at one time or another. I'm not talking about the kind of feedback that will go on a performance appraisal. I'm actually talking about the kind of criticism that should be ongoing and that *shouldn't be a surprise* when it appears on the performance appraisal.

When you offer criticism, remember to keep it strictly professional. Most people know when they've made a mistake, and you don't want to lower their confidence even more. Besides, a personal attack — "You are so inept!" — is rude, unprofessional, and accomplishes nothing.

Say, for example, that Mary is monopolizing your team meetings and criticizing the suggestions of others (when she even lets them speak!). You don't want to say:

> *Mary, you dominate the meetings and are rude and overbearing. You've got to let others speak.*

Instead, you can make your point without being offensive and offer suggestions for improvement at the same time. Start with something positive and make the feedback more performance-based — for example:

> *Mary, you always have a lot of great ideas at our meetings, and I can tell you've really researched the topic. But I've noticed that some of our other team members aren't speaking up as much, and I'd like to give them an opportunity to do so.*

And be sure to do this in private, not in the middle of the meeting itself.

Body language can cue you in on how the person is receiving your feedback. A drooping face, crossed arms, and slumped posture can be bad signs.

No sugar, please

Sugarcoating sounds like such a nice word. And it is. And that's the problem. When you sugarcoat something, you're not describing how things really are. You're making them sweeter than reality. And that's not good when you want someone to behave a certain way based on the message that you're trying to give him or her.

If you have negative feedback to give, don't sugarcoat the issue. Although you need to find a tactful way to express yourself, make sure that you don't dilute the problem.

And the same is true with your employees. If a problem is occurring — say that you run a sandwich eatery and you're out of bread because one of your employees did not plan ahead — you need to address the problem directly. Don't just say, "We had a small setback." (When sandwiches are your business, not having bread is a huge setback!) Instead, say, "We need to work on your planning skills because the bread crisis Tuesday shut us down for the afternoon and has had an adverse effect on our repeat clientele."

Here are some other things to keep in mind when you deliver criticism:

✓ **Focus on facts, not feelings.** Don't just say, "Tom, you're always late, and I'm tired of it." Say, "Tom, I'm concerned because of your tardiness lately. On the mornings of August 8, 11, and 17, you were an hour late."

✓ **Be specific.** Don't say, "I need you to shape up." Instead, say, "Starting tomorrow, I must have your weekly status report on time."

✓ **Be timely.** You want to be calm when you deliver feedback, but you don't want to wait for so long that the person has forgotten the incident and you're blindsiding him. Discuss a situation as soon as your emotions cool.

✓ **Be direct, but tactful.** Make sure that you use the words that you actually mean, instead of searching for a softer word that doesn't really make your point. For example, don't say, "Your lunch break is a little long" when you mean "I've noticed you're gone for four hours every afternoon." You need to make your point clear. Sugarcoating what you're trying to say may only make matters worse. But at the same time, you can use nice words — "I want to talk to you about an error on the Stanley project" versus "You totally blew the project" — to make your point.

✓ **Give feedback in private.** You don't need to embarrass someone with an audience. Take the person aside and speak with him or her one-on-one.

✓ **Consider any training opportunities.** Maybe Samantha missed her deadline, not because she procrastinated, but because she lacked the training to do the project efficiently. Don't forget to consider the person's skills. If you find them lacking, provide mentoring or training.

✔ **Know what you want to say.** You may even want to write down key points so that you don't forget anything or get sidetracked.

✔ **Listen to what they have to say.** After you've had your say, listen to the other side of the story. You may not be aware of some circumstances. Keep an open mind, listen, and be sure to communicate regularly.

Realize that everyone makes mistakes. How you handle those mistakes helps determine your relationship with your employees. Placing blame and pointing fingers is counterproductive. Yelling and screaming are unprofessional under any circumstances. Does it really matter who made the mistake? The *why* of a mistake matters most, and every mistake should be a learning opportunity for your staff.

Say, for example, that an employee didn't know she was supposed to send a review copy of an important press release to the company CEO who had expressed an interest in it. As a result, she mailed the release out as she usually does, and it turned out that it contained some inaccurate information that only the CEO would have been able to correct. At this point, it doesn't matter who made the mistake. If you or someone in your company asks questions like, "Did anyone tell her to send it to the CEO?" or "Who should have told her?" or "Shouldn't she have known?" then you may have a problem. Yes, you need to find out what went wrong so that you can ensure it doesn't happen again. But first resolve the issue, and then look for a way to prevent it from recurring. Pointing fingers without any desire to learn from the problem accomplishes nothing and only creates an environment of fear. You need to recognize mistakes for the learning opportunities that they are.

In fact, your goal should be simply to make sure that the mistake (or one like it) doesn't happen again. Find out how the mistake occurred and then take measures to ensure that the mistake isn't repeated. In the example I just used, a simple routing slip would have solved the problem.

In other situations, maybe the company's training is the problem. If that's the case, you have the opportunity to revamp the training program so that everyone will benefit.

No matter what the mistake, try to put yourself in the other person's shoes. What were they thinking at the time? Remember, you have more information than your employee does, and what may seem like an obvious bad decision — given the information that you have — may have been the best choice that a person with less information could have made.

One for All and All for One: Building a Consensus

For an organization to truly succeed, it needs to have a common goal that's frequently communicated. In fact, employees should be able to trace every decision an organization makes back to that common goal.

That's where consensus building comes in. When you build consensus, you're getting a group of diverse individuals to agree on an issue or solve a particular problem.

Consensus building does not mean stifling viewpoints, initiatives, or alternative solutions. Your team members may have very different feelings about an issue, but it is possible to get everyone's genuine support.

To build a consensus:

1. **Define your goal.**

   Are you trying to develop a new product? Are you designing a marketing campaign?

2. **Choose your players.**

   Who should be involved in the process? Identify the decision makers, but also consider inviting those who may be impacted by the goal.

3. **Set the ground rules.**

   Everyone should be able to express his or her opinion, unless it ventures into a personal attack. You also will probably want to establish that the final outcome needs to be consistent with the values of your company.

4. **Test the waters.**

   How far apart are the members' views and attitudes? If they're polar opposites, you need more time to reach a consensus. (Does this remind you of jury duty?)

   Silence is not agreement. Your goal is not passive acceptance.

5. **Discard invalid assumptions.**

   Find out why someone is opposed to, or in favor of, a position. That person may have an incorrect assumption, so ask questions to clarify viewpoints.

6. **Encourage reasoning.**

   You don't want people simply to disagree. Ask questions that lead people through logical steps of, "If this, then that."

Convince me

Once you have an action plan, you need to persuade senior management of its worth. Persuasion skills are a powerful asset, especially when your plan is innovative and out of the box.

Effective persuasion doesn't rely on tricks, ploys, or other deceptive practices to win people over. Persuasive people rely on fact-based arguments, delivered clearly and concisely, to call others to action.

If your powers of persuasion need a little work, try these tips:

✔ **Define your goal.** What are you trying to convince the other person to do?

✔ **Prepare your argument.** Don't forget to explain why a decision is in the best interest of the company.

✔ **Acknowledge people's concerns.** Think ahead to potential areas of disagreement and address these issues.

✔ **Remain focused, no matter how unconvinced they are.** Don't let people's reactions — or lack thereof — throw you off course.

✔ **Be honest.** Persuasion is built on trust. If you offer misleading information, you may initially win support for your proposal. But all your future attempts to sway will have a giant obstacle to overcome — a lack of trust.

7. **Keep emotions in check.**

    If emotions are running high, take a break and meet individually with the team members who are locking horns.

8. **Reach a consensus.**

    As a last resort, if your team truly cannot reach a consensus, go with the majority opinion.

Encouraging Employee Suggestions and Feedback

Employees are a company's richest resource. They work in the trenches every day, so they know what the problems are. If sales are flat on your most recent product launch, they probably know why. If a procedure is more cumbersome than helpful, they know that, too.

The challenge is getting that feedback from your employees. You want them to feel like they can come to you with good or bad news without ramification. You want them to know you listen and care.

Here's employee feedback at its best: A new manager at a nonprofit organization inherited some less-than-inspired employees. By just listening to her employees, she discovered that some of the department's processes were more than 50 years old. Customers were angry and the employees were taking the brunt of it. The manager acted on the employees' suggestions, and the employees were energized because they found out that something they thought would never change actually could change for the better.

Actively solicit suggestions. And then don't just stand there — act on them!

Seeking out suggestions

If you think getting suggestions is easier said than done, you may be right. Your employees must feel that you will listen to them — otherwise, why should they make the effort?

If you're short on suggestions, try these tips:

- ✔ Respect others ideas, no matter who the idea is from.
- ✔ Create a suggestion box.
- ✔ Conduct small focus-group meetings.
- ✔ Develop a written survey.
- ✔ Meet with employees to talk about work concerns.
- ✔ Never react poorly to something you didn't want to hear.
- ✔ Ask open-ended questions.
- ✔ Write about implemented suggestions in the company newsletter.

Asking open-ended questions

If you've ever encountered an employee who doesn't like to volunteer information, then you know how quickly a conversation can be cut short. Asking *open-ended questions* is the way to go if you want to get any real answers.

Open-ended questions are simply ones that require more than yes or no answers. For example, you might ask, "How did that project work for you — what were the successes in your opinion?" Closed-ended questions are ones such as "Do you agree?" or "Is that true?" Unless the employee wants to, he or she doesn't have to offer any additional information to answer these questions; a simple yes or no will suffice.

By asking open-ended questions, you can gather the information to help you avoid jumping to conclusions about what the other person does or doesn't think on a given subject. And you also present him or her with an opportunity to go beyond the question asked and fill in any other details he or she feels are relevant.

Fielding complaints

You want your employees to be able to come to you. But you certainly don't want them to give you a laundry list of what's wrong with the company and then expect you to solve all the problems.

Some of the "problems" on your employee's list may not be problems at all. But keep in mind that, for many employees, their perception is their reality. So if they see something as a problem, you may need to provide more information and explanation so that they can see the big picture.

When you receive complaints from an employee, the first thing you should do is listen. (See the section earlier in this chapter on listening.) If your employee is complaining about a cramped workspace, find out why. Does he want a new office, which may mean he craves additional recognition? Or is he bothered by the loud neighbor in the next workspace?

After you listen, you should also:

✔ **Make sure that the employee can see the big picture.** Maybe the employee doesn't understand why something has occurred because he doesn't have all the facts. As a manager, your role is to clarify the situation and put his concerns in context. You should acknowledge his concerns and then provide any additional information that you can.

✔ **Ask for suggestions or solutions.** One way to eliminate whine sessions is to turn them into brainstorming sessions. Don't discourage your employees from coming to you. Instead, encourage them to give you possible solutions. For example, if Alex thinks there's a problem with the company's dress code, ask him to research it and come up with suggestions to fix it. That way, employees will come to you only with problems that they care enough about to solve.

If you're dealing with a constant complainer, ask him or her to write down some ideas. If he really cares about his complaints and he's not just being petty, he'll take the time to write them out.

✔ **Provide parameters.** When you ask your employees to come up with suggestions or solutions, let them know about any restrictions you have. For example, if your staff person Alex is planning to research possible dress codes and develop a proposal, you may need to indicate that the recommendations need to be in line with other firms in your industry or fit within a particular definition of "professional." In other situations, you may need to indicate budget restrictions, work-flow constraints, and time limitations.

✔ **Try reasoning with the person.** If the suggestion isn't feasible, walk through your line of thinking. "You've said that your current workspace is too cramped and have suggested moving into the open office down the hall. Here's the difficulty: I'm in the process of trying to hire a senior manager for our xyz division, and I need to leave that office open for that individual. But here's what I can do for you . . ."

Look for compromises. Explaining your reasoning is important so that your employee knows that you truly considered her idea and want to help. Just think how you'd feel if you proposed an idea to your supervisor and only received a yes or no response.

✔ **Solicit feedback regularly.** Hold a monthly or weekly meeting where you're available to address any concerns. If something big comes up, consider holding a brainstorming session.

When you clash with an employee

Maybe you think Clara is a real complainer. She's negative and bossy, and even more, you just don't like her style. Personality clashes at the workplace are a common problem. The good news is that, in many circumstances, they can be overcome.

If you have a pattern of personality conflicts with your employees or bosses, you need to ask yourself what role you're playing in the situations. Patterns are not coincidences.

If you've done all you can to deal with Clara, then you may indeed be working with a true problem employee. If that's the case, then you'll want to check out Chapter 19, which tells you what your options are. If she's not the problem so much as you are, then perhaps you need to reexamine your day-to-day behaviors. And before you automatically criticize Clara for any mistake — regardless of whether your criticism is warranted — be sure to take some time to look at the situation objectively. Carefully plan out what you will say — write it down. Ask yourself if these are the words you would want to hear if the tables were turned. Or pretend that you have to deliver that feedback to a friend — is that the way you'd phrase it? If not, keep revising it until it meets these criteria.

Chapter 8

Encouraging Creativity

. . . .

In This Chapter

▶ Discovering the skill of creative thinking

▶ Brainstorming — in all kinds of weather

▶ Undertaking risks for the sake of an idea

▶ Benefiting from mistakes

. . . .

*Y*ou've probably heard tales of creative workers who were fired because they wouldn't walk the line. Then, these very same workers went off and created a thriving business based on the ideas that their former employers ignored. And, of course, now they're millionaires.

These stories are abundant for a reason. Creative workers are often seen as a threat because they challenge the status quo that exists in a company.

But if you ignore your innovative thinkers, you stifle your business and ultimately drive away some of your most valuable employees. You may have a great product, or even several great products. But there comes a time when the appeal of your product declines. Times change, and unless you adapt to these changes, you can be quickly left behind. To be prepared for the future, you need to have employees who constantly think of fresh ideas.

When you create an environment in which employees feel their ideas can truly make a difference, you motivate your staff. People don't want to feel like trained animals that punch the clock, labor, then go home. Encouraging your employees to be creative shows that you value their intelligence and originality — and helps your employees smile when they come to work in the morning.

Keep in mind that creativity is not just spontaneous combustion. It's a process that you manage. Not all ideas are created equal and, as a manager, you don't want to waste time running up and down dead-ends. But how you respond to those zany or sometimes-unrealistic ideas — not whether you actually follow them — can either dampen or spark further creativity.

In this chapter, you find out how to inspire creative thinking among your employees. You also discover how to conduct successful brainstorming sessions and encourage risk taking in your staff. And you see how your team can benefit from its mistakes as well as its successes.

Fostering Creativity: It Starts with Your Environment

If your employees aren't coming up with innovative ideas, you need to take a look at your company's culture. Are you discouraging great ideas by ignoring them or criticizing them? Or do you nurture creativity by encouraging people to take the best approach possible, even if it's untested?

Ask yourself the following questions to find out whether your department's culture is helping or hindering creativity:

- ✔ **Are authority and responsibility delegated?** Not many people can be creative for creativity's sake. Employees need to be empowered before they can start coming up with great suggestions. You'll find that even the most unimaginative worker becomes creative when he has a stake in the outcome of a project.

- ✔ **Are employees aware of the company's vision?** To come up with creative ideas, employees need a few guiding principles. Make sure they know your company's vision and keep it in mind when they're developing ideas and solutions.

- ✔ **Does your team brainstorm regularly?** Brainstorming capitalizes on synergy. If you conduct brainstorming sessions properly, your employees should be able to come up with better ideas, working as a group, than they would on their own. If you brainstorm with them, they'll also get a feel for just how far out of the box you want them to think. (See the section "Brainstorming Effectively" for more information.)

- ✔ **Do you venture offsite for creative sessions?** Sometimes, an office space — no matter how creativity-friendly it is — can still be stifling. For a change of pace, try venturing offsite: a state fair, a restaurant, a park, the beach, you name it. You may be surprised at the ideas you or your coworkers come up with in a relaxed environment.

- ✔ **Are employees allowed to decorate their workspace?** Although decorating office space is not as critical as empowerment, it does help foster an environment where creativity can flow more freely. Freedom in decoration allows your employees to be inspired by what means the most to them. Maybe one person will see a photo of his favorite getaway place and feel a sense of calm in a stressful situation. Or maybe someone else works best when surrounded by plants and flowers. As long as decorations don't negatively impact day-to-day business, allow a little leeway and let your employees add personality to their workspaces.

Discovering the Path to Creativity

Are you discouraged because your employees aren't coming up with new ideas? When you ask for suggestions, do they just sit and stare at you? If you're offering the right environment and you're willing to coach your team, you can coax creativity out of them.

Your employees will have their creative ups and downs. You need to let people develop their ideas to a point. (What that point is depends on your company's philosophy and mission.) When they fail, you need to encourage them to try again.

Here are some ways to foster creativity:

- Encourage others to speak their mind.
- Don't allow interruptions, even if the person pauses.
- Encourage questions.
- Ask "what if" questions to encourage employees to think through their answers.
- Don't dismiss an idea without discussing it.
- Argue both sides of an issue.
- Attend seminars on innovative practices and concepts both in and outside your industry.
- Require an idea as admission to a routine meeting to get your employees' creative juices rolling.
- Ask the right questions so that you'll get the answers you need.
- Have patience.
- Challenge the status quo.
- Laugh.
- Carry a notebook to jot down your employees' ideas.
- Be thankful for small ideas.

Overcoming Creative Blocks

Even if you're doing everything right, you're going to reach a point when you and your team come up dry in the creative ideas category. That may be a sign that you're working too hard.

In a recent survey of advertising executives commissioned by The Creative Group, 36 percent of the respondents said a timeout from work is the best way to avoid a creative block.

You can try a number of approaches to keep the creative juices flowing. The following advice for preventing a creative impasse was offered by advertising executives. Remember that the little things — especially those that are out of the ordinary — can really jog your creative juices.

- Change the music and colors in your work environment to inspire creative thinking.
- Think out loud.
- Keep an idea log that contains every creative idea that comes to you, whether you use it or not.
- Maintain your sense of humor and laugh often.
- Follow business trends and learn from them.
- Don't allow interruptions. If you can, forward your phone calls while working on key projects.
- Allow time for personal rejuvenation. Spend time on outside hobbies and interests.
- Start a project well in advance and stay one step ahead of the game.

Brainstorming Effectively

Brainstorming is when you get a group of people to think together and come up with a solution that builds on each other's ideas. It's often associated with purely creative endeavors, such as developing a marketing plan. But brainstorming can become a regular part of how your business does business if you look for ways to integrate it.

Do you have a new employee joining your team? Brainstorm ways to welcome and orient her to the department. Does your group have a big project looming that everyone dreads working on? Brainstorm ways to make the project more fun, and maybe even more streamlined!

Good morning, creative thinking!

Coffee isn't the only thing flowing in the morning — so are good ideas, suggests a recent survey. Believe it or not, morning is the most creative time of day for two-thirds of ad executives — and it's their job to be creative!

Because people feel refreshed and relatively free of distractions at the start of the day, morning is usually an ideal time for brainstorming sessions.

According to the nationwide poll, 66 percent of advertising executives find the early hours to be the most conducive to creative thought; only

5 percent said they were most creative during lunchtime or the afternoon, while 14 percent preferred evenings.

The survey was developed by The Creative Group. It was conducted by an independent research firm and includes responses from 200 advertising executives with the nation's 1,000 largest advertising firms.

Remember, though, that morning may not be the most productive time for everyone. Make sure that you have an open-door policy, so that your night owls can contribute original ideas.

Although brainstorming is a widely used technique, it's sometimes mishandled or mismanaged. When you brainstorm, you say the first thing that comes to mind. You do not edit yourself and you do not edit others. The whole point is to come up with as many ideas as possible. The group builds off of each other's suggestions, working toward the best possible idea. Depending on what problem you're trying to solve, you may need more than one brainstorming session.

You don't want your brainstorming sessions to be too long or include too many people, or they'll become counterproductive. Try to keep the meetings under an hour and the number of participants to ten or fewer.

Some ideas may seem downright corny. Don't dismiss them. They may just be the launching point someone needs to reach that great idea.

To come up with the best ideas possible, the group needs to feel comfortable with each other. Mocking other people or criticizing their ideas should be out of the question. When you listen to your employees and value their opinions — even their off-the-wall ideas — then you're creating a trusting environment.

Here are some tips for creating a positive brainstorming session.

  ✔ **Choose a comfortable location without distractions.** The company breakroom is not necessarily your best option! An offsite location helps create a more relaxed atmosphere. Although you probably can't find a place that meets the needs of everyone in the group, make sure that at least the lighting, temperature, and layout are conducive to creativity. If your employees are bothered by bright lights in a hot, cramped room, you're probably not going to get their best ideas.

- ✔ **Schedule brainstorming sessions.** Some employees may prefer creative sessions in the morning because they won't feel worn out by the distractions of the day. But if your team suggests a late afternoon session, give it a try. Your goal is to find a time when most of the participants feels energetic and innovative.

- ✔ **Closely define the objective.** People need to know what they're brainstorming about. Instead of providing a general topic, such as how to improve business, focus instead on a specific issue, such as how to accelerate your response time to customer requests.

- ✔ **Don't get sidetracked.** Sure, you may come up with a great idea about employee retention, but if you're there to discuss response time, save the other idea for a later meeting.

- ✔ **Don't judge.** Create an atmosphere in which there's no such thing as a bad idea. That philosophy may sound unconstructive on the surface, but if you continue to build on a seemingly silly idea while you brainstorm, it may lead you to the solution you're looking for.

  You could even have people toss in a quarter every time they make a critical remark — and then use that money to buy snacks for the next brainstorming session.

- ✔ **Build on each other's thoughts.** Any one idea may not be a workable concept, but it can take you toward the goal. Take that suggestion and find a way to tweak it so that it fits with the ultimate objective. Each person plays a part in moving the idea along, like passing a soccer ball down the field.

- ✔ **Think quantity, not quality.** The more ideas you have, the better the odds are that you'll stumble across one that will work. Encourage participants to come up with as many concepts as possible, regardless of how outrageous they may seem.

- ✔ **Play.** You can even use toys — they may help you regain some of your childhood creativity. Maybe you start the session with a team-building exercise where groups work together to build a prototype of your company's next great product. Or perhaps participants draw their visual images of the current state of customer service. Whatever you do, encourage participants to play their way to ideas.

- ✔ **Bring on the food.** Snacks and beverages can satisfy hunger cravings and boost brainpower at the same time. Who knows? Maybe that bag of chips will lead you to the next big thing!

- ✔ **Have fun.** You want your employees to enjoy and look forward to brainstorming sessions. With a fun atmosphere, who wouldn't come up with a great idea?

✔ **Focus the discussion.** Participants shouldn't be having side conversations; the purpose is to listen to what everyone is saying and build on those ideas. If people aren't listening and involved, encourage each person to contribute an idea or build on the previous suggestion — make it a game, but keep everyone on track.

✔ **Ask questions.** By asking open-ended questions, you can clarify suggestions and help lead the discussion. Likewise, you don't want to lead your employees into giving a certain response, so make sure that you're not asking something like, "You didn't really think that would work, did you?"

Encouraging Smart Risk Taking

When you're striving to have a creative workforce, you need to accept that there are some risks. A truly innovative idea can spark your team to pursue a new adventure with many opportunities — but also pitfalls. Not all risks are created equal, of course. Sometimes the potential pitfalls outweigh the possible gains. What you need to do — and what you should encourage your team to do — is take smart risks.

But evaluating risk is not an exact science. So here are some ideas to encourage risk taking:

✔ **Ask for your employees' input.** Suggestion boxes are one way to get input. Even comments like "Buy better coffee for the breakroom" can be helpful. If you acknowledge those suggestions in a team meeting (and explain why purchasing better coffee may not be possible!), employees realize that you're taking their suggestions seriously. And you can build the trust necessary to encourage their input through other channels, such as one-on-one meetings.

✔ **Don't be afraid to hire someone outspoken.** Every company needs a person who can shake things up and offer a reality check. When you're looking to hire a new employee, be sure to evaluate candidates on both their qualifications and their confidence levels — the more confident a person is, the more likely she'll speak her mind.

✔ **Reward risk taking, no matter how it turns out.** Even calculated risks fail some of the time. Let your staff know that you understand that not every risk yields success. And let them see by your words and actions that taking a smart risk won't be reprimanded.

A smart risk is well thought out. Employees have looked at other options and genuinely believe that the risk is worth the gain. A not-so-smart risk, on the other hand, is taken without serious thought to the potential consequences.

If your employee takes a smart risk and fails, there should be no negative consequences. Unless your employees are willing to take smart risks, your company won't thrive.

Learning from Successes and Failures

Making a mistake isn't a terrible thing. Everyone does it. And even the most calculated risk has a chance to fail.

But no matter what the outcome, you shouldn't punish employees. Instead, ask yourself or your employees the following questions:

- **What went wrong?** Maybe your project had a costly delay. Was it caused by something no one could anticipate, such as a blizzard shutting the company down for a week? Or maybe it was something your team should have thought of — like the annual slowdown at the manufacturing plant during the holidays? Whatever the explanation, you can learn from the experience and plan for the future. In this example, you may decide to add a cushion of a week or two to the timeline to accommodate potential delays.

- **Did you explain things well enough?** You may have thought what you said was crystal clear, but your employees may have heard a message that wasn't what you intended to deliver. Make sure that you ask your employees if they understand your directives. And remember: Sometimes you have access to confidential information that they do not have. Be sure to share what you can with your team so that they not only know what needs to happen, but also why and in what context.

- **Did you point your employees to the right resources?** Maybe your employees really needed to contact key players to get the proper information to make a report complete. In the future, make sure that you give your employees all the resources you can. If you don't know whom they should contact, then give them the names of people who can point them in the right direction. Resources aren't limited to just people. You may need to make sure that your employees have the proper equipment to get the job done.

- **Was the project poorly planned?** You may want to take a look at the project plan when things go awry. Did a plan exist? Were team members following protocol or were they skipping steps? Do practices need to be revised or just reinforced? Learn from this unhappy experience and make the necessary changes for the future!

If you make a mistake, set an example: Admit to it. Mistakes can be excellent teaching and learning moments. The first step in learning may be to concede that your pet project or great new idea was actually a miscalculation. Then, try not to make the same mistake again!

Chapter 9

Tapping the Power of Organizational Communications

· ·

· ·

*A*s a manager, how you communicate with your employees affects whether you motivate them or demotivate them. Whether you planned for it or not, you are now a professional communicator — among your other job descriptions. So make the best of it!

In this chapter, you discover tools for effective mass communication, helpful guidelines for communicating bad news, and how to cope with the company grapevine. You also find out how to gauge and tap into your company's formal communications channels. (For more general tips on communicating with your staff on an everyday basis, see Chapter 7.)

Knowing Your Communication Choices

Whether you're communicating with a few employees in a small company or hundreds of employees in a large company, some things are the same: You want to establish a primary communication vehicle and you want to share news fast.

Every one of your team members or employees contributes to the success of the organization, so you must reach all of them when communicating news.

All companies should have a primary communication method — a reliable channel that you almost always use to distribute information. If employees are wondering what's happening with the latest product rollout or what the repercussions of last week's restructuring will be, they should be able to count on hearing some news through a source that they know will deliver the information. Here are some options:

- ✔ Weekly voicemails
- ✔ Weekly e-mails
- ✔ Memos
- ✔ A company newsletter or magazine
- ✔ Brownbag lunch meetings
- ✔ Company-wide meetings
- ✔ CD-ROM or videotape presentations
- ✔ Intranet postings
- ✔ Weekly team meetings

Managers in small companies have a lot more opportunity for face to face contacts, while managers in large companies need tools for mass communication. The key — in either scenario — is to choose the appropriate vehicle for conveying the type of information that you typically share with your employees.

Although you need to have a primary method of communicating, you also need to use alternative methods. If your favored method of communication is to have a weekly meeting, you may have to use a different method to let people know about an urgent development. Likewise, the company newsletter may provide a great forum for going into issues in more depth than would be appropriate at a team meeting.

Each of your communication channels should complement one another to create a unified but multidimensional whole. Your employees should respect and depend upon the sources of information your company provides — and not rely on rumors.

Weekly voicemails

One option used by a number of companies to communicate urgent news is the firm's voicemail system. Voicemail is particularly useful for broadcasting messages from senior executives to all intended recipients. This can be followed up by a face to face meeting with line managers, who then can address the news in team meetings.

Say, for example, that a hurricane has severely damaged your Miami production plant — and the rumors are already flying. First, use your voicemail system to alert your employees. This allows you to send one message with the same information to all recipients without inadvertently leaving out some critical piece of news, as may happen when retelling the story from person to person. Then you can follow up with face to face communication to answer any questions or address any concerns.

Here are some other situations where you'd want to use voicemail:

✔ Top-level, immediate organizational changes

✔ Unexpected product or employee crises

✔ Updates that may hit the news the next day on recent company activity

✔ Good news announcements and holiday greetings

E-mails

You can use e-mail to communicate urgent information or simply to make general announcements. Assuming that everyone in your audience has access to e-mail, this channel works best when you want to:

✔ Briefly remind a large group of people about a meeting, event, or an action that's needed.

✔ Initiate a vote or feedback on a relatively simple matter with a small group of people. (For example, "Where should we go for the next offsite meeting? A, B, or C?")

You can also use e-mail for communication during a crisis, promotion announcements, and short updates and reminders. However, in the event of a legally sensitive crisis, be sure to get your legal department's sign-off before sending any e-mails.

In fact, you can launch an entire e-mail communication campaign with pre-view e-mails, actual announcements, and follow-ups. For example, if your company is launching a new benefits program, you can send an e-mail teaser, saying something like, "We're expanding your benefits options — more news to come!" Then you could follow up with actual announcements and in-depth materials. One warning, though: Don't bombard your employees with e-mail or they'll start to tune out.

The top challenge with e-mail is that most people receive too many messages that are too long. If you decide to use this tool as one of your communication channels, remember these tips:

✔ Keep messages clear but concise.

✔ To help recipients prioritize e-mail, highlight at the top of the message whether your e-mail requires any type of action — for example, type "Only for your review" or "Action required."

Memos

Memos are effective for making important announcements from executives and explaining the rationale for decisions that top management has made. Through memos, employees can hear the information straight from the decision makers. Memos may be the best way to communicate a lot of in-depth information that isn't necessarily time sensitive. You can then send that memo to your staff as an e-mail attachment or forward hard copies to those employees who don't have access to computers.

Company newsletter or magazine

A newsletter or magazine can be a helpful tool in a company's quest to educate and communicate with employees. The great results companies get when using this communication tool often justify the effort.

Your corporate communications department normally has someone who heads up this project. She or he coordinates information from all company departments and reinforces corporate messages within the newsletter. The publication can come out as often as your organization wants. Some companies publish once a week, while others distribute their newsletters or magazines quarterly. The key, however, is to make sure that the newsletter or magazine is distributed on a regular schedule, so that your employees know when to expect it.

Although a company newsletter or magazine is usually a high-priority communication method for most organizations, it alone cannot accomplish the goal of spreading your company's vision. Because this tool is feature oriented and only appears from time to time, you must use it in conjunction with the other tools described in this chapter. Otherwise, you won't have a way to handle late-breaking news that your employees need to hear immediately — from you, not the newspaper or grapevine.

No matter how small your budget, you can afford to have a company newsletter. It can be as simple as a one-page, two-sided piece of paper that you photocopy in your office, or as elaborate as a glossy, four-color magazine-processed quarterly. And you can save printing costs by e-mailing it or posting it on your company's intranet if you don't want to print it and distribute it in the traditional way.

Your company newsletter shouldn't be too flashy. Your employees will wonder why so much money is being spent on it! However, if you're in an image-conscious industry, such as high-tech, you may need to have a flashy newsletter to be in line with your corporate image. Your newsletter should be in line with the rest of your corporate materials.

To make the most of your newsletter, it should be more than a laundry list of who recently had anniversaries with the company, celebrated a birthday, or became a parent. You want to use the newsletter to reinforce your company's values and goals — for example, if one of your goals is great customer service, you could run a feature story on a staff member who went above and beyond for a client. Stories should be fairly in-depth. Here are some things that you can include in your newsletter:

- ✔ A letter from senior management — or perhaps the CEO

- ✔ Success stories highlighting organizational goals (excellent customer service, collaboration, innovation, and so on)

- ✔ Human interest articles, such as those about charity events

- ✔ News of promotions, new employees, new office openings, and so on, but placed in the context of their relation to business goals and ideals

- ✔ A quarterly review of the organization's finances in lay terms (what the numbers really mean to the company and employees)

Remember that what you include in a newsletter needs to be tailored to your company. Every organization's newsletter contains a different mix of content.

The challenge with a company newsletter is to treat it as a public document while at the same time targeting your employees. Give your employees company news of interest, as well as a snapshot of what other people in the organization are up to. But realize that the information may find its way to competitors or the media.

Whatever you do, don't spin any messages in your newsletter — employees will see right through it. If you can't include an honest account, maybe now isn't the right time — or this isn't the right communication vehicle — to convey the message.

You probably don't determine the contents of your newsletter, but you can still use it to your advantage. For example, you may want to contact the newsletter's managing editor to suggest possible story ideas. Most corporate communications staff members are eager to hear from front-line managers about what information would be most helpful and interesting. Consider your team's most significant accomplishments and successes — do you think other teams could benefit from your experience? And wouldn't it be nice to publicly recognize your employees' efforts through a story in the company newsletter? Share your best practices with your company's corporate communications team and they can help tell the story that both motivates your team and inspires others.

Brownbag lunch meetings

Brownbag lunch meetings are great for casual discussions with small groups or for brainstorming sessions. By keeping the attendance to ten or twenty employees, the meetings can be informal and relaxed. These meetings are also a great way for managers to find out their employees' concerns.

If you decide to hold brownbag lunch meetings, follow these tips:

- ✔ Focus the meeting on a specific topic.
- ✔ Keep the number of attendees under control.
- ✔ Provide time for a question and answer session.
- ✔ Hold the meeting in a relaxed setting.
- ✔ Consider bringing in an expert from within the company to discuss his or her job. This discussion can help employees see the big picture.

Company-wide meetings

If you want everyone to hear the message at the same time and everyone is in one location, then hold a company-wide meeting. Don't forget to hold a follow-up question and answer session, particularly if you're making a major announcement. You can also hold these sessions to motivate your employees and have senior managers share department reports.

CD-ROM/videotape presentations

For something exciting and different, try a CD-ROM or videotape presentation. These presentations are more personable and interesting than memos, voicemails, or e-mails, and they allow you to provide the visual images not possible with other communication channels. Employees can gather together at specific times to view the presentation or watch it at their convenience. These presentations can be a powerful motivational tool, getting your employees excited about the company's vision and ideas. CD-ROMs or videos can be expensive to produce, so select this method only if your budget allows. These kinds of presentations are best for:

- ✔ A visual tour of company headquarters or a branch location, as part of an overall orientation package.
- ✔ A motivational message from the CEO (particularly if your organization is so large that onsite visits are logistically challenging).

Videos and CD-ROMs aren't appropriate for every situation or every company. As a manager, you should know your staff well enough to determine whether they'd prefer a motivational message from an actual face to face meeting, e-mail, voicemail, or memo.

Intranet postings

An *intranet* is an internal Web site where your employees can access pertinent company and personnel information. Only your employees can see the information that you put on an intranet. In essence, your intranet centralizes your company's communication.

If you have an intranet, make sure that someone in the company monitors the postings. You want them to be useful and appropriate.

Here are some things you may include on an intranet:

- Company newsletter
- Company directory
- Links to sites related to the company business
- Weekly team minutes
- Stock quotes
- Senior management messages
- Organizational charts
- Product updates
- Employee benefits and human resources information
- Online versions of your newsletter (perhaps with breaking news stories)
- Training information, including interactive professional development courses for employees
- Best-practices information (particularly appropriate since competitors do not have access to your intranet)
- Positive media coverage and financial highlights

Weekly team meetings

If you want to hear from your employees and share news at the same time, schedule weekly team meetings. You can get immediate feedback from your staff members after you deliver important news. If your team members know they'll get the real scoop from you every Friday, then they won't waste their valuable time hunting down "information" in the hallways or speculating.

If you have a team meeting, consider bringing in internal guest speakers. These individuals can be from a different department and might speak about how their processes work. If you do so, your staff will be able to see how their jobs relate to other groups in the company and you foster interdepartmental collaboration.

Communicating Change and Not-So-Good News

In business, you'll inevitably need to communicate news of change. Whether it's a public offering, corporate merger, or layoffs, you want to be prepared to communicate effectively.

The key to communicating change is simple: Do it quickly and accurately.

One of the biggest drains on employee morale is when staff members hear or read company news from someone outside the company before they hear the news internally. Therefore, you should make sure that communicating with your employees is a priority — *especially* during times of change. Your employees are the company's prized asset, and you need to treat them that way. Be sure to share information with them immediately!

Whenever you're conveying bad news, you should assume that your staff members may already be discussing it. Your goal is to set the record straight and provide an opportunity for interaction and discussion. Not only should you communicate the news quickly and honestly, but you also need to pinpoint and address employee concerns. Make sure that you use all appropriate communication methods to keep the information flowing.

In some cases, the best way to communicate news of an impending crisis is face to face — a company-wide meeting or department-wide session if appropriate. You should provide opportunities for a question and answer session. If you think some employees will be afraid to speak up, let them submit questions anonymously. You should also have senior management involved; their presence and willingness to answer questions will lend credibility and reinforce that they're committed to the welfare of employees.

Say, for example, that you're communicating news of an impending layoff. You probably want to hold a big group meeting where everyone receives the news at once from senior-level executives. Then you'll want to follow up with smaller group sessions where your employees can voice their concerns and ask questions.

Whatever you do, don't ignore bad news. By not addressing tough situations, you risk exacerbating the problem. *In bad times, you cannot over-communicate.* If you fail to address the situation, rumors will spiral.

Also keep in mind that employees not only want to know what's happening in the company, they want to know *why* it's happening. It's human nature to second-guess, and not-so-good rumors may run rampant along the company grapevine — without enough information to prevent the spread.

For more information on motivating your employees through difficult situations, see Chapters 18 and 19.

Counteracting the Grapevine

When you think of the grapevine, you may think of gossip. And gossip, of course, is normally bad — that's what makes it so appealing for some! But the grapevine can also carry good news.

Whether you like it or not, a grapevine exists in your company and it always will. But you do have the ability to limit its potential for demotivating staff by feeding it accurate information that reinforces corporate messages.

To stimulate the flow of good news, start sharing important information faster. As soon as big news happens in your company, someone, somewhere knows about it. And soon the number of people in the know multiplies. You need to acknowledge what's going on before the message becomes distorted.

Just think about the game where one person whispers a message in the ear of the person next to him, who then repeats it to the person next to him. By the time the message travels through the chain, it ends up totally distorted. If you don't address communication issues, then this misinformation can happen at your company — with serious consequences.

To help manage your company's grapevine:

- ✔ **Provide accurate information.** Set the record straight by proactively communicating to all employees. Otherwise, distorted half-truths will make the rounds — so nip these destructive rumors in the bud.

- ✔ **Share information quickly.** Your employees are more likely to trust and believe you if you don't hoard information. If you take a while to convey news, people will wonder if you have a hidden agenda.

- ✔ **Provide a question and answer session.** If employees know they can ask questions, they'll be more likely to wait for an answer before spreading rumors randomly.

> ✔ **Hold periodic group meetings.** Your employees should be able to count on receiving information at regular intervals. If so, they'll spend less energy looking for information elsewhere!
>
> ✔ **Avoid spin.** Keep your content straightforward and concise. Everyone knows when they're hearing *spin* — half-truths and propaganda-like messages — and the only thing that spin accomplishes is decreased morale.

If the grapevine has taken on a life of its own, no one will believe any messages that contradict it.

Part of controlling the grapevine is handling speculation. When someone comes to you with questions, be honest. Tell him what you know. If you know what might happen, say so. If you know something is under discussion but nothing has been decided, let him know that too. You don't want your employees to have the perception that one group knows something that another one doesn't. Employees do understand that some things are confidential; in those cases, reveal as much as you can and then let them know that the rest of the story is confidential.

And Now, a Word from Your Communications Team

Have you ever been in a job where you learned more about your company in the morning paper than in the corporate newsletter? If so, you know how easily that can chip away at your trust in the organization. You may have wondered, "Is management withholding information from employees? What's the real story?"

That's why good corporate communication is crucial to employee motivation. If your company is large enough to support a separate corporate communications function, members of that team can help you speak to the troops effectively. This central channel for employee communication allows you to reinforce your messages and avoid sending mixed signals — or no signals at all!

Your corporate communications team typically develops a strategic communication plan, which outlines how information will be conveyed to both internal audiences (employees) and external audiences (media, clients, and so on).

Corporate communications professionals can help reinforce your company's vision. If an employee did something you'd like others to emulate, then tell your corporate communications team so that it can write it up in the company newsletter. If you want to introduce a new benefits plan to employees, then coordinate with your corporate communications team to develop a company-wide information campaign.

Although the corporate communications staff may help determine a quarterly message and the best ways to distribute it, you, as a manager, can suggest ideas that you know would be relevant to your team and perhaps others. In your actions and day-to-day communication, you should

✔ Look for ways to capitalize on corporate communications pieces. If another department was highlighted in the company newsletter, share that department's success story at your weekly meeting.

✔ Encourage your staff members to submit suggestions to your corporate communications department. Let them know their feedback can help the communications team provide more effective materials and focus on meaningful topics of interest.

Management must reinforce the messages being sent by corporate communications, or corporate communication efforts will inevitably fail.

All employees should know your company's mission and values. If they don't, you may need to rethink how you're using your corporate communications department.

To successfully work with your corporate communications team, you need to ask yourself some basic questions:

✔ **Who is your audience?** You want to address anyone who is affected by the information.

✔ **What do you want the audience to take away from the communication?** Don't focus solely on what you want to say; be sure to say what your audience needs to hear. Your audience won't remember everything you tell them or everything you write. Ask yourself what the important point is, and make sure that you highlight that important information in your communication.

✔ **How much information do you want to communicate?** You may want to tell your employees how you made any key decisions that relate to the story or point you're making and outline any anticipated changes.

✔ **Who is going to communicate the news?** If you're making a change to your company insurance plan, the human resource specialist whom employees consult regarding insurance questions is the logical choice to communicate the news.

✔ **How will you distribute this message?** Match the method of communication — e-mail, voicemail, memo, and so on — with the message that you're sending.

How do you measure up?

If you're ready to start maximizing your corporate communications department, start by measuring how well you're currently communicating to your employees. Doing so gives you a baseline for future comparison and makes you aware of what you need to improve.

Through focus groups, surveys, informal conversations, or meetings, try to find out the answers to the following questions:

✔ What tools are being used to communicate?

✔ How effective are these tools?

✔ What information do employees want and need to do their jobs effectively?

Part IV
Building Home-Grown Talent

...and finally, do you feel well connected to the other members of your department?

In this part . . .

*1*f you want satisfied employees, you can't just expect
them to show up for work every day, do their jobs, and
go home. There's more to building your employee talent
pool than that — after all, you're managing your company's biggest asset. In this part, you find out how you
can empower your employees. You also discover how to
conduct a meaningful performance appraisal and develop
training programs that really teach your employees something. Lastly, you explore the role mentors play in helping
your staff members grow professionally.

Chapter 10

Yes, You Can! Empowering Your Employees

*A*dmit it: If your employees were robots, programmed to do the same job day in and day out, a lot of your worries would disappear. Thankfully your employees aren't automated, but as such they need to have an *explanation*. Tell them why what they do matters. Then go a step further and share responsibility. Failing to share information and responsibility certainly doesn't create any benefits for you — and it only hurts the company and your staff.

Ownership is a term that you've probably heard before. Make your employees feel as if they have a stake in the project and their motivation will soar. Think of a boxer in a prizefight — he's probably not going to try very hard if he doesn't get a share of the prize money. The same thing is true of your employees: If they don't understand why their projects matter or what they stand to gain from success, you can expect to see a lot of unmotivated men and women taking extra-long coffee breaks.

People Need Ownership

Remember when you were starting your career and someone asked you to keep the supply cabinet stocked? You probably weren't too excited about the job. Then came the day that every printer in the department ran out of toner. You were able to do your part to keep the department moving ahead because you'd been keeping the toner well stocked. (Unless you learned the hard way, like some people do!) After that, you realized the vital importance of your job and were probably more enthusiastic about it. Similarly, when your team members know how their roles fit into the big picture, they'll value their own contribution more. They'll also be more invested in the results.

Working in a company is a lot like stocking a supply cabinet. You tend to do a better job when you know what the goal is, when you can see (or, even better, feel like a part of) the big picture. If you want your employees to produce extraordinary results, then you need to let them know how those results fit into the scheme of things. If you hoard information or responsibilities, then you're not maximizing your department's full potential.

Ironically, those managers who hoard power and information are usually the ones with the least amount of power. Because they have no say in things, they tend to hoard what little bit of power they sense they have. Learn from their mistakes and take a different approach.

Empowerment is the giving of power, and it's a win-win situation. Delegating responsibility helps you because you're less bogged down by routine tasks and are more available for work that requires your special expertise. It helps your employees because it expands their skill sets and challenges them. And it benefits your company because you'll have an atmosphere of teamwork, which motivates your staff to produce even higher-quality work.

If you hear people in your company saying things like, "I'll have to check with my manager," "I can't make that decision," or "We've never done it that way before," you're seeing signs that individuals are not empowered. Table 10-1 also gives you ways to tell whether a person is empowered or unempowered.

Table 10-1	Are You Empowered?
An Empowered Employee	*An Unempowered Employee*
Doesn't shy away from challenges	Waits for someone else to solve problems
Recognizes and pursues opportunities	Perpetuates the status quo
Has input in decisions that affect his or her staff	Has no input in these decisions
Is able to make some financial decisions on all money matters	Has to check with his or her manager
Isn't afraid to think out of the box	Is a yes person

Sharing power doesn't mean that you have less of it. In fact, it can make you more powerful — you're doing less work in the trenches and coaching more from the sidelines. When you speak, your words are more meaningful and have more impact.

We're gonna do what?

You probably remember a time when your company announced something that you thought was a little bit off the wall. Maybe it was the mandatory company party offsite. ("How can something mandatory be a party," you wondered.) Or perhaps it was the Switch-Jobs-For-A-Day event. Be forewarned that any new empowerment program you adopt may provoke a similar reaction.

Unfortunately, many empowerment programs fail. When managers announce such a program, employees often greet the decision with a mix of skepticism and optimism. Yes, empowerment sounds great, but does that mean more work?

And sometimes, if empowerment isn't done right, it can indeed mean more work. Employees are still doing their same tasks, only they have some of their bosses' projects on their plates now as well. The result is often chaos, with overworked, underpaid employees bucking responsibility. Not a good situation, and definitely not the situation empowerment programs are intended to create.

Taking the first steps toward empowerment

Have you ever been told what to do? Sure you have! Whether it was your big brother telling you to quit following him around or your teacher ordering you to stop talking, you probably weren't too happy with the mandate. There's a time and a place for directives, but they're not the most effective tactic in most situations at work.

Empowerment isn't telling someone what to do, and empowerment is not delegating tasks. It's delegating responsibility with authority. The employee who is being empowered is free to make decisions along the way and to decide how the project is done. When you're told what to do, you're not given that freedom, and, in essence, your creative thought processes don't matter. In empowered situations, creative inspiration is the key.

If you want to truly empower your employees, you need to give them the freedom to do their jobs. By delegating responsibility and authority, you show your team members that you trust them and you give them an opportunity to develop new skills. You can't just delegate projects to your employees and then tell them that they're on their own. You must provide them with the necessary information to do the job. If you let someone drive your car, but keep him blindfolded, you're not empowering him. You're setting him — and your car — up for a disaster. Let him know the rules of the road, coach him on driving the car, and then let him drive.

Mistakes are inevitable. How you respond to a mistake is what's crucial.

If you like the idea of empowerment (and you should), then the first step is to look at your daily project list. What do you do day in and day out? What should you be doing? Then, decide which aspects you can train someone else to do — it should be a job that doesn't require your special skills.

You're getting paid to do a certain job because you have special talents that others may not have. If you're wasting your time on daily tasks that others can do, then you're hurting your company. In essence, you're being overpaid. Don't try to do someone else's job and yours!

If you're having trouble adjusting to the idea of empowerment, then start small. For example, instead of letting someone produce the company's annual report that goes out to stockholders, start with the internal four-page company newsletter project.

Here are some other tips to keep in mind if you're new to empowerment:

- ✓ **Match the project with the person.** After you've decided what responsibilities you can share with others, decide who you want to give the responsibilities to. Make sure that the person has the skills to do the job, even if she hasn't tackled a similar project in the past. If the individual doesn't have the skills, then give her the training to do the job. You don't want to set her up for failure. If you have a new employee, assign her smaller projects so that you can evaluate her skills and abilities.

- ✓ **Give 100 percent responsibility.** Each project should have a task owner who is entirely responsible for the result — and everything along the way. If an employee isn't responsible for coming up with the process and each step along the way, then how can you hold her responsible for the result?

- ✓ **Explain the big picture.** Your employee needs as much information as you have. Why is the project important? How does the employee fit into the big picture? What's the goal? What outcome would you like to have?

- ✓ **Tell all.** You also need to tell her all you can about the project. You want your employee to make informed decisions. How can she do so without access to critical information? You should offer insight about such things as long-term business strategy, competitor activities, interdepartmental activities, or anything else that impacts the project.

- ✓ **Offer other resources.** If you can't answer some questions or don't know certain information, then direct your employee to the individuals who can help her. Even make introductions, if necessary, or have her attend key meetings with you if it will help move the project along.

  Your goal is to make sure that your employee has what she needs to do the job well.

Are you underworked, overqualified, and overpaid?

If you're spending all your time double-checking memos and reports that your company is paying someone else to do, you're wasting your time — and your company's money.

Try taking your cue from Warner-Lambert Co., a worldwide pharmaceutical and consumer healthcare products firm based in Morris Plains, New Jersey. When the company started evaluating its operations in 1996, it found that operations weren't as efficient as the company had hoped.

Instead of focusing on big-picture work, managers at Warner-Lambert spent 76 percent of

their time on administrative functions. Clearly, someone else needed to be doing the administrative tasks.

The company rose to the occasion, creating and outsourcing a call center. It also created an in-house, shared service organization to handle tasks such as filing, record keeping, and scheduling interviews. Lastly, Warner-Lambert utilized its corporate intranet to enable employees to access data more efficiently and to reduce paperwork.

✔ **Don't be a dictator.** You and your employee are a team. Together, you should come up with ideas for the project. The project itself, not you, should govern how the project is run. (See the section on letting the task be the boss, later in this chapter.) You shouldn't tell your employee how to run the assignment; she should tell you what the project needs. Frustration and helplessness are demotivating. Don't create these feelings.

✔ **Set a deadline and check in periodically for status reports.** You don't need to micromanage the person, but you do need to be aware of what's going on. You need to know if something isn't going the way it should so that you can help everyone avoid last-minute crises. (You can find some advice on avoiding micromanagement later in this chapter.)

✔ **Give your employees decision-making power.** The more input the person feels he has in the project, the more invested he is and the better the results are. In addition, requiring approval for minor details sacrifices time and efficiency — probably things you can't afford to lose. For example, as an owner of a store, you can authorize workers to do whatever is necessary to make a sale, such as offering a discount up to 20 percent.

Practicing empowerment daily

Empowerment is not just handing a project to someone else; you still need to be involved, just not on a daily basis.

It's all about options — and I'm not talking stock

How you empower your employees is up to you. Take Hewlett-Packard's Vancouver campus, for example. Experienced employees can work at home if they'd like and use company-provided Internet accounts and voicemail. The work is what matters most; how they do it is up to them.

Follow these tips to ensure success:

✔ **Be available to your staff.** Your employees should be able to stop by or schedule meetings to discuss suggestions and solutions. You function as an advisor.

✔ **Give feedback.** You shouldn't just point out things that could be done better; you should tell employees, on a regular basis, what they're doing well.

✔ **Ask for feedback.** Communication has to flow both ways. Ask your employees about any concerns they may have or ideas they'd like to propose.

✔ **Learn from mistakes.** If your parents had taken away your bike the first time you ever fell as a child, you probably wouldn't have learned to ride. Mistakes shouldn't be a time of reprimand and punishment; you should view them as the learning opportunities they really are.

Employees are more satisfied with their jobs when they can take pride in the final product, knowing that they were direct contributors.

Believing in Others

Empowerment is about more than simply sharing power. It's about believing in others. If Manager A tells Mary, "Here's an important project. You'd better not mess it up," then Mary doesn't exactly believe that her boss has faith in her.

But think about what Manager B could say: "Here's an important project, Mary. I know you've never done anything like it, but I can tell from your performance on other projects that you'll be able to do this well." Now that makes you feel good if you're Mary, doesn't it?

If you have confidence in your people, they'll have confidence in themselves. As long as you provide proper training (see Chapter 11) and fully explain the project, then you shouldn't have to worry. But if you've done all this and the performance is still unacceptable, you need to consider whether this individual is suitable for the responsibility — or even employment with your firm.

Part of believing in others is curing yourself of micromanaging. Do you hover over people? Watch their every move? Read every memo? Want to be in on every decision? Well, you're a micromanager.

But don't despair. Micromanagers are not born; they're created. You need to trust that your employees can and will do the job that they're hired to do. If someone else's job is to edit and send memos, then you probably don't need to be doing that. After all, aren't you paid to do bigger and better things?

Nothing destroys morale and inhibits risk taking like micromanagement.

You may find yourself micromanaging for a variety of reasons. Perhaps you feel that no one can do as good a job as you can. Perhaps you have misgivings about the employee you've given the assignment to or the employee has made a huge mistake in the past. Perhaps you're afraid that you'll lose power or prestige. Or maybe you even miss your old job and would rather do it instead of manage. None of these reasons are valid, and you'll end up not only hurting yourself and the employee, but your company as well. Don't be a micromanager.

If you're micromanaging an employee because they've let you down in the past, you're actually making the problem worse. Instead of labeling the person as a failure, you need to realize that your actions may have contributed to the problem. Meet with the individual (at a neutral time and place) to discuss the issues and decide what the employee does well and not so well. Then agree on a performance goal and commit to open communication.

Letting the Task Be Boss

Letting the task be the boss is an interesting concept, but what does it mean? Allison explains.

Whenever Allison has a problem on a project or needs a suggestion, she goes to her boss. But instead of just dropping the problem on the manager's lap, Allison presents three to four possible solutions, lists any pros and cons she can think of, and then solicits her boss's opinion to add to the mix. And by doing all of that, Allison takes charge of the task of reaching the decision. But her direction comes from the task, not from her manager.

That's what it means to let the task be the boss.

Your role is to be an advisor — and get out of the way. If you're standing in the middle of the field shouting orders to all the people you've supposedly empowered, then something's not right.

The task itself should dictate how the project is run. As an advisor, you're simply providing the tools and resources to get the job done.

Employees help define the task (the boss) and take full ownership of their assignments. As a result, who does what and under whose command becomes far less important than what gets done and how the customer is affected. This more relaxed, we're all in this together–type atmosphere allows employees to feel safe in vocalizing their ideas. Less fearful of coming up with an inappropriate or "wrong" solution, they can release their creativity and the entire organization benefits. (See Chapter 8 for more on encouraging creativity.)

If you follow a task-is-boss approach, issues such as titles, territorial disputes, and adherence to dated conventions should quickly become non-issues. Productivity and intellectual pride of ownership, though, should rise dramatically.

Chapter 11

Career Mapping — and the Tools for Navigation

● ●

In This Chapter

▶ Conducting a performance appraisal

▶ Developing training programs

▶ Knowing your training options

▶ Mapping your employees' careers

● ●

*P*rofessional development is one of the best — and most overlooked — motivational tools out there. By taking the time to train and develop your employees, you show that you really do want them to succeed within the company. At the same time, you improve your firm's future by investing in talented, knowledgeable employees — your intellectual capital.

In this chapter, you find out about one of your most valuable tools — the performance appraisal. Although this annual review has gotten a bad rap, it's actually an indispensable tool for employee training and development. You discover the many training options available to you and your staff. You also learn how career mapping and cross training can benefit both your employees and your company.

The Performance Appraisal

Employees need feedback on a regular basis. That's why a performance appraisal can be so productive. Although you may not like the process or the responsibility of formally evaluating staff members' work, performance appraisals are necessary for your employees' development. If you're not giving performance appraisals their full weight, then you're depriving your employees of an opportunity for professional development.

Formal performance appraisals help your staff in many ways. If you skip them, you miss out on an opportunity to:

✔ Reflect on past performance.

✔ Reinforce expectations.

✔ Communicate with your employee on a one-to-one basis.

✔ Discuss career goals.

✔ Document what your employee is — and isn't — doing right.

Making the appraisal process a year-round event

Performance appraisals typically require you to sum up a year's worth of per-formance in one review – not an easy task. But it doesn't have to be as hard as you think.

You can change your outlook about performance appraisals by regarding them as a year-round process instead of a once-a-year event. Throughout the year, jot down notes. What are your employees doing well? What do they need to improve? Be sure to write down specific examples. And share these insights with the staff member as often as possible and appropriate. For example, if an individual needs to improve her interpersonal skills to better work with her team, set up a one-on-one meeting with her to discuss the problem as soon as you notice it. And then follow up with her. If you notice improvement, let her know that, too — again, as soon as you notice it.

Performance appraisals should hold no surprises for employees. Employees should already know what they're doing well and what needs improvement, based on your continual feedback throughout the year. They should not be blindsided by poor performance ratings.

Giving feedback

One of the hardest things about a performance appraisal is that you're forced to give feedback to your employees — and it's not always positive. Employees don't always want to hear what you have to say.

Whether you're offering praise or constructive criticism, keep these impor-tant points in mind:

✔ **Prepare your appraisal in writing.** Your company may provide a two-page form to complete or you may decide to develop your own (check with your human resources department first!). Whatever the case, writing out your thoughts and evaluations on paper allows you to keep a record, which may be helpful in any legal dispute.

✔ **Deliver your feedback in person.** Schedule a meeting that's at least an hour long so that you can deliver and discuss the performance appraisal. If you don't use the full hour, that's okay. But at least you know you won't be interrupted by someone else during an important discussion.

✔ **Relate the appraisal to the company's business goals.** Point out how achievements and areas that need improvement are tied to company performance.

✔ **Engage in a two-way dialogue:** Although you've drawn up the appraisal, you need to make sure that the meeting is a conversation, not a lecture. Encourage your employees to comment. You may even want them to complete a self-appraisal before the meeting (see the sidebar in this section).

✔ **Offer specific examples and discuss actions, not perceived attitudes.** Your employees need to know when they didn't meet expectations before they can change their ways. So be polite and tactful, but be direct when you're talking about areas that need improvement. Instead of saying, "You didn't try as hard when you were working on the last project," which is an interpretation, spell out what actually happened: "The last report you submitted failed to mention two key points."

✔ **Emphasize opportunities for improvement.** Although you may need to cite specific examples of failures, focus on what the person can do to prevent such problems in the future.

✔ **Don't say *never* or *always*.** If you find yourself reprimanding an employee because they're never on time or always rude, censor yourself. These words are rarely accurate.

✔ **Set goals for the coming year.** Outline objectives in line with the employee's career aspirations or spell out the steps necessary to improve in certain areas. This is the information staff members can take away from the meeting and focus on over the coming months.

If your company policy is to announce pay increases during the performance evaluation, you may want to sever the two and schedule a separate meeting to talk about money issues. If the two topics are discussed in the same meeting, employees may be more concerned about hearing and reacting to the amount of the raise than discussing their performance. In addition, you want a performance discussion to include the employee's perspective and feedback. And if pay is based on performance, then an increase should not be decided until that conversation has taken place. Say that you have rated an individual poorly in a particular area of performance, but during the meeting she points out other accomplishments that may have been overlooked. You may need to adjust the overall performance evaluation, and, therefore, her pay increase. You can't do this as effectively if both topics are discussed in one meeting. And employees will be less likely to feel that their pay increases are a foregone conclusion.

Setting goals

As a manager, one of your main responsibilities is setting goals for your department and staff and making sure that they're achieved. Setting goals not only gives your employees something to strive for, but it's also a way to gauge their performance. Performance appraisals are the primary venue for you and your employees to establish individual objectives.

Good performance appraisals don't just review employee performance throughout the year. They include an action plan for achieving future success.

All employees — even stellar ones — should have goals and guidelines, so that they know what's expected of them and know how to produce what's expected.

Here are some general tips to keep in mind when you're setting goals:

- ✔ **Make it a two-way process.** Work with your employees to establish goals, so that your staff members are more invested in the outcome and understand how the goals were created. Don't just tell them what their goals are without asking for input.

- ✔ **Write down the objectives.** For whatever reason, seeing the goals in writing — as on the performance appraisal — makes them seem more real and important. Your employees will give them higher priority because they know they are recorded for future reference.

- ✔ **Set challenging, yet realistic goals.** Whether the objectives you and your employees agree on are short term or long term, they should be achievable. Nothing is more discouraging than looking at a list of goals and feeling like it's a lost cause.

- ✔ **Be specific.** If an objective can't be measured, it's probably not specific enough. Make sure that you and the employee know precisely what's expected and when it's expected.

  You may think it's almost impossible to set specific goals in more subjective areas, such as writing or customer service. Au contraire. You can set goals for fewer drafts within the process or improved customer feedback on surveys. Think creatively.

- ✓ **Establish a deadline.** If you don't set a deadline, the goals will become lost in the hectic routine of your employees' daily responsibilities.

- ✓ **Make sure the goals support an employee's career path.** Goals should be in line with each employee's long-term career plans. For example, if an employee tells you she'd like to move into a management position, be sure to include objectives that help her acquire the necessary experience, skills, and knowledge.

- ✓ **Set a stretch goal.** In addition to the realistic objectives, set a goal that requires employees to stretch their skills and abilities. If you need to, give them the tools or training that will help them accomplish that goal. Show your staff that you believe in them.

- ✓ **Don't make the mistake of setting too many goals.** Your employees won't be able to give each one the focus it deserves. Two to three goals at one time is a good general rule.

Goals are a great motivating tool. They show employees where they need to go and can let them see the smaller steps they need to take to make it a reality. Say that an employee is facing a huge project. He can divide that project (the goal) into smaller, more manageable tasks — such as outlining a report, researching the topics, writing the report, and gathering feedback. Although the employee may feel that the goal is far away, each step he completes places him closer and closer to his objective. And once he reaches his objective, he can look back to where he was a year ago and see his success.

If an employee is overwhelmed by a huge, long-term goal, schedule a meeting to discuss the steps involved in the process.

Try a self-evaluation

One technique you may want to try is to have your employees complete a self-evaluation of their strengths and weaknesses. Not only must employees examine their skills before you meet, but you discover how well they think they're doing.

For example, Alison may think that she's a wonderful communicator because she speaks up frequently at team meetings. But in your opinion, she monopolizes the team meeting and discourages others from contributing. If you find discrepancies between your assessments, you have an opportunity to discuss them during the performance appraisal. And these differences may also be a clue to you that you need to improve your communication with that staff person. After all, if you provide clear feedback on successes and expectations throughout the year, you shouldn't have major discrepancies during the actual review.

The 360° evaluation

If you find typical performance appraisals too one-sided, you may be fond of the *360° evaluation* that's gaining popularity. In this type of review, managers are evaluated not only by their boss, but by their coworkers and subordinates (sometimes of the manager's choosing) as well.

If done correctly, a 360° evaluation can boost productivity in many areas. Employees discover skills they may need to improve — such as running the team meeting more effectively or

involving all staff members in discussions — that may not have been otherwise noted. They also receive affirmation of the things they are doing well from many sources, not just their boss.

One key to the process is that the reviewees should be anonymous. Another key is that peer reviews should not be used to decide pay increases or promotions. These evaluations work best when their sole purpose is for employee development.

Training and Development Programs

Most employees realize that how well they do on a job has a lot to do with the kind of training they receive. Today's new recruits are particularly hungry for career-growth opportunities. So don't be surprised if, during a job interview, someone asks you a lot of questions about your training and development programs.

Training and development can meet multiple needs. Although the words *training* and *development* are usually used in tandem, they actually relate to two different things. *Training* addresses immediate needs, such as using computer software or finding a better way to do a task. *Development* is more long term and centers around career development — for example, gaining the skills necessary to get the next promotion.

If an employee isn't performing well on the job, take a look at the training you've provided. Did you let him know when he didn't meet expectations and how to avoid the problem in the future? Did you pair the individual with a mentor to help him learn the ropes? You may discover that you haven't done all that you can to help the employee succeed within the company.

As a manager, you're responsible for staff development. Development doesn't just happen on its own. No matter how talented and motivated your employees are, they need training to help them achieve their full potential within your company.

Determining training needs

Before you can jump in and start training your employees, you need to figure out who needs what. Remember that training is not a one-size-fits-all situation. Each staff member may have individual needs, and it's your job to determine what those are. Thanks to performance evaluations, you should already have a head start. But don't just rely on your own sense of who needs what.

Discuss with your employees any areas in which they'd like to acquire additional training. Perhaps their computer skills are adequate enough to get the job done, but a course in a particular software application would help them do their work in half the time. Or maybe you're grooming someone for a leadership position, but he doesn't feel ready to lead group meetings. A public-speaking course may be just the solution.

Don't forget to look at soft skills as well. Your employee may be a technical whiz, but is she a team player? How does she communicate with the rest of the staff? These areas can be addressed through training.

When assessing staff training needs, don't just focus on weaknesses. Consider your employees' strengths and aspirations as well. If Brian is a fantastic writer, you may mutually agree that he could oversee your department's internal communications. But maybe he needs some formalized instruction to round out his innate abilities and reinforce his confidence.

Whatever you do, address immediate training needs first and then focus on long-term development issues.

If you don't feel comfortable assessing your staff's training and development needs, you may want to consult with your human resources department or hire an outside source. These experts can use employee focus groups, surveys and questionnaires, and other tools to evaluate your department's training needs.

Selecting the right method

After you determine that your employees require training in a particular area, you need to decide what method of training is appropriate. For example, if your entire department needs training on new software, the most cost-effective solution may be in-house training. But if only one or two staff members need training — say, on project management skills — you may opt to send them to an outside seminar.

Distance learning

A new trend that is catching on is *distance learning*. In this type of training program, employees at various locations can be part of the same seminar or training path, thanks to high-tech delivery systems such as videoconferencing and the Internet.

Distance learning has many benefits. Because employees don't need to be together in the same location, you're able to reach more people in your training effort and eliminate or reduce travel and lodging expenses for participants. Employees are also able to work at their own pace and convenience, establishing individualized objectives. And instructors are able to do more one-on-one consultations.

Here are three common distance learning options:

✔ **Video teleconferencing:** Employees at different office locations can take the same seminar, which is typically transmitted at predetermined times.

✔ **Internet:** Staff members select programs to work on as their schedules and needs determine. Employees and instructors can communicate via message boards and e-mail.

✔ **Internal networks:** This increasingly popular option converts classroom-based training information into coursework available on your company intranet. Be warned, though, that this does require set-up time and lots of expertise to develop an effective training curriculum.

Take time in choosing your training sources. Don't let cost be the only consideration. You also may want to do post-training surveys, so that you can discover how useful the type of training you chose actually was to your employees.

Some of the more common training options include

✔ **In-house training:** Depending on the company, your human resources department may be able and willing to offer or arrange training on given topics, such as sales techniques or time management. Your IT department may be able to provide workshops or tailored seminars on particular software applications. Not only is in-house training cost-effective, but you may be able to arrange several short training sessions to accommodate schedules as well. Doing so helps minimize work disruptions.

✔ **Outside seminars and conferences:** Seminars and conferences are a great way to provide training when no one in your company has the particular expertise. Held at a public site, such as a hotel or conference center, most seminars require that you preregister. The cost can range from less than $100 per person to as much as $500 or more for a one-day session, depending on the topic. Typically, the more people you register, the bigger discount you receive.

You get what you pay for. Because seminars are targeted to a large audience and often cover broad topics, the training that participants receive may be somewhat generic. In addition, the presenter's skill and experience often dictate the ultimate value of the session.

✔ **Tuition reimbursement programs:** Tuition reimbursement programs fall more under the development category: They address long-term training needs of career development, such as leadership or advanced certification in a given area. Typically, a company reimburses employees for a percentage (or all) of the expenses related to courses that the employee takes. Some companies reimburse registration fees but not books. Others pay for only those courses that relate to an employee's job duties. Others pay 100 percent of all costs, as long as a certain grade point average is maintained in each course.

Using career mapping

If you want your employee to enjoy what he's doing, feel challenged, and stay on board for the long haul, you need to offer career planning, also called *career mapping.* Career mapping involves setting long-term goals for employees, and then developing a plan to make the goals happen.

Career mapping involves *career development plans.* You list specific goals and deadlines and provide standards for the measurement of those goals. You also cover the tools, such as outside seminars or tuition reimbursement programs, that will help your employee get the training and development he needs. Career mapping is the perfect complement for the goal section of your performance appraisal.

Table 11-1 covers some things your employees should consider when working with you to develop a career plan. You and the employee need to consider the person's interests, values, working habits, personality traits, and skills. The first column lists categories. The second column is where your employees rate them on a scale of 1 to 5, with 5 being the most important. How many items your employees list will vary from person to person, depending on individual values and interests. Even if they have ten items listed, they can still use the 1 to 5 measurement here. (Yes, in that case, more than one item will have the same score.) Here's what each category encompasses:

✔ **Values** includes items such as salary desires, training interests, working on teams versus working more independently, and family time. Your employees should list their values and then rank them in order of importance.

✔ **Working style** includes the type of work your employees like, as well as the amount of diversity they need on the job. It also covers how much challenge they want on the job, as well as their need for creative outlets and stability.

✔ **Strengths and weaknesses** are based on past on-the-job performance. The category should help employees identify what they're good at, as well as the areas they need to improve (which may be potential action items) A one score would me a minor strength or weakness; a five would indicate a pronounced strength or weakness.

As they complete Table 11-1, ask your employees to think about whether they'd like to work for the same company in five years, what kind of salary they'd like to make, and how much decision-making authority they'd like. Employees should also think about the type of environment they'd like to work in, as well as the skills they'd like to be using.

For example, one employee may decide that her goal is to end up as a director within the current company. To accomplish that goal, the staff member may need to gain experience in other departments, serve as a manager, acquire additional financial knowledge, and perhaps take a stint as a trainer for a while. As a result, action items may include researching other positions within the company, attending a management seminar, or even acquiring an MBA.

After you've settled on a career plan, you need to help your employees update the plan as necessary. You should also set a time to review the action items — for example, once a month — as well as develop a timetable for each action item. Remember to be realistic.

For your employees to arrive at their career destinations, they must first know where they want to end up. That's why mapping out a career plan is so crucial to employee development.

You should also encourage your employees to discuss their career plans with you. Obviously, if one of your staff members wants to end up as a manager but balks at decision making and working with executives, you may need to talk to him about the reality of these plans.

In addition, remember that a career plan needs to be flexible to accommodate unexpected events or life changes.

Table 11-1	Developing a Career Plan
Category	*Your Answers*
Values	

Category	Your Answers
Working style	_____
	_____
	_____
	_____
Strengths	_____
	_____
	_____
	_____
Weaknesses	_____
	_____
	_____
	_____

Cross training

In years past, employees were defined by their job descriptions and did only specific tasks relating to that job. But those times are long gone, and *cross training* has become increasingly important.

Cross training involves orienting staff members to do other jobs within a department. It also may mean that employees receive training in jobs in other departments within the company.

At companies that employ cross training, it's not uncommon to find technical employees occasionally working in non-technical departments or sales staff working inside the office to create the product. Cross training can take a few hours each day or perhaps months over the course of a year.

The advantages of cross training include

- ✔ Employees better understand the responsibilities, pressures, and priorities of their coworkers.
- ✔ The potential exists for decreased territorialism and increased teamwork and collaboration.
- ✔ Employees have a firsthand understanding of how each job fits into the company's overall vision.

✔ Staff have a better knowledge of how things work and also have an increased skill set.

✔ Companies are less likely to overstaff because all employees are trained to do multiple jobs and a slow department can help one that is temporarily swamped.

✔ Employees experience increased motivation and renewed interest in their jobs.

✔ Staff members appreciate one another's abilities more.

✔ Companies are better able to maintain productivity when employees leave the company.

But cross training isn't all positive. It has its downsides as well. If you decide to implement cross training, keep in mind that you need to put thought and effort into the project. You can't just suddenly decide to swap employees' jobs for the afternoon. Here are some of the challenges you face when cross training:

✔ **Implementing cross training, whether it's for a day or a few months, takes time and effort on the part of managers.** You may discover that your employees don't know the jobs they're cross training on well enough to make decisions. As such, they'll need your constant direction and attention.

✔ **If your company really takes cross training to heart — with employees swapping jobs for a quarter, for example — you may discover that you're creating a group of generalists.** That's okay for some companies, but you need to consciously decide whether your organization is more productive with a group of generalists or with a group of specialists.

✔ **Your employees may not know what you expect of them when they're cross training.** What kind of decision-making powers do they have? Are they expected to jump in and perform or sit down and observe? You need to establish this criteria upfront, not when the time comes to make decisions on the job.

✔ **Cross-training may not match some of your employees' career goals.** If your current employees are doing their dream jobs and have no interest in sales, for example, forcing them to train in the sales department, however sporadically, may create demotivation.

In short, cross training as a way of life may not be the road you want to lead your organization down. However, cross training for a day or so is a good way to promote teamwork within your organization. It's definitely a motivational option you should consider for your employees.

What about lateral moves?

In the past, lateral moves were often seen as a bad thing — as if the employee performed poorly in his former position and was no longer on the promotional track.

No more. Lateral moves are seen as a good way to gain the experience that can help a person ultimately attain his or her career goals. For example, in order to become department manager, Jane may need to be experienced in each of the sub-departments. Once she has gained hands-on knowledge, she'll be better prepared to lead the entire group as a whole.

Managers who have worked in several different departments realize how the company works together as a team to get the job done. They can better see the big picture. And they can make suggestions that help improve processes.

A lateral move may also be a way to retain a valued employee who no longer feels challenged in his job.

Even *downward* moves may pay off in the long term. Sometimes employees lack the crucial experience that's necessary to thrive in their current position. By taking a step back and gaining that experience, they can ultimately go forward in their careers. However, before demoting a staff member, be certain that the move will indeed give him or her the skills and training needed to ultimately succeed. Otherwise, you may not be addressing the problem.

Realizing the benefits, some companies have even encouraged current managers to make lateral moves by enticing them with pay raises. Managers can gain new perspectives, meet new contacts, expand their skill sets, and better understand the company's business.

Chapter 12

Mentoring for Professional Growth

- -

- -

*F*ormally or informally, you've probably had a mentor to look up to or served as a mentor for someone else at one time in your life. A *mentor* is a person who has more experience in a particular area who offers advice and expertise. Whether your mentor was your big brother or a teacher, that person helped you learn the ropes. Likewise, as a mentor for someone else, you probably provided insight that the person needed to navigate unfamiliar territory.

Mentors are as important at work as they are when growing up. Employees benefit from the guidance of more tenured staff members. Mentors gain fulfillment by sharing their knowledge with less experienced coworkers. And companies reap the rewards all around. In this chapter, you discover the many benefits of mentoring. I even show you how to set up a mentoring program, if you don't have one already.

What Are Mentoring Programs?

Mentoring programs pair more experienced staff members with employees who want to gain experience in a particular field or skills area, or they pair veteran employees with new staff members who just need a helping hand to show them the ropes. Mentors may offer friendly tips (what that "casual" dress code really means) or professional advice (no, you don't want to make that lateral move if your goal is to be a manager). Mentors sometimes help their mentees just by being a source of encouragement.

The mentor and the mentored work together, sharing experiences and insights. The best mentors offer both encouragement and honest criticism. But they don't direct: They guide. The mentor-mentee relationship may even last the entire duration of the participants' careers. In a survey by Robert Half International, 82 percent of the executives polled said they still keep in touch with their mentors.

Mentees should never be paired with one of their supervisors. Mentees need to be able to talk freely with their mentor about a range of topics, from office politics to career aspirations, and may not be able to do so if their mentor is their supervisor — or even if their mentor is a member of the same team.

Mentoring isn't a new concept. In the same Robert Half International survey mentioned earlier, 75 percent of the respondents said they personally have had mentors. The difference now is that people don't always have to find their own mentors — sometimes their companies facilitate the process.

If you currently have a mentoring program, don't think that it'll just run itself. New hires may perceive that their assigned mentors are busy and be reluctant to ask questions, and mentors may be afraid they'll ruffle their protégés' feathers by offering advice. As a manager, you need to encourage the process of mentoring.

Mentoring Pays Off

Mentoring is a crucial practice for transferring wisdom, fostering talent, and promoting the best practices within the firm or your department. More and more companies are recognizing the rewards of establishing a mentoring program and are making mentoring a formal part of their organizations.

Helping new hires acclimate

In the Robert Half International survey, 94 percent of executives said mentors are important for professionals just beginning their careers. More experienced staff members can provide advice on how the corporate culture works and give guidance on charting a career path. Mentors can also help new hires feel like they belong by introducing them to coworkers, answering questions, and offering an additional source of support.

Think about your first few months at your present company. Didn't you wonder what the protocol for casual dress on Fridays was? Or whose unofficial sign-off you needed on your first important project? If you were one of the lucky ones, you had a mentor within the company whom you could go to for guidance. If you weren't so lucky, you probably felt like you were left alone in the deep end to either sink or swim.

Although your employees can discover mentoring relationships through organizations outside of the office, corporate programs work best because they help develop loyalty toward the company and cultivate teamwork.

Promoting professional development

You don't have to limit participation in mentoring programs to new employees. Professionals at any stage of their careers can benefit from the wisdom and expertise of a mentor. For example, you may have a manager in a field office who has been with your firm for several years. He could benefit from being paired with a more senior employee: Maybe he could gain additional insight into being a better manager, or maybe he'd like to move up the corporate ladder to become an executive himself.

Enhancing the mentor's leadership

Keep in mind that the person doing the mentoring gets almost as much benefit from the mentor-mentee relationship as the person being mentored. Staff members whom you choose to be mentors are recognized as having qualities worth emulating and experience worth sharing. Being handpicked as a mentor is an honor as well as a responsibility. Mentors get to pass the torch, so to speak — and they know it's a compliment that they've been asked to fulfill that role.

For many employees, being a mentor may be a step toward a promotion. Mentors develop supervisory and training skills, not to mention leadership qualities.

Another thing to keep in mind: Just about everyone likes to assist others. By being a mentor, staff members contribute to the development of less experienced employees. Most mentors enjoy the responsibility, and employees who enjoy their work normally are — you guessed it — motivated employees.

Facilitating corporate growth

So what's in it for the company? Are mentoring programs only good for the participants, both mentor and mentee? Not at all. Mentoring programs are important to an organization's success, too. A mentoring program helps your firm:

✔ **Enhance productivity.** New employees who get up to speed more quickly are able to contribute more quickly. Because they have someone to go to for guidance, they're also less likely to make errors in judgment or delay decisions.

✔ **Increase intellectual capital.** By encouraging mentors to impart your firm's best practices and wisdom to other employees, you create your own homegrown talent. When job openings occur and you're searching for qualified candidates, you may find that you don't have to look beyond your own backyard.

✔ **Support recruitment.** When you're competing with other firms for qualified candidates, your organization may hold the advantage if you can tout the benefits of a great mentoring program that the candidates could participate in initially as a mentee and then again, down the road, as a mentor.

Establishing a Mentoring Program

Have you ever wanted to clone one of your top employees so that the rest of your staff could be just like her? With a mentoring program, you can do that . . . well, sort of. You can't exactly clone your top employee, but you can encourage her to share her knowledge and talent with others. And then, before you know it, you'll have a top-rate team of loyal performers.

If your company doesn't have a mentoring program already, you may want to develop one. The rest of the chapter gives you the information you need to do just that.

What are the goals you want to achieve?

One of the first things you need to think about is what exactly you'd like to accomplish by starting a mentoring program. Have employees been resigning lately after spending only a couple of years on the job? Then you'll probably want to develop a program that works on employee retention. You can do that by pairing relatively new hires with more senior employees.

Or perhaps you've noticed a lack of qualified candidates when it comes to open management positions. Skill building, perhaps even across teams, may be something you'd want to consider. When employees feel like they're doing a good job and have the skills they need, they're more likely to stay with the company.

Will your mentoring program be formal or informal?

A mentoring program can be informal, meaning that you encourage the process but the responsibility for creating a mentor-mentee relationship is really on your employees. Or a program can be formal, meaning you assign mentees to mentors and oversee the relationship.

Although an informal program may give your employees more flexibility, a formal mentoring program usually works best. Your time spent planning a formal mentoring program usually pays off with better mentor-mentee relationships down the road.

Keep in mind that you can't force people to get along. That's one rationale behind having an informal program, in which employees usually choose each other. However, a well-designed and well-operated formal program should be able to consistently pair folks who complement one another.

Which type of program works best for your company?

Like ice cream, mentoring programs come in more than one flavor. In fact, what works best for your company may not work at all for other firms. Here are a few mentoring options that you may want to consider:

- **Traditional mentoring.** In this relationship, a more senior employee is paired with a new or less experienced employee for the purpose of giving guidance and advice.

- **Group mentoring.** In this option, one mentor is teamed up with a handful of mentees. The group decides when and how often to meet. The sole mentor offers insight into corporate culture and decision making and office politics.

- **Team mentoring.** A twist on the group approach is when one mentee has several mentors. The thought here is that one person can't cover everything. Each of the mentors offers guidance in select areas.

- **Cross-skill mentoring.** In this approach, mentees are paired with mentors who have different areas of expertise than the mentee.

- **Consultant mentoring.** In this scenario, someone outside the firm helps employees become familiar with the field. If you opt for this relationship, also consider using an internal mentor to help employees with company-related matters.

✔ **Reverse mentoring.** Instead of more senior employees serving as mentors, more recent hires fill that role. This technique is especially useful when the newer hire has skills that tenured employees don't have. In addition, newer employees can help provide a fresh perspective on current products and practices.

So how do you know which one is right for you? Say that you're a manager in a hospital, and you've got new nurses you'd like to pair with mentors. You may want to consider reverse mentoring if you think that your relatively recent hires are more knowledgeable about some new practices than your more tenured employees are. You may want to consider group mentoring if you have only one or a few senior nurses who have time for mentoring and a batch of newly hired nurses who need mentors. And so on. Match your mentoring program with what you have and what you need.

Matching Up Mentors with Employees

You need to put some thought into which employees you bring together as mentor and mentee. Not every person is suited to being a mentor, and trying to force someone into that role just doesn't work.

A mentor has to be a special person. Not everyone in your organization is well suited for this crucial role. As you decide who to ask to be a mentor, consider that an ideal mentor should

✔ Demonstrate strong leadership, communication, and technical skills.

✔ Show empathy toward others.

✔ Have a positive attitude.

✔ Enjoy his or her job.

✔ Know the position, its responsibilities, and its role within the big picture.

✔ Want to encourage and help others.

✔ Be able to listen attentively.

✔ Give positive feedback and constructive criticism.

✔ Guide, but not direct, coworkers.

✔ Be a good role model.

Even if a person has all of these qualities, he or she may not be a good match for the prospective mentee. Don't forget to take personalities and work styles into consideration when you're pairing participants.

Advising the mentors

You may have a candidate who exhibits all the qualities of a top-notch mentor, but she or he may not be sure how to fulfill that role effectively. Here's some advice you can give prospective mentors to help them develop their mentoring skills:

✔ **Advise, don't command.** The mentor isn't the boss. The mentor can give the mentee insight based on personal experience, but should never give orders.

✔ **Tailor your approach to the learning style.** Some people learn new information best when it's offered verbally. Others prefer

documents. Still others prefer to be shown. The mentor's approach should vary according to each mentee's needs.

✔ **Listen before you speak.** The mentor should listen intently and let the mentee take the conversational lead. Although the mentee may consult a mentor for advice, sometimes the mentor's response should be to encourage the mentee to talk through the solution. The mentor shouldn't try to solve every dilemma or offer expertise at every turn; doing so may hinder the mentee's growth.

If a mentor turns out not to be a good match for a particular mentee, assign a different mentor immediately. You create problems for everyone involved if you delay.

If You Need Assistance . . .

If you want to create a mentoring program, but you don't know where to start or you don't have the time to create a program on your own, then you may want to get some help. Here are three possible sources of assistance.

Menttium

www.menttium.com

Founded in 1991, Menttium helps corporations design and implement mentoring programs. Menttium's goal is to have an immediate impact on an organization's ability to successfully attract, develop, and retain a diverse employee base. Menttium specializes in cross-racial, cross-gender, cross-industry, cross-company, cross-functional, cross-generational, and cross-cultural mentoring.

The company's clients include Fortune 500 and 1000 companies, and it has offices in Minneapolis, Chicago, Detroit, San Francisco, and Dallas.

For more information, call (612) 814-2600 or write to the company's head-quarters at Riverview Office Tower, 8009 34th Ave. So., Bloomington, MN 55425.

Corporate Mentoring Solutions Inc.

www.mentoring.ws

Formerly known as The Mentoring Institute, this company has been around since 1978 and can help start or improve your mentoring program. It has developed more than 120 mentoring programs, specializing in four areas: orienting new hires, career development, executive development, and enhancing existing mentoring programs. It has case studies on its Web site, as well as a program (Online Mentoring System) that helps match mentors with mentees. You may want to subscribe to the company's free monthly newsletter, *MentorInk*.

For more information, contact the company at 11316 Ravenscroft Place, Sidney, B.C., V8L 5R4, or call (877) 955-0314. You can also e-mail the company at sales@mentoring.ws.

International Mentoring Association

www.wmich.edu/conferences/mentoring/

Since 1988, the International Mentoring Association's goal has been to provide a regular public forum for effective mentoring. Located at Western Michigan University, this organization also has information on mentoring strategies and programs, promoting effective mentoring, and maintaining support for the concept of mentoring.

Mentoring program coordinators, mentors, and mentees can become members. If you decide to become a member, you receive

- An annual subscription to *Mentoring Connection,* the association's quarterly newsletter
- Discounted registration for annual mentoring conferences
- A membership directory, which includes member and program profiles
- Access to CONSLT-L, an electronic network for discussion of mentoring issues

For more information, write to the International Mentoring Association, Western Michigan University, Office of Conferences and Institutes, Kalamazoo, MI 49008, or call (616) 387-4174.

Looking for leaders

The ingredients of leadership are much debated; everyone seems to have a slightly different idea of what it takes to be a successful leader. But everyone can agree that a leader's responsibility is to set the example and behave the way the leader wants others to behave and that you want your office leaders to possess a dedication to your company's corporate culture and values. You may want leaders to also possess the following qualities:

- ✔ Energy and commitment
- ✔ Fairness, honesty, and objectivity in all matters
- ✔ Good decision-making skills
- ✔ The courage to take smart risks

Find these people in your office. They are the ones you want as mentors.

Part V
Paying Your People — and Patting Them on the Back!

The 5th Wave   By Rich Tennant

"I told them it would take more than a pay increase to keep me happy at my desk all day."

In this part . . .

Most people won't work for free. So, obviously, money plays an important role in motivating your employees to show up for work. But there's a right way and a wrong way to compensate your employees for their time, and Chapter 13 gives you the scoop.

No matter how high the salary, you also need to recognize your staff on a daily basis for their efforts. Money isn't the end-all. In Chapter 14, you find out how you can develop a program that gives them the recognition they desire — and deserve.

Chapter 13

Compensation:
It's More Than Money

M otivating your employees requires more than just a series of pep talks. (If only it was that easy!) Motivation requires consistent, hard work on your part. As a manager, everything you do affects your employees' enthusiasm. Furthermore, the way your company operates can motivate or demotivate employees. One of the most important factors in creating an enthusiastic workforce is your firm's compensation package and the way you present it to your employees.

Although you may not be the ultimate decision maker in some of these areas (many may be within the purview of your human resources department), you can be an advocate for your staff. If you think that additional time off would be more beneficial to employees than spot bonuses, for example, you may want to speak to your own manager or provide this feedback to your human resources contact. (For more detailed information on these topics, take a look at my book *Human Resources Kit For Dummies*.)

Assembling the Compensation Package

Compensation doesn't just refer to the money you're paying your employees. It also includes other incentives that you offer, such as bonuses, childcare assistance, and insurance benefits. These are all things that you can't overlook if you hope to be competitive in today's workplace.

Mission critical compensation

Some firms set up compensation scales according to the relationship between a particular job and the company's mission. The more essential a job is to the fundamental mission of the company, the higher its pay range is likely to be.

To determine the hierarchy of positions within your company, follow these steps:

1. List all the jobs in your company.

   Your list should include everyone, from the CEO to the mailroom clerk.

2. Group the jobs into categories based on major function.

   Some examples of categories include sales, management, administrative, and marketing.

3. Rank each job according to its relationship to your company's mission.

   Certain jobs contribute directly to the mission, while others provide support. At a publishing company like Hungry Minds, the editors and writers are direct contributors

to the mission of publishing books, while members of the internal information systems team are indirect contributors.

If you're unsure of where a position fits in, consider asking yourself some of the following questions:

- How closely does the job relate to the company mission?

- How indispensable is the job?

- Does the job require special skills or training? In other words, how difficult is the job?

- Does the position generate revenue or support revenue-producing functions?

The goal is to end up with a hierarchy of jobs based on their importance in reaching your company's mission. Keep in mind that you look solely at the positions, not the individuals who fill the position. You simply determine how important the job is in relationship to your company's mission and strategic goals.

Base wage or *salary,* on the other hand, refers only to the wage or salary that you pay your employees before any deductions or additions. To be specific, *wage* refers to pay for hourly employees, while *salary* refers to the pay given employees who receive a set amount per set period, no matter how many hours worked.

Incentives include any special rewards that you offer your employees — think bonuses. This amount is on top of their base wage or salary.

In addition to incentives, compensation packages include *benefits* such as health insurance, stock options, and retirement plans.

Some of your employees may receive *commissions,* or a percentage of each sale, on top of their salary or instead of it.

If you're offering a fair compensation package, you shouldn't have a problem with other companies stealing your employees because of financial entice-ments. If you're sure your compensation package is fair and yet you are losing employees, you may want to take a look at your managers and their management style or your company's culture.

Making a Living: Setting Salary Scales

One of the first things a company should do is establish pay levels within the organization. Employees should not be hired and offered salaries at random. Your company needs to have a general philosophy about how compensation is determined.

Here are some basic questions to help you begin developing a compensation philosophy:

✔ Will you establish salaries that are merely competitive with other employers in your industry or region, or will they be higher?

✔ Are you going to develop structured pay scales for each job classification or base wages on an individual's value and potential?

✔ Will you offer bonuses, other financial rewards (such as stock options), or benefits? How large a role will they play in overall compensation and how will they be determined?

✔ Are you going to offer increases according to merit or length of tenure?

Building your pay scales

After you determine your compensation philosophy, you need to implement it. The following are the most common methods used to establish pay scales:

✔ **The going rate.** Using the going rate approach, you or your human resources department determines what other companies in your indus-try and region are paying for similar jobs, and structure your pay accordingly. Although this system is easy to set up and administer, find-ing comparable jobs and pay rates can be difficult if any positions in your company are fairly unique or unusual. (See the sidebar for tips on how to find out what other companies in your industry are offering.)

✔ **Job evaluation and pay grading.** Using the job evaluation and pay grad-ing method, you evaluate each job based on several factors, such as how it affects the bottom line, how difficult or dangerous it is, and what kind of training is necessary, and then develop an appropriate pay range. The federal government uses such a system to pay its employees, although the approach isn't currently popular in the business world.

Job evaluation and pay grading works best for large companies that must have some type of structured approach to pay ranges. The downside to the system is that it requires much time and effort to create and maintain. It is also difficult to maintain in a company that has rapid change.

✔ **Management fit.** In this type of approach, a manager or owner decides the amount of pay for each employee, without using any system. As you may expect, the management-fit approach usually results in inconsistent pay. Resentment, hostility, and a lack of teamwork can result when inequities are discovered.

You can also look into alternative structures that are based more on what the employee can do and less on what the job description is:

✔ **Skill-based pay.** In this system, pay scales are determined by skill level, not job title. You create a list of skills necessary for each job and develop the criteria that signify the mastery of each skill. As your employees master the skill, they receive pay increases.

This approach is popular because you can hire new employees at below-market rates, then encourage them to improve their skills. The company usually benefits from increased quality and production. Team-based organizations, in particular, like this approach.

On the other hand, establishing a skill-based pay system takes time and money (you may have to hire outside consultants), and the system must be constantly monitored. Also, if your employees master all their skills, they max out their pay. Make sure that you can justify paying many employees the maximum salary or wage if many employees master all the relevant skills. If the skills required for the job are constantly changing, then you must continuously update your pay system.

✔ **Competency-based pay.** This system bases compensation on an employee's traits or characteristics instead of on specific skills. Salaries and raises are based on how well employees acquire the core competencies needed for their positions. Although this system rewards improved performers and star employees, your employees may think the process is unfair and subjective. To avoid charges of discrimination, you must define competencies carefully.

✔ **Broadbanding.** In broadbanding, you group several related jobs, such as office assistant and receptionist, into one *band* — for example, administrative staff. You assign a pay range to that band, but you don't base it on a job title. Doing so gives you the flexibility of paying based on factors such as job performance instead of job title. You're also able to transfer employees among the same jobs in the band without battling red tape. On the downside, broadbanding can result in inconsistent compensation across departments and leave you open to charges of favoritism or discrimination, unless you follow clear, established guidelines.

 ✔ **Variable pay.** This system links a percentage of an employee's pay to performance and accomplishments. You first establish a base pay rate, and then define group and individual objectives as a variable salary component. On the plus side, you're paying your employees a stable base income while also giving them financial incentives for superior performance. On the downside, your employees can become discouraged if they're not meeting performance targets. This system can also be difficult to administer.

Factoring in individuals

After you determine a particular pay scale for each job, you need to decide what to pay each person who has that position. Some of the things you want to think about are job performance, seniority, and advancement potential.

With most positions, the more experienced or educated an employee is, the more productive he or she is. Although this generalization isn't always true — for example, sometimes over-qualified employees are less productive than other employees — you want to take this factor into account when evaluating pay levels.

You need to determine how you'll gauge your employees' performance if job performance is one of the factors that influences pay rate. You may also want to pay certain employees more than others based solely on their potential to be stellar performers.

In the past, *seniority,* or length of service, has been a major factor in determining pay. However, seniority and productivity don't always correlate, so you may want to think carefully before basing raises on tenure alone.

Offering Benefits

If you want your company to retain its employees, you have to offer desirable benefits on top of fair salaries. Although you're not required to offer a full range of employee benefits, you may need to do so to attract and retain employees.

Benefits run the gamut from basic insurance packages to coveted options such as dependent care spending accounts, tuition reimbursement, and even in-house concierge services. Different companies offer different benefits; there is no one right combination. Chapter 6 describes benefits relating to work/life options, while the following sections in this chapter describe standard benefits that you don't want to do without.

Finding out the going rate

When you're working on setting a salary scale, one of the first things you should do is find out what other companies in your industry are offering their employees. Although this may sound like a difficult assignment, it doesn't have to be.

To find out what other companies are offering:

✔ Talk with specialized recruiters and human resources consultants.

✔ Talk with representatives of other companies.

✔ Review industry salary surveys.

✔ Carefully inspect classified advertisements in your daily newspaper, industry publications, and on the Internet.

If you're in accounting or finance, you may also want to look at the annual *Robert Half/ Accountemps Salary Guide* booklet. This booklet, which is used by the U.S. Bureau of Labor Statistics as a resource for its widely read *Occupational Outlook Handbook,* features salary levels for a wide range of positions and provides information on current and future hiring trends. To request a free copy, call 1-800-803-8367 or visit the Web site at www.rhi.com.

Keep in mind that compensation differs by region and company size. The number of qualified candidates, the growth of particular industries, and the cost of living in certain geographic areas all affect salary levels as well.

In general, your company should offer benefits choices to its employees. People's needs are different; therefore, giving your employees a menu of choices and letting them select the benefits that best fit their needs is helpful.

Insurance

Perhaps the most sought-after and common benefit — and the most expensive — is health insurance. Although the traditional *fee-for-service* plans are still available, most companies now offer *managed care* programs. Another option is a program that uses *health maintenance organizations (HMOs)*.

Fee-for-service plans reimburse members (employees and dependents) regardless of what doctor or hospital they go to. Managed care programs (including HMOs) focus on preventive health and are generally less expensive for both employee and employer. These programs offer many of the same benefits as fee-for-service, but your employees are limited as to which practitioners and facilities they can visit to receive maximum benefits. If your employees opt to go outside the network, they may not receive any benefits at all.

In addition to health insurance, you may provide dental insurance and vision care. Dental insurance generally covers all or part of the cost of routine checkups, fillings, and other regular dental procedures. Vision plans generally cover routine eye exams and pay a certain amount for eyeglasses.

Retirement plans

Retirement plans include traditional pensions and 401(k)s. Retirement plans differ in how much employees are required to contribute, as well as when employees are *vested,* or eligible for the money.

Although you're not required to offer a retirement plan to your employees, you're at a significant disadvantage in hiring and retention if you choose not to. If you do decide to offer a retirement plan, you need to pay special heed to the Employee Retirement Income Security Act (ERISA) of 1974.

In general, ERISA says that if you decide to offer a retirement plan, you must include all employees older than 21. You cannot require more than one year of service as an eligibility requirement. You must fund the plan annually, and you must purchase ERISA's government insurance to protect employees from the possibility of a pension plan dissolving. You also must not invest more than 10 percent of the assets in your pension plan in company stock.

Pensions

Years ago, employees usually stayed with one company and then received a retirement *pension,* or a fixed benefit amount. If they moved to another company, they generally lost their pensions. They had no say in how their pension money was invested.

Pensions were generally calculated based on salary level and length of service. Employers could fully fund *noncontributory pensions* or require employees to contribute to *contributory pensions.*

Pensions were popular because employees could count on receiving a fixed amount when they retired. In exchange, companies received employee loyalty and retention.

Unfortunately, pensions weren't able to move with the employees when they changed jobs and were expensive to administer. Today, many employers offer more flexible retirement benefits, such as 401(k) plans.

401(k) plans

If your company provides 401(k) plans, employees have their own accounts and can take the money with them when they switch companies. They can contribute as much as 15 percent of their income into the fund. The company may choose to match a percentage of that money — or even dollar for dollar — with its own funds. Taxes in 401(k) plans are deferred until withdrawal. Some plans even allow employees to borrow against their own accounts.

Employees themselves get to choose from investment options, ranging from very safe investments to slightly more adventurous ones. They're generally allowed to change these options or their contribution amounts at set times during the year, such as at the end of a quarter. By law, all employees are immediately vested in the money they contribute to their 401(k) plans, although they may not be vested in any employer contributions for several years.

The downsides are that employees do not know what their eventual payoff will be (their amount depends on the success of the stock market) and they receive a stiff tax penalty for most early withdrawals.

Time off

Even though you're paying your employees a salary, you can't expect them to work every day out of the year. That's why it's important that you pay employees for holidays, vacations, sick days, and personal days.

You should offer your employees a fixed number of paid holidays every year. Typical holidays include New Year's Day, Memorial Day, July 4th, Labor Day, Thanksgiving, and Christmas (and perhaps an extra day before or after the latter two holidays). Some companies also offer additional paid holidays.

The amount of vacation generally depends on the employees' length of service. In general, companies give employees more vacation than sick time. Most companies offer one to four weeks paid vacation, adding more time each year until a maximum amount is reached. In addition, some companies allow employees to carry over only a minimum number of vacation days each year to ensure that they take this important recovery time.

You should also offer your employees a certain number of sick days per year. Unlike vacation time, you generally offer the same number of sick days per year to each employee.

Personal days are generally designated for personal use, such as doctor appointments. Employees usually are given two to six per year, depending on the company. Usually, organizations require that employees use their personal days by the end of the calendar year or lose them.

Some companies choose to lump all their days off — vacation, personal, and sick days — into one pool of *paid time off (PTO),* giving employees the freedom to use it as they want.

You may even want to consider providing paid time off for jury duty, National Guard duty, and birthdays, as well as bereavement leave.

Leaves

If you've been in business any length of time, you've probably had an employee inquire about a leave of absence.

A *leave of absence* occurs when an employee is off work for a specific amount of time, usually without pay, but is still employed by the company. When the leave ends, the employee returns to his or her old position.

Employees may request a leave of absence because of the birth of a child, illness, to care for a parent or other family members, for military service, to travel, or for other personal reasons. Generally, they're required to submit a request in writing. The immediate manager or human resources department decides whether to grant the leave, and arranges the particulars of insurance and pay if it decides to allow the leave.

If you're a company with 50 or more employees, you are required by the Family Medical Leave Act (FMLA) to grant employees up to 12 weeks unpaid leave for the following reasons:

✔ To allow both mothers and fathers to care for a newly born or adopted child

✔ To care for a child, parent, or spouse with a serious health condition

✔ For a serious health condition that makes the employee unable to perform the job

Some states have additional requirements on FMLA leave. Consult an attorney familiar with the law in your state.

Childcare assistance

Because of changing family dynamics, more and more families have two working parents or only one parent. As a result, childcare assistance has become a very enticing benefit. (See Chapter 6 for more on childcare as a work/life issue.)

Here are some of the ways many companies are assisting employees with childcare:

✔ **Dependent care reimbursement accounts:** You can establish accounts that enable employees to use pretax dollars for dependent care.

✔ **Care referral sources:** These sources do the research to help employees find child and adult care services that match their needs.

✔ **Onsite care:** Some companies create onsite daycare facilities for their employees. Although it can be costly, employees see this as the ideal scenario because they can drop in on their children as needed.

✔ **Contracted daycare:** In this option, a company contracts with a childcare provider that holds slots for the employees' children.

✔ **Vouchers:** These subsidies reimburse employees for all or part of their childcare expenses.

Taking Advantage of Financial Incentives

Incentive programs are designed to inspire employee loyalty and increase productivity over the long term. Examples of incentive programs include stock options and profit sharing, which are covered in the following sections.

Although raises and bonuses aren't considered true incentive programs because they aren't designed to be long term, they do have an effect on employee motivation.

For all programs, whether they're short term or long term, you need to make sure that your employees understand the criteria for receiving the incentives and how the amount is determined, and know who will judge their performance. You should also make sure that you've set specific targets or quantifiable goals. Doing so discourages arguments and misunderstandings. Goals should not only be worthwhile, but attainable.

Never promise a financial incentive and then fail to deliver.

Stock options

When you grant your employees *stock options,* you give them the right to purchase company stock at a fixed price over a certain amount of time. This price usually is below market value.

Stock options are now common in employee packages offered by public companies, although they may only be available to employees who have worked for the company for a certain period of time. Most stock option programs include a vesting schedule, as well as a date at which the options expire.

Stock options encourage staff members to operate more as business partners, tying personal reward to the company's financial success. They also have the potential to, over time, generate significant wealth for employees and give staff members a sense of ownership in their company, therefore increasing the likelihood that they'll stay with the company for the long term.

If you're interested in setting up a stock option program for your employees, consult with an attorney who specializes in the area.

Profit sharing

Companies that have profit sharing programs set aside a percentage of their profits for employees. The better the company does, the higher the profits and the more money the employees receive. When employees have a financial stake in the company, they tend to work harder and smarter. Like a 401(k) plan, employees do not need to pay taxes on the money until it's withdrawn.

Profit sharing plans can be a good alternative for small companies who do not have enough employees or assets to find a good 401(k) plan provider.

If you're interested in starting a profit sharing program, you may want to check out the Web site of the Profit Sharing/401(k) Council of America at www.psca.org.

Raises

In most companies, raises are a once-a-year event greatly anticipated by employees. The amount generally varies depending on the individual's performance and the philosophy of the company.

No matter what method you use to award raises, make sure that your employees understand the guidelines. No quicker way exists to cause mutiny among your employees than to confuse them on the basis for the salary increase.

Several types of raises exist. If you base raises on seniority, they become pretty much automatic. *Seniority step-up* raises are commonly found in union contracts and are fairly rigid.

You can base your raises on superior performance. These *merit raises* reward employees who have done a superior job or who have acquired additional education or training. Merit raises are granted during a formal review process.

Another type of raise is known as a *cost-of-living adjustment* (COLA). These raises are designed to keep pace with inflation.

Bonuses

Bonuses occur one time per year or at a certain number of predetermined times each year. This extra cash is by no means guaranteed and can range from as much as several thousand dollars (or more, depending on the job) to nothing at all. Employees should never rely on their bonuses, even if they're quarterly, as part of their annual income.

Bonus amounts are usually based on company, team, or employee performance, or a combination of all three. They're usually in the form of cash payments, although stock options and deferred compensation are also possibilities.

Spot bonuses are another popular strategy to quickly recognize superior work. An employee is awarded a predetermined sum, typically ranging from $250 to $1,000, preferably within 24 to 48 hours of a certain achievement. This type of instant reward not only encourages additional contributions by the employee, but motivates others in the department as well.

No matter what form your bonus takes, you need to make sure that it follows three main principles:

- ✔ Employees receive bonuses based on specific results.
- ✔ The rules for bonuses are clear and fair.
- ✔ Bonuses reward extra effort and superior performance.

Bonuses don't need to be tied only to job performance. You can offer them for employee or client referrals, suggestions that enhance company goals, or for completing a successful special project.

Chapter 14

You Did Great! Recognizing Your Employees

*H*ave you ever experienced the power of a simple thank-you from your boss? Chances are, the phrase made you glow with pride. You knew that your hard work was appreciated.

A *sincere* thank-you means a lot. You can hand out a dozen job-well-done trophies, but unless you make the recipient feel that the reward is heartfelt, you're not truly recognizing the individual. In fact, cookie-cutter thank-you methods may even harm your relationships.

A manager needs to do more than simply make sure that things are running well. You need to be your team's general manager, coach, and cheerleader, encouraging team members whenever possible. You also need to actively support the recognition program. If you're not on board, this particular ship will sink.

In this chapter, I show you why a thank-you is so powerful and I give you some ideas on how you can show your employees that you truly care. In addition, you discover recognition ideas that show your employees how much you appreciate them — without breaking your budget.

Knowing Why Recognition Is Important

Whether you're the CEO of the company, the head of a department, or a middle manager, you can't afford to be above giving gratitude and recognition. Sure, your employees are getting paid to accomplish a certain task. But if they do it with record speed, exceed your expectations, come in under budget, or do anything else that sets them apart, you need to recognize their success . . . or you risk losing your team members to a more grateful company.

A recent national survey by Robert Half International shows that limited praise and recognition is the primary reason employees leave their jobs today, ahead of compensation concerns, limited authority, and personality conflicts.

A small thank-you note can enhance your company's corporate culture. Great corporate cultures encourage a team spirit, and thanking your teammates and employees for their stellar performances is vital. A positive corporate culture helps your retention efforts, lifts your employees' spirits, and (drum roll) increases your profit margin.

If you want to foster teamwork and create a positive work environment, try saying "Thanks." You feel good, your employees feel appreciated and valued, and your department is invigorated.

Creating a Recognition System

Just because your company has a long-standing employee-of-the-month program, don't think that you're doing all you can to recognize your employees. You should make an attempt to recognize your employees informally, personally, and spontaneously, on an everyday basis. A sticky note that you leave on an employee's desk to compliment her on her organization skills can energize and motivate that employee. However, your company should also have a formal recognition program.

In fact, a recognition program that — however well intentioned — is no longer in line with company goals can hurt your efforts. For example, if you're telling your employees that quality comes first, yet you're only rewarding them for quantity, your recognition program is actually hindering your true goals.

A successful recognition program doesn't have to cost a lot of money. A box of doughnuts for your team after they finish a minor project doesn't break the bank.

Even though you want to be able to recognize your employees on a moment's notice, you don't want a haphazard recognition program. Instead, put careful time, thought, and effort into designing your recognition plan.

The first thing you should do is evaluate your current methods of recognition. How well do they work? Are they meeting your goals? Do your employees like and value these methods?

'Tis the season to recognize employees

The winter holidays. Ahhh, good cheer, the spirit of giving, and lots of extra food in the break-room. But that's not all the holiday season brings. This time of year gives you the perfect opportunity to recognize your employees for all their hard work.

Some companies host extravagant holiday parties. Some offer all-expenses-paid trips to Hawaii. And one company even leased new BMWs for its 45 employees — from administrative staff to managers.

You don't need to go to extremes to acknowledge your employees during the holidays. Some ideas you can try include

✔ **Tie special rewards to the holidays.** You may want to consider timing your distribution of bonuses, stock options, and increased company contributions to retirement programs to coincide with the holidays.

✔ **Schedule a mid-December all-employee meeting to announce these rewards.** Don't forget the complimentary goodies! This meeting can be in addition to the traditional holiday party or part of it.

✔ **Recognize extraordinary achievements and announce special awards.** To motivate your staff, hand out awards that are based on productivity and initiative.

✔ **Offer casual dress days or more flexible schedules.** Relaxed business attire and an occasional Friday off can help your employees manage the hectic holiday season.

Your recognition program should change as your company changes. Continually reevaluate the effectiveness of your efforts by getting feedback from employees.

The following sections take you through some of the steps to running a successful recognition program. Figuring out the best way to recognize your employees is an ongoing process. You shouldn't try to walk into the office tomorrow with a brand-new recognition plan — your plan should develop slowly and evolve.

Establish your goal

If you feel that your current recognition program needs a makeover or you need to create a new one, decide what you hope to accomplish before you do anything else.

For example, say that you've noticed that your employees are only concerned with numbers. As a result, the quality of your products or services has decreased. You should consider a recognition program that rewards improved quality and not increased quantity.

Table 14-1 lists some common goals that managers seek to achieve through a recognition program, according to responses from a 1999 study by the Incentive Marketing Association and Ralph Head & Affiliates Ltd.

Table 14-1	Common Recognition Program Goals
Goal	*Percentage of Companies That Use Recognition Programs to Achieve This Goal*
Increasing or maintaining sales	84
Building morale	65
Building customer loyalty/trust	51
Increasing market share	51
Building employee loyalty/trust	49
Improving customer service	49
Creating new markets	44
Fostering teamwork	42
Developing contracts	40
Demonstrating concern for workers	32

Think about your audience

You're not creating or revamping your recognition program in a vacuum. You need to think carefully about your target audience. Who are you trying to reach through the program and what methods will you use to reach them?

Include everyone, from managers to support personnel, in the recognition program. Failing to be inclusive creates resentment and can undercut your motivational efforts. Although rewards can be different for each role within the team or company, all the rewards should encourage teamwork. You may even want to hand out awards to teams or groups of people in addition to individuals. Whatever you do, make sure that your reward program doesn't unintentionally promote the lone ranger approach. Also, you may want to include employees in the design phase of the program for optimal success.

The size of the audience helps you determine the amount of money you should budget for the program.

Some of your employees who need to be a part of the recognition program may work offsite. Remember to include them as well. Out of sight should not mean out of mind.

Establish the criteria

Decide how to determine who receives rewards. Careful thought should be given to this part of the plan. You want the goals you set to be attainable through hard work and dedication, but you don't want them to be so easy that they lose their meaning. And the goals you reward should be ones that reinforce the company's mission as a whole, not necessarily the individual's personal goals. (For more information on setting goals, see Chapter 11.)

For example, you decide to set up a recognition program that awards those employees who best provide exceptional customer service. When outlining the criteria, be sure to list clearly defined and measurable actions or attitudes that would merit the award, such as proactive communication with customers; commitment to problem solving; a positive, can-do attitude, even in times of stress; and so on. You need to set the bar low enough that it can be reached, but high enough to be a challenge.

Don't be inconsistent or haphazard with employee rewards. You need to make clear to employees which behaviors will be rewarded. And when any employee performs up to the standards for recognition that you've set, she needs to be rewarded. You don't want to play favorites. If you overlook significant achievements and reward mediocre efforts, your recognition program will breed dissatisfaction and discontent among your staff.

Plan your budget

You don't want to start your program only to run out of money halfway through. Like your department budget, your recognition budget should be well planned and well utilized.

The amount you set aside for your program depends on several factors:

✔ How many people are eligible for a particular program? Is it your entire company or just a part of it, like your sales force? (You may have more than one program, in order to recognize appropriately all the different levels of employees in your organization.)

✔ Is your program open ended or closed ended? *Open ended* means it's ongoing and permanent. *Closed ended* means it runs for a set length of time, such as one quarter only. If the program is closed ended, you need to decide how long it will run.

✔ What will you be purchasing? If the recognition program revolves around gifts of flowers and free lunches, you'll have to set aside less than if the recognition program involves weekend trips to tropical getaway spots. (See the end of this chapter for tips on how to have a low-budget recognition program.)

Determine your rewards

Rewards work best when they're meaningful. Don't give everyone the same reward — and certainly don't give something meaningless.

A special company jacket is a better reward than something that doesn't last, such as a cake. Rewards don't have to be extravagant. A plaque or engraved paperweight can become a coveted reward — not because of anything inherent in the paperweight, but because of what it means. The reward should convey to the recipient that she's truly valued and respected.

If you can, try to give your employees options for their rewards. Some may prefer lunch with the CEO instead of something material. (Just remember to snap a photo of the reward winner lunching with the CEO. Give it to her so that she has something to remember the event.)

For more reward suggestions, see the section later in this chapter, "Matching Rewards to Performance."

Administer your program

Even an established recognition program doesn't run itself. You need to make sure that a point person — or group of people — is in charge of the program.

One of the key duties of the program administrator is to make sure that people know about the program. A recognition program isn't any good if your staff doesn't know about it. Publicize the program in your company newsletter or on the corporate intranet. Take the time to listen to feedback about it as well.

After your program has been in place a while, take a step back and evaluate it. Did it do what you intended? Remember that it's never too late for improvement.

Table 14-2 lists some common ways to communicate with employees about your program, according to responses from a 1999 study by the Incentive Marketing Association and Ralph Head & Affiliates Ltd.

Table 14-2	Ways to Communicate Your Program
Method	*Percentage of Respondents Using the Method*
Mailings to employees	62
Company newsletter	50
Memos (internal or external)	48
Company meetings	48

Method	Percentage of Respondents Using the Method
E-mail	44
Word-of-mouth	38
Voicemail	37
Bulletin boards	30

Knowing What Behavior to Reward

If you want a behavior repeated, reward it.

Good attendance — which should be expected — should not be rewarded. And you certainly don't want to encourage the wrong behavior. For example, don't reward timely service if health, safety, or ethics are compromised in the process.

Here are a few times when recognition may be appropriate:

- ✔ Project milestones reached
- ✔ Completion of difficult or long projects
- ✔ Promotions
- ✔ New contracts or business secured
- ✔ Surpassing of sales quotas

You may also decide to recognize your employees' birthdays and anniversaries. (If you do, don't forget to celebrate their anniversaries with the company as well.)

Be careful not to celebrate everything, or your revelry may lose its impact.

Matching Rewards to Performance

After you decide what behavior should be rewarded, you need to come up with an appropriate reward. Keep in mind that this recognition doesn't need to be expensive. In a recent survey by Robert Half International, employees ranked a personal thank-you as the most sought-after recognition, followed by a handwritten note of appreciation from their boss.

Facing a challenge? Make it a game

One of the management teams at the California Public Employees Retirement System sure knows how to have fun — even when faced with a not-so-fun project.

The team's managers were asked to eliminate a backlog of files — the equivalent of a month's work — in only three days. Realizing that they needed to motivate, encourage, and recognize their employees, the management team created the Option 4 (the name of their team) World Series.

The department was divided into the majors team (red) and minors team (blue). Each team scored when certain tasks were completed.

They also scored points for dressing in baseball attire and decorating the work area. Quality was rewarded in addition to quantity. If something had to be redone, a run was deducted. And no one went hungry during this busy time. The staff had plenty of ballpark-themed foods, such as hot dogs, chips, peanuts, cotton candy, and soda. Both teams earned the same reward — trophies and series rings.

Not only did the department get rid of the backlog in the allotted time, but the members felt more like a team and enjoyed increased motivation as well. What a game!

Don't hesitate to be creative when you're brainstorming rewards. Here's what some other companies have done:

- At Busch Gardens in Tampa, employees received scratch-off cards. They scratched off the gray areas and then redeemed the tickets for the prize revealed.

- At Trinity Services, Inc., a nonprofit agency serving people with disabilities, employees receive the frog mascot, Lillie Leapit, to symbolize their leap ahead.

Be creative with your rewards. Your employees will appreciate it. Here are some other ideas:

- Write a thank-you note.
- Offer a personalized gift, such as a poster or book.
- Buy movie tickets.
- Give a framed photograph of an employee event.
- Hold a lunch in the employee's honor.
- Provide time off.
- Create a bulletin board that contains the photos of top employees.

✔ Bring bagels or doughnuts to a team meeting to honor the employee.

✔ Give fruit bowls or freshly baked chocolate chip cookies.

✔ Hold a meeting just to discuss how good a job the person is doing.

No matter what reward you decide on, don't forget to let your employee know why she's receiving it.

Here's an idea that's sort of like recognizing an employee in advance for all the great work he'll do: Buy lunch and flowers on his first day.

When you're promoted or recognized, acknowledge your support staff. Without them, you probably wouldn't have been able to do the fantastic job that you did. If you want their continued support and enthusiasm, you need to show them your gratitude.

Celebrating alone isn't fun. If someone has done a great job or just finished a project, celebrate as a team.

If you're having trouble coming up with recognition strategies, check out www.recognition.com. This is the Web site for the Chicago-based National Association for Employee Recognition (NAER). This nonprofit organization offers information on recognition, and its sole goal is to advance recognition in the workplace. You can also write to NAER at 1805 N. Mill St., Suite A, Naperville, IL 60563; contact them by phone at (630) 369-7783; or through e-mail at NAER@recognition.org.

Motivating Employees on a Tight Budget

Every company can afford a recognition program. A simple thank-you costs nothing. As long as you're sincere, your recognition program can be based on nothing more than verbal feedback.

If you're up to spending a few bucks, consider the example of one company that gives an inexpensive stuffed koala bear as recognition. The bear is known as the Koala T. Bear Award. (Get it? If not, repeat *Koala T.* over and over.) Believe it or not, it's the award that people in the organization most desire.

Keep your cash in your pocket

Believe it or not, awarding cash may not be the best bang for the recognition buck.

Some employees want something other than easy money. They want personal, genuine recognition — a thoughtful token of appreciation.

Whenever you can, repeat positive remarks that you hear about an employee. If a coworker tells you how much another employee helped out with a project or your boss tells you he particularly liked a project that your employee did, tell the staff member. She'll glow with the praise.

Here are some other ideas for rewards if you're on a budget:

✔ Allow employees to take a long lunch or have a short workday.

✔ Offer a round of applause from the team.

✔ Distribute movie tickets.

✔ Hold a celebration.

✔ Offer interesting projects.

✔ Bring in food.

✔ Give time off or extra vacation days.

✔ Deliver a note or letter of appreciation from the company president.

✔ Provide dinner for two at a local restaurant.

✔ Designate an employee-of-the-month parking spot.

✔ Print a photo and brief article about the stellar performer in the company newsletter.

✔ Host a team lunch.

✔ Hand out special gear with the company logo.

✔ Arrange events that involve family members, such as a children's fair or holiday bazaar.

If you're still searching for the right idea, check out Bob Nelson's *1001 Ways to Reward Employees* (Workman Publishing Company, Inc., 1993).

One of the best ways to reward an employee for her stellar work is to offer her more interesting projects and increased responsibility and authority.

Part VI

Teamwork: Motivating Others to Cooperate and Collaborate

The 5th Wave   By Rich Tennant

"I think Dick Foster should head up that new project. He's got the vision, the drive, and let's face it, that big white hat doesn't hurt either."

In this part . . .

It's common knowledge that a team can create more as a group than team members working individually. Teamwork is a synergistic approach to motivation that you won't want to overlook. In this part, you find out how you can promote teamwork, both onsite and offsite — including your part-timers, job sharers, flextimers, international employees, and telecommuters.

Chapter 15

Promoting Teamwork

· ·

· ·

Teamwork can be hard to foster. Think about your own experiences: If a colleague does a fantastic job on a report, do you think that you have to do an even better presentation on your next project? Or, if another coworker misses an important deadline, do you begin to wonder if you have a better chance at a promotion?

Although friendly competition can be healthy, everyone should focus on the common goal — the company's mission. Whether you're the boss or the administrative assistant, you're on a team that has an objective. You need to keep that objective in mind whenever you engage in a project.

If your coworkers' attitudes are becoming destructively competitive and combative, then it won't be long before your company feels the impact. Communication breaks down, the right hand doesn't know what the left hand is doing, and chaos ensues.

This chapter explores why teamwork is such a crucial part of a successful company. It explains how you can infuse the spirit of collaboration into your department and includes tips on establishing a common goal.

Why Teamwork Is Important

Ever try to host a holiday party? It's kind of hard to do it all — cook, answer the door, mingle, refill the food and drinks, clean up, *and* have a good time. That's where your spouse or significant other or kids come in . . . or, at least, where they're supposed to come in! A holiday party is kind of like a crisis in the business world. (Well, okay . . . so a party is a lot more fun than a work crisis, but you get the idea.) The point is that stressful times in business are when your teammates become even more important.

Think how much smoother your party would go if your spouse or a good friend answered the door and your kids were in charge of the refills and clean up — you may actually be able to have fun. Now that's teamwork!

Think about some other reasons teamwork is so important: Have you ever tried to brainstorm by yourself? You don't have anyone to bounce ideas off of. You don't have anyone to spark your creativity or help you generate your next great idea. Or have you ever tried to get your job done without contacting another department? Even if you have a very isolated job, chances are that someday your computer will go down and you'll need to seek out your technology support group — at the very least. More likely, you interact with members of other teams and other departments constantly.

The crux of teamwork is that a well-organized team should produce better work than individuals working toward the same goal. Think *synergy,* where the whole is greater than the sum of its parts. A team should produce better results, more efficiently, than if unconnected people were to toil on the same project.

The other great benefit of teamwork is that it gives team members a feeling of belonging — something they may not be getting elsewhere. If you've ever been part of a successful team, you know how good it feels to work together to do the best job that you can. You may work alongside people with whom you would never have been friends in high school, but suddenly you have a lot in common . . . and you discover that you like and respect them in the process!

Understanding the Types of Teams

The kind of team that you set up depends on the goal that you want to reach. If your department has been assigned the task of making the workflow more efficient within the department, then you probably won't want to form a cross-functional team. Likewise, if your goal is to improve communication between departments, you wouldn't want to form a team made up of just employees in your department.

When I say *team,* I'm referring to a group of people who are working together on either a temporary or a permanent basis to achieve a common objective. Your team may be your department. Or maybe you've formed a team to develop solutions to a particular challenge, and — after the project is complete — you'll disband the team.

Go, team!

In a survey conducted by Robert Half International, more than 80 percent of the chief financial officers in Fortune 1000 corporations surveyed felt that self-managed teams will increase productivity in the decade ahead. And when the Work in America Institute asked members representing 100 leading American companies what research topics would have the most value to their companies, 95 percent of the respondents chose teamwork.

The following sections describe the three most common types of work teams. Remember that sometimes team types overlap, and each company may put a different twist on the nature of the teams. For example, how long the team works together and how much authority a team has varies from company to company.

No matter what type of team you form, everyone on the team is trying to reach a common goal. This goal can be achieved more effectively by a group of people working together than by an individual, no matter how talented that one person may be. (See Chapter 2 for advice on creating and sharing a common goal.)

Project team

A *project team* is pretty much what it sounds like — a group of people brought together to accomplish a particular project. (Sometimes project teams are referred to as *steering committees* or *task forces*.) For example, your company may ask for volunteers to help solve some issues that were brought to light in an employee survey. Or perhaps you ask a team to handle something more lighthearted, such as the company holiday party. Typically, when the project ends, the team ends.

Not every task demands that you put together a team. For a project team to succeed, you need to make sure that the task is appropriate for a group of people to work on together.

Cross-functional team

A *cross-functional team* is made up of not just employees from your department, but employees from many departments.

Perhaps you work for a publishing company and you've been assigned the task of developing a new process for getting a book to print faster. You could ask members of the editorial, production, and manufacturing departments to be on your team. That way, team members can discuss how each department works and what timetables are negotiable.

Or maybe your goal is to find out why a particular product has stopped selling. Then you would definitely want members of your sales and marketing departments and the department that created the product to be on your team. That way, the key stakeholders can brainstorm together and make improvements to get the product selling again.

Self-directed work team

Like a project team, a *self-directed work team* is just what it sounds like — a team that determines how it will get a job done and has the authority, and often the budget, to carry out decisions.

The phrase *self-directed work team* — or *self-managed team* — doesn't mean that the team doesn't need a leader or manager. It just means that the team is responsible and accountable for its decisions, as opposed to proposing action that will be approved or denied by someone outside the team.

For example, say that a company survey indicates that a particular department is experiencing a lot of turnover. You can ask for volunteers from the department to form a team that helps determine the reasons for the turnover (say, too much work and not enough time) and possible solutions (job restructuring, for example). The self-directed team then makes recommendations for what actions should be taken. The team will also likely implement the initiatives.

Why teams fail

Teams can falter for a number of reasons. Your goal is to identify the problems early and solve them immediately.

A team managed by Olivia includes both Fred and Joan. Here are just a few of the problems the team faces:

✔ Fred and Joan can't agree on anything — whether it's something as minor as where to go for a team lunch or something as major as the direction of a big project.

✔ Fred and Joan are both vying for the same promotion, so they're each trying to outdo the other and toot their own horn at the same time. They're looking out for number one, not the team.

✔ Olivia wants the team to be self-directed, but she can't bear to be the one not making decisions, so she intervenes constantly.

✔ Olivia's team is made up of both exempt and non-exempt employees, whom she's asking to work overtime.

This team probably isn't going to fare too well, is it? But if those problems were identified and solved upfront, then its fate may have turned out better!

Establishing a Common Goal

Whether the team is a small business working toward a company mission or a small team within a department building a marketing campaign, the team needs to have a goal. Whatever the goal is, everyone needs to buy into it. It needs to be more important than individual agendas. In other words, personal recognition ("Hey, that's my idea that we're using!") should be secondary to attaining the objective.

The common goal is what holds the team together and allows it to continue when times are tough.

Team members need to know the objective — why the team exists, what the mission is, and how the mission relates to the company's overall vision. The objective should be made clear at the first meeting.

Consider drawing up a team *charter,* which outlines the team's mission and sets down the ground rules of how the group's going to work together. You may also want to have a team kickoff meeting that is focused solely on communicating the goal and allowing members to interact and get to know one another — especially if it's a cross-functional team. The time invested upfront pays off in better relationships and enhanced productivity.

Promoting Teamwork: "A" Is for Attitude

A good team can get a job done quickly and effectively — even under intense pressure. But you can't just walk into the office and say, "Voila! We're a team." Like most things that are worthwhile, you have to work at teamwork.

Attitude is everything when it comes to building a team. Some of your staff members may not even want to be part of a team. But remember that you're not only striving to reach a goal that's very important to your company, you're also developing camaraderie, gaining knowledge, and sharing an accomplishment with others — all which require a positive attitude. Make sure that your employees know this as well and that you embody this attitude in your everyday actions.

As a team leader, your job isn't to supervise or manage the project. Your main responsibility is to facilitate the team process. If you're a good team leader, you will rarely have to lay down the law.

Whether you need to tap someone else to be a team leader or you find yourself in the role, you need to be aware of the things good team leaders do and don't do.

Do

✔ Listen to everyone.

✔ Play devil's advocate.

✔ Propose solutions.

✔ Prepare a meeting agenda and stay on track.

✔ Ask open-ended questions.

Don't

✔ Criticize others' ideas.

✔ Be overly demanding.

✔ Enforce your ideas.

✔ Be a dictator.

The following sections describe ways that you can mold your disparate elements into a unified team.

Choose your perspective

Enthusiasm is contagious — but in a good way. No matter what task is at hand, don't gripe about it and bring others down. Instead, look at the bright side. As soon as you finish the job, you can cross it off your list and go on to something more appealing.

You can choose to be energetic, passionate, and positive. Or you can choose to be lethargic, apathetic, and negative. You may not love the task you're doing, but you can have fun doing it. And the same is true of your employees. If you're the team leader, the other team members take their cues from you and your attitude.

When you're in a good mood, other people are happier to be around you. (Ever notice how the person who smiles the most in the office always has coworkers gravitating toward her?)

Things aren't going to go well every day. But remember that you can choose how you react to things. You can choose your mood. No matter how the day is going, remain upbeat and positive.

Take pride in your work

Remember when you were in college and got that A on the term paper you worked so hard on (the one that hung over your head for the entire semester)?

Or when you finally stuck with the exercise program that you'd been trying to follow for years? When you do something well, with energy and enthusiasm, you can't help but feel good. So take pride in your work.

When you have pride in what you're doing, it affects both you and the other team members. You know what they say about one person bringing a whole team down — well, the reverse works, too. One person can inspire a whole team to exceed expectations.

No matter what job you're doing, do it well, and others will usually follow your lead. And when everyone on a team is performing well, the team produces stellar work.

Place the team's goals first

Don't just look at your role and make decisions based on your needs. Look at what the team needs and then figure out what you can do to help the group succeed.

Nothing is more disruptive to a team than a glory seeker wanting individual credit.

Getting your team's buy-in

Some people like to work by themselves. The thought of working with other people on a regular basis makes them uncomfortable. Others may enjoy the socialization that teamwork offers, but they're unconvinced of the true benefits of working as a group. Maybe they've experienced some difficulties in past team-based situations.

When you present the idea of working on a team, you need to make sure that you spell out all the good points about teamwork. Doing so can persuade staff members to be optimistic and excited. Point out that:

✔ Each team member was specifically chosen — that's a good thing. Explain the goal of the team and how members can

contribute to that goal. Tell them as much as you can about the type of assignment and their teammates and how they can make the most of this experience.

✔ This task is important. Let employees know the importance of the new project and how they should prioritize it within their current project schedule. Also let them know what to do if they need additional help to handle all their responsibilities.

✔ Remind them not to make snap judgments. Especially on cross-functional teams, team members' beliefs, attitudes, and communication styles may collide. Let everyone know the differing points of view and advise participants to keep an open mind.

A strong team doesn't have a group of participants clamoring after their own personal goals. Instead, it has team members who place the team goal before their own individual agendas.

Think of your team as a choir. (They may not look the part, but try anyway.) The singers must blend all their voices together. One person doesn't outdo everyone else in the choir. Even a soloist can only shine when in harmony with the group. Although you're the leader of the team, you're just one member of the choir, one voice among many voices.

You need to be able to discard your personal agenda. Think instead about the welfare of the project and the team.

Be responsible

If you make a mistake, admit it. If you don't, others will doubt your credibility in the future. Your personal accountability will encourage others to be equally accountable.

Encourage idea sharing

If everyone participates on the team, especially in meetings, then everyone feels ownership and has a responsibility to help the project move along. If you're the team leader or manager, don't rush to answer a question or solve a problem. Encourage teammates to work together to come up with a solution — whether in a meeting or informally. If the team is struggling for a resolution, though, lend a hand.

Top performers may take on more responsibility than others or participate more in team meetings. That's okay. Just make sure that other team members aren't being squeezed out and that your star isn't feeling overwhelmed. The ideal situation is that each individual has equal participation, so each person is just as invested as the next person. The next best thing is to encourage everyone to chip in, even if some members of the team dominate the discussion.

Communicate, communicate, communicate

For a team to succeed, one person can't disappear to do his own thing. Everyone needs to report regularly to each other, even if it's just to say, "Hey, I found the data we needed on the Web, and we were right on target with our estimates." Until your team is functioning at peak performance, you may need to establish some guidelines for regular communication. Schedule weekly meetings, send biweekly e-mail updates, or plan monthly teleconferences. Just make sure that information flows freely and often.

How well you communicate within your team may mean the difference between success and failure.

Roll up your sleeves

As a leader, you should be willing to work right alongside your team. Need someone to make photocopies of the report to distribute at the meeting tomorrow, but your assistant is sick? Do it yourself. When your team members see the boss pitching in, they're apt to redouble their own efforts.

Although you shouldn't routinely be caught up in tasks that you're not getting paid to perform, when the team's in a bind and something needs to be done, roll up your sleeves and get busy. You shouldn't ask your team members to do anything that you yourself aren't willing to do.

Work hard

Don't just do your job halfway. Your team will notice and follow suit — "Well, Miranda came in an hour late on Monday, so maybe I can, too."

Do the best job that you can in the time that you have. If you truly can't produce quality work in the time period that you're allotted, tell your manager and ask for more time for your team. If you need to arrive early and stay late for a few weeks, then try and do so. (But if this situation is the norm, you and your team may be on your way to burnout — see Chapter 20.)

If you're really overwhelmed — say that you have to verify the URLs of 10,000 Web sites in a few days — consider hiring a temporary employee. Don't push your team members to achieve the impossible. They'll achieve even more if you give them the support they need.

Promote chemistry and caring

Chemistry is more than just team spirit — it's about the team caring about each other, looking out for one another, and working well together. Say, for example, that Mia is going through a hard time due to a serious illness in the family. As a result, she's usually running late in the morning, although she always shows up on time at work. Muriel notices that most mornings Mia hasn't had breakfast, and one day, Mia shows up to find a nice big muffin on her desk — compliments of Muriel. That's one example of how caring and chemistry can be manifested.

If a team has good chemistry, everyone is comfortable with one another. They may not agree all the time, but they know they can speak their mind. Because everyone cares about one another, people aren't afraid of making mistakes or being personally attacked.

No group of individuals builds chemistry overnight. Don't try to rush the bonding process.

Establish processes and protocols

The best teams don't wing it; they plan. They also have *protocols* — the etiquette for how you should do something. For example, maybe the protocol is that team members e-mail success stories to one another soon after the success happens, to exchange information and inspire one another.

Team members need to decide early on how they're going to work together. Establish protocols for making decisions, solving conflicts, and providing status reports.

Don't underestimate the importance of little things, like being punctual for meetings and contributing to discussions.

Celebrate

One company I know of honors team members' birthdays by making the celebration a team effort. A volunteer bakes the cake for the first upcoming birthday. Then the honoree of that party agrees to prepare the next cake for the following birthday bash, and so on down the road.

Here are some ideas for celebrations:

- ✔ **Host a thank-you luncheon for your team.** If you've met a big quarterly goal due to extra team effort or your team has finished an important project, consider hosting a thank-you luncheon. Invite everyone who made the project possible, give a small speech, and then serve up something as informal as submarines, chips, and soft drinks. Don't forget dessert, of course!

- ✔ **Send baskets of goodies to your offsite employees.** Just met a big deadline? Then why not send tins of popcorn, baskets of fruits, or bags full of goodies to your offsite team members? They need to celebrate, too.

- ✔ **Have a celebration party.** It doesn't have to be expensive, either. Go outside on the company lawn and enjoy cookies and snacks.

- ✔ **Take your team to an offsite event to relax.** Try bowling, laser tag, or a dinner — whatever helps your employees blow off steam and celebrate.

Celebrating together draws a team closer. Whether it's a birthday, closure of a project, or a holiday, find reasons to celebrate.

Emphasize the mission

Day-to-day tasks can distract you and your team from the big picture. Don't let them. If the daily tedium is discouraging you and your team, take a fresh look at the ultimate goal and consider ways to rejuvenate the team.

For example, say that you work for a nonprofit organization. Your employees are getting bogged down by having to make endless phone calls requesting donations. For every ten calls they make, they receive one donation. Receiving endless no's can bring anyone down if that's what your team is focusing on. In this case, remind your team how far they've come — hey, you've raised $300,000! — and what the result will be when you finish. When your team members are thinking about the new children's home they're helping to fund, they may be able to retain their motivation.

Chapter 16

Motivating Beyond the Usual Boundaries

*N*ot everyone walks into the office at 9 a.m. and walks out at 5 p.m. Thanks to technology, you may have offsite employees who live down the block or live around the world. As a manager, your motivational efforts have to be far reaching, in every sense of the word.

You may also work with consultants who work with you on a project basis or temporary professionals. Or your organization may be paired with another company in a strategic alliance. The firm that was your competition last week may be your partner for success today. But how do you motivate folks who are only on your team for a short time?

In this chapter, I show you everything you need to know to motivate employees who fit into any of these nontraditional categories.

When you're managing an alternative work force, you're often the only person your employees have regular contact with, so what you do and say becomes critical.

Note: If you want information specific to telecommuting, head straight to Chapter 17, which is devoted entirely to that topic.

Starting with You

The basics of managing effectively apply to every employee — full-time or part-time, onsite or offsite.

- ✔ You need to be organized.
- ✔ You need to have good communication skills.
- ✔ You need to be able to motivate the people who work for you.

Motivating part-time employees, temporary workers, telecommuters, or offsite employees isn't all that different from motivating in-house employees. You still need to create an environment where everyone feels challenged, and you still need a system of rewards and recognition.

Conduct the following brief exercise to review your basic motivational skills. Use a scale of 0 to 5 to rate the degree to which each statement describes your current approach to managing. Be honest! If in doubt, think about what score your employees would give you, and go with that number.

After each question, I give you the number of the chapter that contains more information. If you give yourself a 3 or below for any statement, check out the chapter for help developing that aspect of your managerial style.

____ I have developed a clearly defined vision of my department or group, and I have communicated this vision to everyone who reports to me. (Chapter 2)

____ The people in my group understand my values — what I stand for. I go out of my way to make sure that my job performance and management style are consistent with those values. (Chapter 2)

____ I take time to make sure that each person understands his role, recognizes his value to the organization, and collaborates with me to establish performance standards. (Chapter 11)

____ I don't hesitate to give the people in my group meaningful responsibility, and I provide the resources and support they need to meet that responsibility. (Chapter 10)

____ I've done my best to create an environment that fosters enthusiasm, cooperation, and high performance. (Chapter 4)

____ I do everything I can to help people develop, grow, and realize their professional ambitions, even if, by doing so, I help good employees leave my team. (Chapter 11)

____ I keep my word. If I make a promise or a commitment to someone, I do everything humanly possible to follow through on it. (Chapter 2)

___ When I give people responsibility to perform a task, I allow them an opportunity to perform it in the best way they know how. I don't second-guess them if they don't perform the task the way I would have. (Chapter 10)

___ Whenever I'm communicating one-on-one with someone on my team, I devote my complete attention to her and do my best to understand any concerns that she may have. (Chapter 7)

___ I encourage creative problem solving and reward risk takers. When mistakes are made, I look at them as opportunities for everyone to improve rather than incidents that require punishment. (Chapter 8)

Rating your total score:

- ✔ 45 or higher: Stellar leadership abilities

- ✔ 40 to 44: Excellent

- ✔ 35 to 39: Good, but could be better

- ✔ Below 35: Room for improvement

Defining Team Roles and Responsibilities

The success of a team — whether its members work inside or outside of the office — centers on employees understanding how they fit into the big picture. As a manager, you need to tell all employees, onsite or offsite, what their roles are and how they fit into the team's overall goals.

Think of this example. Felix considers himself just one of 20 people who all do the same job. He's sure that he won't be missed if he takes a "mental health" day, even if he doesn't need one. But if Felix realizes that an important report won't go out on time if he calls in sick — because he's the only person with access to crucial information — then he's much more likely to be motivated to come to work.

Employees need to know why they're important to the company's success. A detailed job description is one way you can communicate the importance of a position to employees. Also use weekly team meetings to make sure that everyone knows how their projects affect the team as a whole.

Foster an environment where employees feel comfortable discussing their confusion or doubt about roles and expectations. Doing so prevents a potential source of conflict and, when conflicts do arise, allows responsibilities and expectations to be the starting point of a discussion.

Creating Teamwork when Team Members Are Scattered

Teamwork takes time to really develop. All those impromptu lunches and surprise parties to celebrate coworkers' birthdays develop the bonds that create a strong team. Your role as a manager is also crucial (see Chapter 15).

But what about employees who work offsite or who only work part-time? After all, they're not in onsite for those lunches or parties. They can't always walk down the hall to pop into someone else's office for information.

You *can* integrate these workers into your team. A few general steps that you should take to help you manage and motivate an office where everyone is coming and going on different schedules include

- ✔ **Know your staff's schedules.** After you've established schedules, you then need to share them with your team via a company intranet or another central location.

- ✔ **Encourage all employees whose schedules deviate from a normal workweek to list their hours on their voicemail.** That way, clients and coworkers will know when they can reach the individual.

- ✔ **Make sure that you communicate face to face with your staff whenever you can.** Although face to face opportunities may not occur often when you're dealing with offsite employees, you need to find the time. If geography permits, employees should come into the office for meetings with managers and coworkers.

The following sections outline specific things you can do to motivate offsite, part-time, and flextime employees. Later in this chapter, I cover temporary workers, international employees, and alliance partners.

Offsite employees

Increasingly, workers are no longer linked to each other through physical location. Instead, telephones and the Internet act as connective devices. Even if you're not one of the growing number of *virtual companies,* with employees scattered around the country, you still need to take steps to make your offsite employees feel like a part of the team.

Here are some things companies are doing to make sure that offsite employees feel like they're a part of the group:

✔ **Scrutinizing the orientation program.** This is important not only to cover the basics, such as benefits and the company's philosophy, but also to offer communication training to help staff members learn effective ways to interact in a virtual workplace.

✔ **Bringing offsite employees into the office for the orientation program.** This gives them the chance to meet fellow recruits and get a true feel for the company culture. Even if you have to fly employees in, make sure that your offsite employees spend at least some time at the office. Some virtual organizations schedule a group meeting at a hotel or other site so that employees can meet each other in person.

✔ **Assigning mentors to offsite employees.** Having mentors is especially helpful for offsite employees. (See Chapter 12 for more on mentoring.) Some companies assign a go-to person or point of contact who can be available by e-mail to answer questions and provide guidance to offsite employees.

✔ **Posting photos and biographies of all employees on the company intranet or in a newsletter or special annual publication.** Not only are employees able to put names with faces, but they recognize each other when they finally do meet.

✔ **Responding quickly to phone calls and e-mails from offsite employees.** Offsite employees can't just walk into your office and get your attention, so it's important to respond to them when they need you.

No matter what the working arrangement, communication plays a crucial role in the motivation of the employee and your effectiveness as a manager. In fact, the greater the distance, the more you should communicate.

Part-time employees

Just like full-time employees, part-time employees want recognition, career opportunities, and training. But a few motivational techniques are especially important to keep in mind when managing someone who is not onsite full-time.

✔ **Encourage initiative.** Just because an employee works part time doesn't mean that she can't have great ideas.

✔ **Show part-time employees where they fit into the big picture.** Take some time to let them know how their work and projects make a difference to the organization's ultimate success. This is particularly important when they're not in the office as much as their full-time coworkers, and, therefore, may not have as clear a view of the big picture.

✔ **Appreciate their job.** Yes, a part-time employee works fewer hours than a full-time one, but you wouldn't have the position if you didn't need it. Show your part-time employees that you recognize their contributions and appreciate their efforts.

> ✔ **Include them as part of the team.** Even if it's their day off, invite part-time employees to offsite events. Always make sure that they feel welcome to attend all team functions and after-work events.

Flextime employees

To reduce stress and absenteeism and promote greater work/life balance, your company may offer flextime policies, where employees can vary their respective start and end times as long as they're in the office during certain core hours — for example, from 9 a.m. to 3 p.m.

On the plus side, flextime often results in better time-management on the part of your employees, and increased morale. But when your employees come and go at different times, you may find it hard to communicate with them, inadvertently leaving one or more of them out of the loop. Motivation may also suffer if employees aren't able to meet and interact with coworkers face to face.

To reduce the difficulties caused by flextime, meet with your employees whenever you can. In fact, scheduling regular meetings with each employee is a good idea. Also require that all employees attend a weekly team meeting, which you establish at a set time so that they can plan accordingly.

Working with International Employees

Offsite employees could be living anywhere across the globe while still maintaining employment with your company.

Whether you've transferred an employee overseas or you've hired a permanent resident of another country, establishing and maintaining a strong connection, despite geographic and cultural differences, is crucial. If you're managing international employees, you need to speak to them on a regular basis so that you're human to them.

International employees have become so common that special terms are used:

> ✔ *Virtual expatriation* is when an employee is assigned to another country temporarily.
> ✔ *Traditional expatriation* is when the employee permanently resides in the country.

Employers are realizing that if they want to attract and retain good employees at overseas locations, they need to go the traditional expatriation route. No matter the category the employee falls under, communication is once again crucial to motivation.

If your employees are natives of another country, you need to take into account any cultural differences or language barriers that may exist. Some behaviors that are accepted in your culture may be offensive — and signify lack of respect — to your international employees. (See the sidebar for some specific cultural differences you may encounter.) You should be friendly, polite, and respectful at all times.

If you want to successfully motivate your international employees, you need to familiarize yourself with the *culture,* or acceptable and normal behavior, of their countries.

Also keep in mind that other countries may not have the same level of technological infrastructure. And if you rely on technology such as e-mail or teleconferencing to communicate with your employees on a different continent, you need to make sure that you've provided training on these tools.

Accommodating cultural differences

When in Rome, do as the Romans. That's an apt way to describe how you should conduct business in other parts of the globe. By engaging in behavior that is acceptable in your country but not in the one your employees are in, you may be building fences you can never mend. Here are a few things to keep in mind when doing business in another country or with an international worker:

✔ Americans tend to want more personal space than individuals in other countries. If you back up to retain that space, your international employees may sense rejection. The same goes for backing away from physical contact.

✔ At business meetings in some countries, business talk doesn't begin until everyone socializes. The same goes for business lunches and dinners. The American habit of getting down to business right after ordering food may be a turnoff to some international employees.

✔ Calling someone by his or her first name may be insulting in another country. Some

cultures encourage the use of courtesy titles, even among coworkers who have been working together for years.

✔ Try not to use slang, because international employees will probably not be familiar with the terms — and may even take them literally. Don't try to translate idioms. Err on the side of being too formal when addressing your employees.

✔ In some cultures, exaggerating the details of certain situations is okay. You definitely want to be aware of that fact when you have employees working in a country where this habit is accepted and commonplace.

✔ Kidding around isn't acceptable in some cultures. To be safe, you should avoid this behavior. Instead of setting someone at ease, you may be putting the person on guard.

✔ Although asking personal questions may set your fellow Americans at ease, that doesn't work in all cultures, and personal questions may even be considered impolite.

The best communication plan uses several means of communication, such as voicemail, e-mail, and teleconferencing. Don't rely on just one medium for your long-distance communication.

Making Temporary Workers Feel Welcome

Temporary workers, who are also known as *contingent* workers, work in the office on a temporary basis, such as during busy periods. Growing numbers of companies depend on such workers for their staffing needs. For some organizations, a temporary assignment is a method of screening before offering full-time employment. In addition, contingent workers can offer important skills that may not exist within a firm's existing talent base.

Temporary professionals are part of your team; therefore, their level of motivation can affect the entire group as well as your department's productivity. Although the employees are only with you on a temporary basis, you should hold them to the same standards as a full-time employee.

If you decide that contingent workers are appropriate for your company, don't just pick up the phone to call the nearest staffing firm. You first need to develop a strategy. Consider why you're using contingent employees, what kind of responsibilities you'd like them to handle, and what kind of skills you'd like them to have. You also need to figure out how much you'll pay per position. In addition, try to anticipate heavy workload periods so that you can plan ahead for staffing.

Remember that when you employ a contingent worker, he or she should be a good match not only for your team, but also for the task at hand. Inquire about the person's software skills and industry expertise, if necessary.

To motivate contingent workers:

✔ **Match the task to the individuals' skills.** Give them work that taps their experience. If you have an assignment that involves filing and photocopying, don't ask for a seasoned project manager. Keep in mind that temporary work has evolved in the past decade or so, and it is not uncommon for a company to bring in a temporary CFO for a major initiative.

✔ **Set out the welcome mat.** Although your contingent workers are only in the office temporarily, introduce them to their coworkers. Nothing is more disconcerting than being ignored day after day and not being treated as a valued contributor. In addition, you should make sure that your staff knows that contingent workers will be in the office, and why, before they actually appear.

- ✔ **Make their responsibilities clear.** Know what the workers will be doing before they arrive, not after, and let them know to whom they should direct questions.

- ✔ **Prepare a workspace.** Make sure that they have everything they need to perform the job, such as a phone and a computer, or an office, depending on the task.

- ✔ **Offer guidance.** Because contingent workers are new to the office, they'll have more questions than full-time employees will. Don't just leave them hanging. Not only should you be there to answer questions, but you should try to anticipate them as well.

- ✔ **Brief them on corporate culture.** Even if they're only in the office for a few days, contingent workers need to know how things get done. Let them know how lunch breaks work, for example, or any security procedures they need to be aware of to get back into the building.

- ✔ **Don't take contingent workers for granted.** Keep in mind that you may want them to come back someday. If they've done a great job, tell them. If their work needs improvement, offer constructive feedback.

- ✔ **Think of contingent workers just like you would any other employee.** These workers aren't a permanent part of your team. But they do work with your group to achieve results. If you want top performance, then you need to apply the motivational skills described throughout this book to your contingent employees as well as your full-time staff.

Collaborating with Alliance Partners

Alliances may consist of several partners or just one, and may be formal or informal. They may involve sponsorship agreements (where money changes hands) or in-kind services, in which a firm donates non-monetary assistance to an organization, most often a nonprofit. Their overall goal is to achieve mutual benefit to the parties that have formed the alliance.

Say that a publishing company would like to do more than just publish books. It may decide to pair up with a company that has expertise in the area it would like to get into, such as Web publishing, audiotapes, or music CDs. For the arrangement to be an alliance, both companies need to benefit from the relationship. The publishing company gains expertise and experience in venturing into new areas, while the second company may get a percentage of the revenue, a larger clientele base, or anything else that the two companies agree on.

Working with alliance partners can be a bit challenging. After all, they aren't your employees and they have their own agenda.

So, what did you think of the office?

A temporary worker's impression of the corporate culture is often similar to what your current employees think. Your current staff may be reluctant to share their true feelings about things that need improvement, but contingent workers often feel freer to offer constructive criticism. So when you're saying adios to temporary professionals, you may want to take that opportunity to ask them how everything went.

You may want to ask how well they understood their responsibilities and encourage any suggestions they have for improvements. Oh, and of course, you don't want to forget to ask them this important question: "What do you think of the corporate culture?" You may discover some things you need to fix! And who knows — the answer may be "I loved it."

If you find yourself working with alliance partners, keep the following tips in mind:

- ✔ **Manage your projects superbly.** When you're working with someone outside the company, you need to pay even more attention to your projects. Don't underestimate the resources you need and don't let deadlines pass.

- ✔ **Let bygones be bygones.** Even if you were rivals before or still are in certain geographic areas, you work together now.

- ✔ **Try to complement each other.** Let your partners play roles that complement their strengths and minimize their weaknesses.

- ✔ **Define all goals.** Otherwise, you and your partner won't know what you're working toward.

- ✔ **Designate a decision maker.** When two companies are involved and a potential standstill may be the result of a disagreement, you need to agree on one person who has the power to make decisions.

Chapter 17

Keeping Telecommuters Motivated

● ●

In This Chapter

▶ Understanding telecommuting

▶ Planning a successful telecommuting program

▶ Setting telecommuting guidelines

▶ Managing telecommuters effectively

● ●

*W*ith increased numbers of people telecommuting, either because they're on the road or work full-time at home, the issue of motivating these workers has become increasingly important to managers.

Chances are that your company already permits some form of telecommuting. As a manager, you may have already discovered that it doesn't work for every employee. You first have to make sure the job responsibilities are conducive to working offsite. A staff member may not be able to telecommute if her job requires the use of equipment that's found only on company premises or extensive interaction with other employees. Even if a job can be done out of the office, you still face challenges managing the worker who fills the job. How do you motivate workers who aren't always onsite? How do you ensure that they still feel like a part of the team?

In a survey by OfficeTeam, telecommuting received mixed reviews from executives. Although 36 percent of those polled saw no difference in productivity levels between telecommuters and onsite workers, more than a quarter (26 percent) felt the arrangement compromised job performance.

Although the tips in Chapter 16 apply to telecommuters (as do almost all the motivating tips in this book), employees who work remotely do create special concerns. In this chapter, you discover the secrets to keeping telecommuters motivated.

So What Is Telecommuting?

Employees who regularly work outside the company's offices for any length of time — from one day a week to every day — can be considered *telecommuters*. Although they work from home or a *satellite office* — think of a district sales manager periodically working in a small, suburban office to write reports and check in with the home office — they perform the same job they would if they were onsite. Thanks to technology, they're able to access the tools they need from home or other locations.

The operative word in the preceding definition is *regularly*. Telecommuting doesn't refer to sporadic instances when someone works from home — to take care of a sick child, for example. Telecommuting refers to a structured routine — when an employee works from home or a remote office one day a week or more.

Although some telecommuters may never come into the office, many come into the office several days a week and work from home just once or twice in a week. This arrangement enables them to remain an active part of the team while still reaping the benefits of working from home.

When Telecommuting Is a Go . . .

In 1999, 28 percent of all companies offered telecommuting arrangements, according to a report released by the Employment Policy Foundation, a non-profit economic policy organization. That's an increase from 1996, when that number was 19.5 percent. If you're not already managing a telecommuter, you need to be prepared for the possibility in the future.

Telecommuting isn't something that you can implement without preparation. You need to invest time upfront to consider some of the big issues involved, such as computer and phone access and office hours, before you welcome your employees into the telecommuting age.

Nothing is more demotivating to employees than being given something that they've wanted — telecommuting — only to have it taken away. Don't jump into a telecommuting program without thinking about the issues outlined in this chapter. A poorly enacted program may actually demotivate employees, and a telecommuting program that has to be cancelled because of glitches will certainly demotivate employees.

Need additional information?

If you decide that telecommuting is appropriate in your workplace, you may want to pay a visit to two Web sites that provide more information about the practice:

✔ www.telecommuting.org, which is maintained by the Telecommuting Knowledge Center (TKC). The nonprofit TKC's goal is to help telecommuting users, vendors, consultants, and other relevant parties form mutually beneficial relationships. The organization prides itself on providing unbiased information about telecommuting technologies and has an online sourcebook and information center devoted to telecommuting topics. To access the material, you simply need to register online. There is no fee to access the information.

✔ www.gilgordon.com, which is maintained by Gil Gordon Associates, a consulting company that provides telecommuting tips. The site gives you lots of information on telecommuting. Better yet, the site is updated every two weeks. You can even use its search engine or site map to find what you need. The company specializes in the implementation of telecommuting programs.

Deciding who pays

Say that you and Elizabeth agree that she will work at home a few days out of the week. But Elizabeth doesn't have a computer at home. So who's responsible for paying for the computer (and other supplies) that Elizabeth needs in order to work at home?

Unfortunately, no easy answer exists. Telecommuting is such a recent practice that established norms regarding financial arrangements have yet to be established.

If an employee must use a particular piece of equipment (like a computer or fax machine) to perform a job and that piece of equipment is one that the company would provide if the employee were working in the office, the company often pays for the equipment. The company may also decide to pay for e-mail access and a dedicated phone line.

Depending on the situation, firms can work out an arrangement in which the company agrees to share some of the expense and the worker pays some.

Making the transition

Before implementing a telecommuting program, meet with each participating employee and decide how many days (and which days) he or she needs to come into the office. That may range from a few times a month to two or three times a week. Whatever the number, the transition should be gradual.

Give everyone — you, your manager, your coworkers, and, most of all, your employees — ample time to adapt. Consistency is the key. Your employees should establish a routine and stick with it.

Telecommuting arrangements should be contingent upon business needs — which may change down the road. If you discover that you really need your employee in the office three days out of the week instead of just two, be prepared to discuss your concerns with your employee. The two of you should be able to reach an amicable resolution that's satisfactory to all parties.

Understanding insurance

Hannah returns home from a weekend vacation to discover that her apartment has been burglarized. The computer that she uses for work is missing. So whose insurance company will reimburse her?

It depends on how diligent Hannah's employer was when it established the telecommuting program. An accepted principle of employment law is that employers are responsible for the health and safety of their employees regardless of where the employees are working. However, most company insurance policies that relate to *property* are limited to equipment located on company premises. Some firms, though, do have policies that cover computers and other equipment located in the homes or apartments of employees.

To find out where your organization stands on issues of insuring a home office, check with your legal counsel or insurance carrier to see what coverage your firm carries and what additional coverage it may need.

Dealing with telecommuters' injuries and illnesses

Your employees are covered by workers' compensation when they become ill or are injured on the job. But what happens when "on the job" is actually "on the job at home"?

Questions of workers' compensation coverage become very complicated because telecommuters frequently have daily activities that are a mix of work and personal activities. For example, your employee falls down the stairs while walking from his home office (where he was making a business call) to his kitchen (where he plans to relax and read the paper).

As the employer, you're typically required to provide a safe and healthy workplace. Your company could be liable for safety hazards in your employees' home offices, such as fires resulting from overloaded outlets. In California, under Cal-OSHA rules, the employer may be required to inspect an employee's home office to insure that it doesn't have any safety hazards.

Consult with your company's lawyer and insurance carrier and the state workers' compensation agency before implementing a telecommuting program. That way, you're familiar with the rules before your employees begin their new work arrangement — and you can fill your employees in on the details as well.

Protecting company work

If your firm controls valuable information, employees who work out of their homes create a security issue. Breaking into someone's house is often easier than intruding onto company property. Likewise, a home computer may be unprotected by your firm's network security, so files and transactions are exposed to potential theft.

If you have intellectual property — and you probably do — don't forget to discuss security arrangements with your information technology department and your telecommuting employees. You may even want to ask your telecommuters to sign a written agreement that spells out the company's confidentiality policies and guidelines.

Navigating tax issues

Even though your employees work for you, they may still encounter tax problems when they work out of the home. The reason? Home office deductions.

Employees cannot deduct anything for which they are reimbursed. They should check with a CPA or attorney for additional guidance. And for more information on the home office deduction, they may want to refer to the current edition of *Taxes For Dummies* (Hungry Minds, Inc.) by Eric Tyson and David J. Silverman.

Signing on the dotted line

After you've thought about all the issues outlined in the preceding sections and you're ready to begin your telecommuting program, you may want to prepare an agreement that any employee who telecommutes will sign. (Be sure to check with an attorney first to help create this document.)

In general, the agreement should cover

- The telecommuting schedule
- The equipment the company is providing and how the company will install and maintain it
- Status reports, such as how often the telecommuter is expected to call and check voicemail
- A term, if this is a trial arrangement
- Confidentiality requirements

Helping Your Employees Work Efficiently at Home

If you decide a telecommuting program is appropriate for one or more of your employees, here are some suggestions for helping them establish a home office:

- Set up their office in a separate room, if practical.
- Establish protocols for answering their business phone.
- Arrange for voicemail or an answering machine to pick up when they're not available.
- Consider putting a lock on the door of their work area.
- Set up a routine for backing up electronic files.
- Designate their computer for business use only.
- Create a work schedule and stick to it.
- Coordinate tech support.
- Plan their telephone system carefully — they may want multiple lines.

Special Concerns

Telecommuting arrangements may require creativity on your part to make sure your offsite workers are motivated. Following are some tips:

- **Interact in person whenever you can.** Without personal contact, misunderstandings are more frequent. Sometimes a one-on-one meeting is the best way to reach an agreement on an issue.

✓ **Pay special attention to employee evaluations.** Remember that performance appraisals should hold no surprises, so you should be providing your telecommuters with year-round feedback, just as you would any other employee.

✓ **Know your employees' schedules.** You don't have to memorize them, but you should have a list that helps you know when each one will be in the office.

✓ **Encourage your employees to maximize office and at-home time.** For example, your employees may want to arrange meetings and phone calls for their office days and save their solitary computer work for at-home days where they will likely have fewer interruptions.

✓ **Be organized.** As a manager, your goal should be to operate proactively rather than reactively. You will be able to avoid many last-minute meetings if you spend time upfront anticipating problems and paying attention to details. When you're organized, your telecommuters won't have to miss out on as much.

✓ **Be willing to reevaluate.** Telecommuting may not work for every person, even if it may work for his or her position. Telecommuting can be a time of self-discovery for your employees — "Hey, I didn't know I was a people person!" — so you may need to reconsider the arrangement if it's not working out. No decision is carved in stone.

✓ **Consider each employee.** Is he or she motivated and disciplined enough to work alone?

Part VII
Overcoming Challenges to Motivation

The 5th Wave By Rich Tennant

STOP WORKPLACE GOSSIP

"What do you think the _real_ reason is for putting up these posters?"

In this part . . .

Perhaps you bought this book because you have some specific motivational issues in mind. You need to do more than motivate your employees. You need to solve some specific challenges. Have no fear. This part offers suggestions for dealing with some common challenges, such as staffing shortages, chronic lateness, stress, and office politics.

Chapter 18

Managing through Change

● ●

In This Chapter

▶ Understanding change

▶ Enduring staffing shortages

▶ Accommodating growth

▶ Dealing with mergers and acquisitions

▶ Surviving downsizing

● ●

Successful companies continually evolve. Evolving may mean providing same-day delivery, offering 24-hour customer service, or trying, in some other way, to stay one step ahead of the competition. Whatever the particulars, change is a constant in the business world.

These changes may be accepted or even embraced by some of your employees, while other workers will resist even the slightest modifications to the status quo. Even those employees in favor of change experience stress during the transition. You can imagine what those *opposed* to the change feel.

In this chapter, you find out what to do when your company is facing change, including painful changes such as downsizing. You also discover ways to make the transition process easier for your employees.

Poorly managed change is a guaranteed motivation killer. Employees need to feel like they know what's going on and that their company has a firm foundation. They should never feel as if changes are being made just for the sake of change or because upper management is subject to whims.

Making Sense of Change

Whether you like it or not, *you can't avoid change.* As a person, you age, you enjoy different things at different stages of your life, and your friends and acquaintances come and go.

The same maxim holds true for business. As a company grows, it has different needs and objectives. A start-up company in the beginning stages of development may only expect to break even and may long to see that first month of profit. Ten years later, that former start-up may be looking to expand its products and client base into new markets.

Perhaps your company has to change because it's facing increased competition. Other common reasons for change include adapting to new technology, the flattening of organizational hierarchies, and downsizing. (See the last section of this chapter for more on the last point.) Another catalyst for change in the workplace is the changing workforce. As a manager, you need to adapt to a new type of employee.

The four stages of change

No matter what the change is or when it occurs, people respond to it gradually. The four steps that people go through when dealing with change are

- **Denial:** At the first signs of a coming change, many people go through denial. They don't believe change is necessary or that the proposed changes will even work.

- **Resistance:** After people realize that change will almost certainly occur, they still continue to resist it. They refuse to accept that the change makes sense. No matter how fantastic a manager you are or how cooperative your employees are, resistance is an unavoidable part of the process. Successful managers discover how to get their team past this stage. If you discover that you or your employees are having trouble with resistance, then it may be worth your time to pick up a copy of *Managing Business Change For Dummies* (Hungry Minds, Inc.) by Beth Evard and Craig Gipple.

- **Exploration:** In this stage, people begin to realize that the change may actually make sense. They start looking at the pros and cons of the change.

- **Acceptance:** People may realize that the change does work and has improved things. If nothing else, they accept the change and begin to regard it as the status quo.

To help your employees deal with change, you need to inspire trust and create confidence. Your employees need to feel that they'll be told what's going on. Feeling like they're a part of the team can also help workers deal with change, so do your best to reinforce these connections. You should offer training, if necessary, so that they can continue to perform their jobs competently.

Make an effort to see the change through your employees' eyes. How does it really affect them?

Strong leadership, effective communication, teamwork, and training all facilitate smooth and efficient change.

Entering change with your eyes wide open

After you decide to introduce a change, make sure that you follow through with it. Otherwise, you convince your employees that you're afflicted with *flavor-of-the-month syndrome.* People use this phrase to describe organizational initiatives that are introduced with much enthusiasm but then fizzle because of a lack of planning or support. Your employees will become suspicious and unlikely to support future initiatives if you introduce a change and then fail to follow through.

Don't enter change lightheartedly. After you introduce a new way of doing things, your employees can't help feeling confused, worried, and uncertain. These feelings may affect your company's productivity for the worse in the short term. Make sure that the change is worthwhile enough to justify a period of confusion and inefficiency.

Handling Staffing Shortages without Destroying Morale

Staffing shortages shouldn't sneak up on you. As a manager, you should be aware of when your department will be busy, either because of seasonal fluctuations or the introduction of a new product.

When you plan ahead for staffing shortages, you anticipate your department's needs, help your team members avoid burnout, and make sure that you have adequate human resources in place to get the job done without overburdening your staff.

Here are some clues that your company is currently experiencing staffing problems:

- Frequent mistakes or missed deadlines
- Excessive overtime
- High turnover
- Absenteeism
- Stressed employees

Don't understaff. Doing so causes increased employee stress, decreased customer service, higher turnover, and increased errors.

Strategic staffing

One key to managing staffing shortages is to be *proactive* rather than *reactive*. When you're proactive, you anticipate important dates, deadlines, and demands. If an employee submits a resignation, you don't just accept it and move on to other tasks. You think about the repercussions, such as who will take on those responsibilities, and you immediately ask the person to train another employee before departing. If the staff person has already moved on to greener pastures and you realize no one knows the job and a training manual doesn't exist, you now need to be reactive — and fast!

You can also use temporary employees to get through a peak workload or manage a special initiative requiring skills or expertise your current full-time staff members don't adequately possess. In addition to using temporary help, here are some other do's and don'ts for successful management of a staffing crisis:

- ✔ Don't ignore the need for additional support, hoping that your employees will somehow catch up with all the work.
- ✔ Do think the problem through.
- ✔ Do be flexible when implementing change.
- ✔ Do maximize your resources by strategically partnering with other departments, if possible.
- ✔ Do get others' opinions, if necessary.
- ✔ Don't avoid making a decision.
- ✔ Do establish a plan and goals.

Calling on temporary staff

If you find yourself faced with a staffing shortage, you may want to turn to temporary staff. Not only can you find employees to assist with office support — answering phones, filing, data entry — you can also bring in temporary engineers, programmers, and even senior managers and executives. You can work with a staffing firm to help you find professionals in the specialty areas you need.

For more on working with temporary workers, see Chapter 16.

Empowering full-time employees

If you find yourself overwhelmed by major responsibilities as a result of increased business demands, you may want to create opportunities for your employees by delegating more responsibilities to staff people who aren't as busy and would love the opportunity for additional learning. Discuss career goals with them beforehand to help you match the right tasks with the most appropriate employees. For more on empowerment, see Chapter 10.

Dealing with Fast Growth

Growth isn't easy to manage, especially when it happens quickly. One day you work for a company with 20 employees, flexible policies, and informal procedures. Everyone knows everyone, and it's fairly easy to implement change or bend the rules for a coworker or customer. The next day you work at a 500-employee company with detailed processes and procedures. You don't even know most of the employees on other managers' teams.

With rapid growth, employees — especially the ones who've been with your firm a while — sometimes pine for the way things used to be done. If they express their preferences too vocally, they can bring down the rest of your staff. Keep in mind that some employees are just more suited to working in a small company. However, you can take small steps to help all your employees grow accustomed to the changes caused by fast growth.

If you want your employees to hang around, you need to:

- ✔ Communicate, communicate, communicate.
- ✔ Let your employees know where the company is headed.
- ✔ Explain why changes are necessary and how they're going to happen.
- ✔ Express your company's vision and values whenever you can.
- ✔ Encourage employees' involvement in planning change.
- ✔ Answer their questions about upcoming changes.
- ✔ Pay special attention to your corporate culture.
- ✔ Make sure that all employees know their roles during the transition as well as the goals once the change is complete.
- ✔ Encourage ownership of projects.

Handling Mergers and Acquisitions

As American corporations seek to become more competitive in the global economy, the number of mergers and acquisitions continues to escalate. In a nationwide survey of financial consultants with Robert Half International, 68 percent said they believe the current level of mergers and acquisitions will increase over the next three years.

Companies are opting to consolidate for many reasons:

- ✔ To gain strength in dealing with competitors
- ✔ To gain efficiencies
- ✔ To tap new markets
- ✔ To expand

Although mergers and acquisitions do have benefits, employees of the companies facing these changes view them with trepidation. Managers need to do whatever they can to ensure a successful integration.

If you find yourself swamped with work that relates to the merger and you have little time for your employees — who really need you now — consider bringing in a consultant who specializes in the transition process. These individuals can analyze financial ratios, develop forecasts, and assist with complex tax compliance issues. If you hire such a consultant, your hands are free to focus on helping your employees through the transition period. See the sidebar for more information.

Coping with Downsizing

The downsizing trend began in the business world in the early 1990s and continues today. Companies usually downsize in an effort to reduce expenses, increase profits or productivity, improve cash flow or decision making, and reduce bureaucracy. Sometimes this strategy works, sometimes it doesn't. Even when staff reductions do produce the desired fiscal results, the toll on a company's remaining workforce may be much heavier than anticipated. Downsizing affects employee morale, company productivity, and long-term processes. It goes without saying that you should downsize only when it's absolutely necessary.

Deciding who to let go can be tough. Some companies opt to lay off their recent hires. Others decide to release their poorest performers. Either way, downsizing is certainly no picnic. It can also expose your company to legal claims by employees who are let go.

Hiring a transition professional

Transition consultants can make major contributions to companies involved with a merger or acquisition. In fact, their involvement can have a lasting positive effect because they help your organization think through problems and solutions.

Here's an example of a transition consultant's effectiveness: The CFO of a company was negotiating the sale of one of its businesses to a competitor. The company was being purchased by an international conglomerate, and the CFO's concern was that his organization would lose people during the acquisition.

The CFO needed a consultant to focus on employee retention and morale issues. The project professional placed with the company was a long-term consultant who also was an effective motivator. The combination of strong interpersonal skills, technical expertise, and knowledge of purchasing account issues, budgeting, internal reports, and final regulatory reports made him an ideal fit. In addition, he had experience working on pre-sales numbers and post acquisitions.

The consultant utilized many of his financial skills to streamline accounting procedures, develop budget and purchasing reports, prepare the internal and regulatory reports required for the sale of the business, and determine the pre-sale and post-acquisition values of the company. He also was able to address retention and morale issues, including redefining roles and responsibilities and implementing a mentoring program.

If you like the idea of hiring someone who focuses solely on the administrative process of the merger or acquisition, then you need to look for a consultant with certain skills. Here are some of the areas of knowledge that companies look for when hiring consultants during a time of transition:

- Financial systems implementation
- Business process improvement
- Personnel management
- SEC reporting
- Due diligence
- Back office integration

If you find yourself in the unfortunate position of laying off employees, here are some tips to get you through the process:

- **Start by consulting an attorney familiar with the employment law issues that arise with layoffs.**
- **Manage the message.** Determine when you will notify your workforce about layoffs and make a game plan. Legal, practical, and other factors will need to be considered.
- **Make sure that you really have no other options to laying off employees.** When you focus on streamlining your operations and trimming your spending, you'll be amazed at the many opportunities you'll find. (See the sidebar on alternatives to downsizing.)

- ✔ **In advance, prepare a list of the individuals you'll be releasing in the order you plan to let them go (for your eyes only, of course).** That way, you can easily decide who should stay if you discover that you don't have to lay off as many individuals as you once thought.

- ✔ **Decide, with fellow managers, the criteria for laying off employees, and be consistent.** If you do so, your employees can see that all departments were fair and consistent in determining who would be released.

- ✔ **After you've decided who's to be laid off, schedule private meetings with each employee to relay the news.** Don't forget to offer outplacement services to assist them in finding new jobs.

After you've downsized, your remaining staff will feel the repercussions. In fact, employee morale may be at an all-time low among your employees. You want to reassure them that you're doing everything in your power to avoid future layoffs. Whatever you do, don't overlook motivating your remaining staff — or you may end up losing them, too.

In addition, make sure that you pay special attention to the career development of your remaining employees. For more information on career development, see Part IV.

If your company is downsizing, standards of fair employment practices still apply. Consult with your legal counsel or an employment attorney when making cutbacks. All downsizing decisions should involve sound legal advice.

Alternatives to downsizing

Although you may think that the easiest way to cut costs is to downsize your staff, you may be surprised by the number of options you really have. Before taking such a serious step — one that can devastate your employees' and their families — consider some of these alternatives:

- ✔ Retrain employees to do other jobs within the company.

- ✔ Rethink business processes to eliminate cost and redundancy.

- ✔ Ask employees to volunteer for reduced hours, part-time work, job sharing, unpaid sabbaticals, and so on.

- ✔ Examine each position when someone resigns and analyze whether you really need to hire a new person as a replacement.

- ✔ Develop voluntary early-retirement packages.

- ✔ Use temporary workers if you have a current need but may need to release workers down the road.

Chapter 19

Dealing with Difficult Situations

· ·

In This Chapter

▶ Deciding how to treat chronic problems

▶ Ending perpetual tardiness and absenteeism

▶ Spreading positive thinking

▶ Preventing workplace violence

▶ Terminating employees

▶ Reassuring the rest of the staff

· ·

Y ou already know that being a manager isn't always easy. What do you say to the person who's constantly late? Or one who doesn't bother to show up and doesn't even call? What's the correct way to handle employees who, despite warning after warning, refuse to change? And how do you keep everyone else motivated while one person is dragging down morale?

In this chapter, I show you how to handle these difficult situations. You also discover how to create procedures that are fair to you, your company, and your employees.

This chapter covers some legally sensitive information, and these are not areas in which you can afford to be your own lawyer. Employee disciplinary action, termination, and workplace violence are matters that require advice that applies to your particular company and situation. My recommendation is to consult an attorney.

You should always address performance problems right after they happen — don't wait for the annual performance review that may be months away.

Establishing Procedures

No matter how great your company is and how wonderful a manager you are, sooner or later you will have to deal with a problem employee. How you respond determines if the situation is quickly resolved or if things get worse and the problem behavior spreads from one employee to affect your whole team or department.

Hopefully, you won't have to fire anyone. But you need to be prepared for that possibility and you need to know the proper steps to take to be fair to everyone involved.

As the immediate manager, you are responsible for that problem employee; you're the one responsible for handling his or her poor workplace conduct. So take the time now, before problems arise, to figure out how you're going to handle these situations. If your human resources department doesn't have written procedures in place, you need to work with them to establish some.

Problems don't go away if you ignore them. Ignoring a problem sets the stage for other employees to disregard performance standards because they think that you don't care.

Although the following sections outline some basic things to consider when disciplining employees, you may want to check out my book *Human Resources Kit For Dummies* (Hungry Minds) for more detailed information on this topic.

Putting fairness first

Whatever process you have in place to discipline employees needs to be fair. For example, if you tell an employee that he or she has an opportunity to correct the problem behavior before being fired, you need to provide that chance.

Here are some other tips:

- ✔ **Clarify expectations.** Your employees need to know what the standards are for an acceptable performance and how their efforts (or lack of efforts) affect the company's productivity.

- ✔ **Outline the consequences.** Staff members should know the consequences of their failure to meet these standards.

- ✔ **Address problem behavior as soon as possible.** Otherwise, you send the message to other employees that a certain behavior is acceptable.

- ✔ **Match the discipline to the offense.** How serious was the offense? What does the individual's employment record look like? Has he or she been a problem employee before, or is this the first time that there has been a performance issue?

✔ **Be consistent.** Being consistent limits the possibility of being charged with discrimination.

✔ **Document, document, document.** Remembering what you talked about in a performance review meeting last year with a staff member can be difficult. To be fair to everyone involved, you need to take notes and keep a record of your discussions and any problem behaviors. That way, at a later time, you won't inadvertently think the person said or did something he didn't say or do; likewise, you can't be falsely accused of statements or actions. And you will likely need this documentation in the event the person's behavior — or termination — becomes an issue in litigation sometime down the road.

Knowing the basic steps to take

You need to follow some general steps when handling any difficult situation. You may need to skip or add steps, depending on the circumstances. Always check with someone in your human resources or legal department for guidance in difficult or sensitive situations, because your company may have a specific policy in place. The rest of this chapter also has additional tips that may be appropriate for particular circumstances. The following are some general guidelines:

1. **Notify your employee that he or she is not meeting company standards.**

   You should give this warning verbally, in a one-on-one meeting. Make a memo to yourself about what was said.

2. **Issue a second warning.**

   If the behavior hasn't improved, have another one-on-one meeting. This time, deliver a memo that outlines areas that need improvement and explains how the employee's actions are negatively affecting business.

3. **Issue a final warning.**

   If the individual's conduct doesn't improve, ask your human resources or legal representative to guide you. In some instances, a final warning is appropriate. In other cases, termination without a final warning may be the right step.

4. **Terminate the employee.**

Handling grievances

The procedures that you follow in case of a problem employee need to do more than simply guide your actions. They also have to give your employees a chance to have their say. In other words, you should have some form of *complaint procedure* in place. It doesn't have to be very complex, although it sometimes is if you're a unionized company (in which case the formalized steps are known as a *grievance procedure*.) Again, check with an attorney for specific advice on these matters.

In general, your complaint procedure should:

✔ **Allow communication options.** Typically, employees should report problems they're having to their supervisors. But if the situation involves the supervisor — or the complaint is serious in nature, such as harassment or discrimination — individuals need to be able to go to someone else, such as a human resources representative.

✔ **Encourage a quick response.** If someone comes to you with a complaint, address the issue as soon as possible. Ignoring any complaint — especially those related to workspace safety or health violations, sexual harassment, discrimination, or criminal activity — can increase your company's exposure to legal action. Report such complaints immediately to your human resources or legal department. In many instances, you may also want to report back to the employee to say where the situation stands or what action is being taken.

✔ **Investigate with an open mind.** Remain objective while looking for facts and consider all pieces of information to be important, until you have reason to believe otherwise. However, don't launch an investigation on your own without first checking with your human resources or legal department.

✔ **Protect employees from reprisal.** Assure your staff members that if they follow the company's recommended procedure for filing complaints, they will not be penalized in any way. Be sure to counsel managers against any actions that may be perceived as retaliatory.

Dealing with Habitual Lateness

Ask people what their pet peeve is, and you hear a variety of answers. But if you ask enough people, you'll hear *tardiness* again and again. No one likes to wait for others to show up. And when tardiness is habitual, insult is added to injury.

Those who are left waiting often feel that the late person's tardiness shows a lack of respect for them, their time, their feelings, and the event, whether it's a meeting or a lunch date. After all, if one person is 15 minutes late to a meeting that includes six people, that's 15 minutes lost by each person — collectively, one and a half hours. No wonder tardiness can raise such ire.

No matter what's causing the problem, chronic lateness is something you will have to address. Okay — so sometimes bad things happen, and even your best, most reliable employee is occasionally late. But you know it's the exception, not the rule. If lateness is something you've come to expect from certain employees — you're already planning excuses to the vice president for your staff member who you know will be late to a meeting — then you have a problem.

How do you deal with chronic lateness? For starters, you stop it before it becomes chronic. Even if your best employee shows up late — for the first time — call her on it. You don't have to read her the riot act; you just need to let her know that you noticed. For example, Martha shows up 15 minutes late one day. You could take her aside privately and ask her if everything went okay that morning. Doing so gives her the opportunity to explain her tardiness without feeling like she's under attack. Then you can respond with something like, "I thought something like that had happened. You always set such a good example for our staff by being on time every day." If you do so, you show Martha that you notice and are concerned, and also that you appreciate the standards that she sets for the rest of the staff.

You need to make sure that you set the example that you want your staff to follow. If you want all of your employees to be at their desks, ready to work, at 8 a.m., then you should be at your desk, working, by 8 a.m.

If you address tardiness the first time, and the first time turns into the second, and the second into the third, then the tardiness has become a performance issue. Handle it like any other performance issue. (See the section, "Establishing Procedures," earlier in this chapter.)

If you ignore an employee's tardiness, he or she will think that punctuality is unimportant. That's just the message you want to avoid sending. By responding quickly to one employee's tardiness, you send a message to all your other staff members as well. Every company has a grapevine, and you can bet that your late employee will tell at least one other person of your actions, who will tell one other person, and so on.

Coping with Absenteeism

Late employees are bad enough, but what about employees who just don't show up?

Of course, everyone gets sick. Most people call to let you know they won't be at work on a given day. But what if days turn into weeks, or the absences exceed acceptable limits over a period of time? Once the problem is apparent, you need to take action.

If your employee doesn't come to work and doesn't call, catch it the first time it happens. Call the individual that morning and ask whether he or she plans to come in. Find out why the person is out of the office. Is it a medical condition, such as an illness or injury? If it is your regular practice to do so, ask for a doctor's excuse and for guidelines for when the employee can work. Is it a personal emergency, such as a death in the family? Offer your support and find out when the individual expects to return to the office. Once you've uncovered the reason for the absence, remind him or her that you need and expect all employees to call in as soon as possible, regardless of the situation.

Changing Negative Attitudes into Can-Do Attitudes

If you want your company to be successful, you need to make sure that you have employees who motivate, encourage, and inspire their coworkers. In other words, you need employees to think positively. In fact, in a recent survey of executives commissioned by Robert Half International, more than a third of the respondents cited a positive attitude as the single most valued interpersonal skill among job candidates.

Just as a smile can be contagious, so can a negative attitude. Some people aren't doing anything particularly wrong; they just have a cynical, negative perspective that is pervading the halls of your company. So what do you do?

For starters, sit down with the employee to talk about what's wrong. You could start off with something like, "I've noticed that you don't seem very happy lately. Is something at work contributing to this?" That way, you open the door for him to tell you that he isn't satisfied with the job, dislikes a coworker, or has issues in his personal life. (With any luck you won't hear all three!) If your employee has a valid complaint, then do what you can to address it.

To improve the level of optimism at your workplace, keep the following in mind:

- ✔ **Acknowledge concerns.** Don't gloss over complaints or present a Pollyanna view of things. If appropriate, acknowledge the other person's point of view and provide clarification on any misunderstandings. Try to avoid sounding defensive or angry, which only makes the situation worse. Instead, be open to the possibility that your employee may have a few legitimate gripes.

- ✔ **Be part of the solution.** Instead of allowing your employees to present only problems, encourage them to propose solutions. Ask them to offer at least one resolution to any complaint.

- ✔ **Encourage humor.** Humor can diffuse tension and ease stress. But don't confuse humor with sarcasm. Humor should be positive and light-hearted, and should never occur at the expense of others.

✔ **Make time for others.** As a manager, you should have an open-door policy and be approachable. This encourages employees to be open and upfront about problems and concerns. Workers feel anxious and uneasy if they perceive you as inaccessible or oblivious to the interpersonal dynamics of the workplace. As a result, they are less likely to communicate with you — about both positive and negative issues.

✔ **Watch your body language.** Smile, establish eye contact, listen attentively, and nod in encouragement. Use your physical actions to send a positive message to your staff.

✔ **Suggest privacy if appropriate.** If a major setback or crisis occurs at work for an employee, encourage the person to take a few minutes to be alone. That way, the individual can work through strong emotions and avoid scenes or actions that he or she may later regret.

✔ **Praise, praise, praise.** When successes occur, share them with others and praise those who made them happen. When an employee delivers an outstanding presentation, say so. Recognizing achievements makes everyone feel good.

If you can't cheer up your downtrodden worker, and other employees come to you complaining about the person, then encourage them to distance themselves. Let them know that it's natural to want to sympathize with someone who's unhappy, but that they shouldn't do so at the expense of their own morale. See "Helping Your Staff Cope," later in this chapter, for more information.

Handling Threats and Potential Workplace Violence

Although it's not an easy topic to discuss, you can't afford to ignore the issue of workplace violence. And for the majority of businesses, violence is not an issue. However, you should still take steps to prevent violence and prepare your firm to deal with it if it does occur. The stakes are too high to completely ignore the issue.

Your goal is to provide your employees with a safe, secure workplace where violence is unlikely to erupt. Some concrete ways you can do this, depending on the type of business that you have, include

✔ Limiting access to the office through the use of passwords or cardkeys

✔ Making sure parking lots or garages are well lit and monitored

✔ Providing a place where employees can store valuables

✔ Limiting the amount of cash on the premises

✔ Establishing protocols for emergencies

These items address dangers that may come from outside of the company. To protect your staff from threats from within, you should

✔ **Implement a strict policy regarding violence.** Make sure your employees understand that certain behaviors — physical and verbal threats, aggressive gestures, harassing behavior — will never, under any circumstances, be tolerated.

✔ **Watch for volatile situations.** The chance always exists that an upset employee will react violently to disciplinary action, notice of suspension, or termination. To minimize the likelihood of trouble, always review problematic discipline issues with an expert in your human resources or legal department.

✔ **Conduct thorough reference checks before hiring.** Be very careful in your screening process of candidates. Check references, and if something suspicious comes up, get as much information as possible before making a hiring decision.

✔ **Provide counseling or similar assistance.** Let your employees know that they can seek counseling or consult with your company's employee assistance program, if you have one. When contracting with healthcare providers, check whether their benefits include a toll-free crisis line or access to seminars that help employees deal with the stresses of life in and out of the office.

Watch for these signs that may be precursors to violence:

✔ Alcohol or substance abuse problems

✔ Frequent displays of anger, abusive language, or threats of violence

✔ Any attempt to bring a weapon into the workplace

✔ Extreme behavior

If you see any of these signs, address the situation right away, and seek legal counsel.

It's better to be safe than sorry. If an employee threatens violence — whether or not any violence is actually carried out — you can fire the person immediately.

Dealing with Confrontations

If an employee confronts you or is verbally abusive in a meeting, such as during a performance appraisal, you need to know how to respond. Here are some tips you should read over before you find yourself in that uncomfortable, and sometimes dangerous, situation:

- **Listen.** Don't interrupt as your employee blows off steam, and don't respond while the employee is still upset.

- **Be calm.** Becoming agitated just makes the situation worse.

- **Don't agree automatically.** Here's a common remark made by managers to employees: "I can understand where you're coming from." Unfortunately, you may not understand and you shouldn't say that you do. You should, however, acknowledge valid complaints.

- **Call for help if you expect violence.** If you suspect the situation may erupt in violence, call the police immediately. Don't try to handle the situation by yourself, and don't allow other employees to become involved.

Verbal abuse that rises to the level of threats or insubordination is a cause for immediate termination.

Terminating Employees

The proper approach to some difficult situations — such as theft, highly inappropriate behavior, or evidence of substance abuse — isn't hard to determine, because these situations are fairly extreme. In other instances, deciding to terminate an employee is a difficult decision. For example, you have an employee whose attitude is upbeat and whose work style is compatible with the company's culture, but who just doesn't have the skills she needs for the job. She's aware of her deficiencies and tries extra-hard, but with no improvement. Her coworkers, who try to help her and pick up the slack, are getting behind in their own work. Although you've been aware of the problem for some time, you've wanted to give her a chance to get her act together. By now, though, it has become apparent that things aren't going to change.

You've reached the point where it's time to consider termination. Firing an employee is always difficult, especially when you're dealing with a problematic employee who is a likeable person. But you must be fair to your entire staff. By keeping a poor performer in her current role, you're ultimately increasing the workload of the rest of the staff. And, by doing nothing to solve the problem, you're also sending the message that quality work is not that important.

If the worker with inadequate skills may fit better in another position, you might try a transfer first. If this isn't feasible, and keeping her on board is detrimental to your other employees, it's probably time for a parting of the ways.

As a manager, you must accept the hard fact that sometimes things just can't be worked out. If you've warned an employee, both verbally and in writing, spoken to the human resources department, and asked your boss to talk with the individual, you have every reason to expect a change in behavior. But when nothing changes and your staff is becoming demoralized, termination is often the only option left. (Read more about helping your staff cope later in this chapter.)

If you must fire an employee, you need to respect the person's rights and dignity. But, you also need to make sure that your company will not be the target of retaliatory action in court — and if it is, that it will not lose the case. Once again, my advice is to consult an attorney for guidance specific to your situation. And for more information on termination, refer to my book *Human Resources Kit For Dummies* (Hungry Minds).

Understanding employment-at-will

Most employers in the United States operate under the policy of *employment-at-will*. Employment-at-will means that as long as your company does not have a contractual agreement that guarantees employees certain job protections, you have the right, as an employer in the private sector, to fire any of your employees at any time and for any (or no) reason. In other words, you don't need an excuse to fire someone. Likewise, your employees can quit your firm at any time, without reason and without notice.

Keep in mind the following exceptions to employment-at-will:

- ✔ Unionized employees have contractual guarantees and are therefore not employed at will. Not only must you have a reason to terminate union employees, but you also must follow the disciplinary and termination policy.

- ✔ If you have a certain number of employees, your policies must comply with federal laws, such as Title VII of the Civil Rights Act of 1964 and the Americans with Disabilities Act. Talk to your human resources representative.

- ✔ Although you technically employ employees at will, you should not terminate them recklessly. You can fire employees who don't do their jobs or meet certain standards, but you need to use a reasoned approach.

Terminating without prior warning

Sometimes behavior is offensive enough that you can skip the typical process of written warnings and other formalized procedures. Here are some of the offenses for which human resource professionals usually agree you can terminate an employee immediately:

- ✔ Verbal abuse or obscenities directed at a supervisor

- ✔ Incompetence

- ✔ Insubordination

- ✔ Violence or threat of violence

- ✔ Theft

- ✔ Intoxication on the job

- ✔ Falsification of records

You don't want your company to become embroiled in a wrongful discharge suit. If such a suit reaches trial, you'll probably lose; most juries tend to favor employees over employers. So if you're going to terminate someone, keep the following points in mind:

- ✔ **Make sure that your company literature doesn't guarantee employment.** Words such as *permanent* or *probationary* should be avoided.

- ✔ **Follow documented performance standards for all company positions.** You need to make sure that the performance standards are easy to understand and that all employees are aware of these standards.

- ✔ **Take detailed notes regarding all performance and disciplinary issues.** You need to be able to prove poor performance and prior warning.

- ✔ **Ask for legal help if you're uncertain.** Find out if you're following procedure correctly before you terminate an employee.

As the immediate manager, you will likely be responsible for delivering the news to your employee. (In some cases, a representative from your human resources department may be handling the situation.) Schedule a one-on-one meeting and, in a sensitive, concise manner, tell the person why he or she is being terminated. The person has the right to know.

In the termination meeting, you need to

- ✔ **Deliver final payment.** Your employee, in an ideal situation, should leave the meeting with a check that pays everything: prorated salary, any severance pay, any expense reimbursements, and money for accrued time off (vacation, sick days, or personal days). Check with someone from your human resources department because requirements for final pay vary from state to state.

- ✔ **Eliminate access to the company.** Ask for company-owned items, such as keys, access cards, and badges. Ask your information services department to terminate the employee's computer password, and don't forget to end credit card privileges.

> ✔ **Supply COBRA information for medical plans.** If your company is subject to COBRA regulations, you're obligated to extend the employee's medical coverage — with no changes — for 18 months. Who pays — the company or the employee — is your call.
>
> ✔ **Discuss any outplacement arrangements.** Depending on circumstances, you may want the outplacement counselor onsite, so that he or she is available to talk to the employee immediately.

Helping Your Staff Cope

A difficult situation doesn't have to be dramatic to have a destabilizing impact on your staff. Even an employee who's chronically late to meetings can disrupt workflow, create stress, and cause resentment among his or her colleagues. As a result, after you deal with a problem employee, you must then address your staff.

The best way to do so depends on the situation and how it has affected other employees. Obviously, you should keep matters of confidentiality in mind when telling your staff about the termination of another employee. But an even more delicate situation arises when you're handling matters concerning an employee who remains on staff — for example, when you're dealing with an employee who frequently calls in "sick." What, if anything, should you tell his or her coworkers about the steps you've taken to resolve the problem?

Checking with your company's legal counsel or human resources department is always wise. You don't want to divulge private matters or create a situation in which the employee who has been privately disciplined feels publicly humiliated. Representatives from your legal or human resources department can help guide you in what to say and whom to tell.

Because of potential legal complications or the discomfort you may feel in discussing staffing issues with other employees, you may be tempted to just avoid making any kind of statement about the situation. Avoiding the issue is a mistake. Your employees expect you to be fair and consistent in your enforcement of policies. As such, you need to keep them somewhat in the loop as you handle a difficult situation.

You can't expect employees to communicate with you if you don't communicate with them. At the same time, you must be sensitive to each individual's need for privacy and respect. After all, a person who's always tardy isn't a criminal and hardly deserves to be treated like one.

Here are some do's and don'ts to guide you when you speak with your staff about your responses to difficult situations:

Do

✔ **Be brief and straightforward.** A simple acknowledgement of the problem ("I know there have been some difficulties because of Pam's repeat absences") and a general assurance that you're taking care of things ("We've spoken about it and she's going to correct the problem") should suffice.

✔ **Tell only those who absolutely need to know.** If an employee's behavior or poor performance creates problems for members of her project team, and no one else, speak just with those employees. Let them know that you've taken steps to improve the employee's performance and, ultimately, the productivity of the entire team. You don't need to inform the entire department or company about the problem or the solution.

✔ **Say the same thing to everyone.** Avoid giving some staff members more details than others. In addition to violating the problem employee's privacy, you create an group that has the scoop. Those people who aren't in this group will wonder why they're being kept in the dark and resent what they perceive as favoritism.

✔ **Let the employee know what you've said.** To prevent rumors and gossip that may hurt the employee and create more problems, you should make sure the difficult employee knows exactly what you said and to whom.

✔ **Assume a mature response from your staff.** Let them know that you're sure they will handle the situation in a professional manner. For example, you could say, "I know you won't allow this to adversely affect your own work or your interactions with Brian." Doing so tells them what you expect and implies that you won't tolerate meanness toward or isolation of the employee at fault.

Don't

✔ **Give details or betray confidences.** If an employee has been habitually absent because of a personal crisis or family problems, that information should stay between you and that individual. Don't tell other staff members details about a problem ("Bill has been out a lot because his kid's in trouble") or your response ("I suggested he see a family therapist").

✔ **Make light of the situation.** This is one instance in a manager's life in which humor is inappropriate. Joking about an employee's problems just isn't tactful or considerate. Avoid flippant statements like "Let's all chip in to buy Pam a new alarm clock" or "Remember Steve? He's not coming back!"

✔ **Leave staff members to speculate about the future.** If an employee has been terminated, let his or her coworkers know how this is going to impact them — will you expect them to divide his responsibilities among themselves or do you plan to hire a replacement? If a problem employee is still on staff, briefly explain what, if anything, will change — for example, if the individual will be assigned to a different work team or given other duties.

✔ **Turn it into a public trial.** Do not speak to your other employees about the problem employee in the presence of the one you had to discipline. Doing so would only create even more problems and conflicts. By the same token, don't call all your staff members and not the problem employee into a meeting, or afterwards you'll have a group of people who are embarrassed to make eye contact, let alone work together. The best strategy is to have a brief, closed-door, one-on-one meeting in your office with only those staff people who have been directly affected by the poor work habits or behavior of a colleague.

✔ **Talk about it if you don't have to.** If the problem has somehow not affected anyone but you, keeping quiet about the matter is best. An example is if an employee works well with others but has trouble accepting your authority as a manager and questions your every decision. This is a problem you need to resolve one-on-one. Don't mention it to the employee's coworkers and create friction where none exists.

✔ **Vent to other employees.** If you're having trouble with one employee, avoid complaining about him or her to other members of your staff. Remember, telling your staff that you're taking care of a situation is not the same as griping about how frustrated or disappointed you are with one of their coworkers. Even a casual negative remark is a sure-fire way to make people uncomfortable and undermine morale. Your other employees will worry that you make critical comments about them too.

By reacting to difficult situations promptly and appropriately, you minimize the impact the employee's actions or behaviors can have on the rest of your staff. Your response can keep you from having to do emergency repairs to the relationships that your staff members have with one another and with you.

Chapter 20

Handling Stress and Beating Burnout

• •

• •

*I*n today's world, stress and burnout are commonplace. Downsizings, corporate mergers, and everyday work pressures create a workforce that wonders what *not* being overwhelmed feels like. According to the American Institute on Stress (yes, such a group exists), 78 percent of Americans consider their jobs stressful. If the majority of your employees feel stressed, you may be in for trouble.

Stress takes its toll on the morale of your workforce. Not many employees stroll into the office at 8 a.m. feeling energetic and excited if they know they'll be overwhelmed once they reach their desks. In fact, approximately 1 million workers stay at home every day because of stress, according to the Occupational Health and Safety News and National Council on Compensation Insurance. The same study finds that 95 billion dollars is lost in productivity every year due to stress.

As a manager, you have to worry about stress as well as its companion, burnout. Stress is sort of like a waterfall, and burnout is more like a slow drip. But burnout, if you don't do anything about it, can turn even your best employees into less enthusiastic, less productive workers.

This chapter helps you identify the signs of stress and burnout and gives you ideas that can help both you and your staff cope.

A Little Stress Is Good for You, Right?

The experts define stress as a physiological response to *stressors,* which are the stimuli in your environment. In other words, stress is how your body reacts — mentally, emotionally, and physically — to the pressures and strains in your life.

Even happy events can cause stress. A promotion, a big raise, or the birth of a child all produce stress as people struggle to adapt to their new situation.

Stress, in itself, doesn't have to be a negative force. Sometimes, it can be motivating. You'd probably have a hard time staying up until 2 a.m. working on that crucial report if not for stress. Stress can help you accomplish things you never thought possible. You've probably heard the stories about people performing amazing feats — like lifting cars — in a crisis situation. In the workplace, stress can prompt a team to accomplish in two days what should take two weeks. That's the good stress, the kind that creates focus and motivation.

And not all employees perceive stress the same way. What one person perceives as stressful is a day at the races to another person. One of your coworkers may dive into the Häagen-Dasz when a tight deadline is approaching. Another coworker may be glued to her computer, adrenaline pumping, having the time of her life.

But then you have the bad stress — the kind that can make you tense and frustrated. If this type of stress is ongoing, it can lead to depression or apathy.

Some jobs are inherently more stressful than others. Table 20-1 lists the ten most stressful jobs, as reported by National Business Employment Weekly.

Table 20-1	The Ten Most Stressful Jobs	
Rank	*Job*	*Stress Score*
1	U.S. president	176.55
2	Firefighter	110.93
3	Corporate executive (senior)	108.62
4	Race car driver (Indy class)	101.77
5	Taxi driver	100.49
6	Surgeon	99.46

Rank	Job	Stress Score
7	Astronaut	99.34
8	Police officer	93.89
9	Football player (NFL)	92.79
10	Air traffic controller	83.13

What stress can do

For your health and well-being, stress should come in small doses. Stress is sort of like vinegar or garlic — great from time to time, but not appropriate for breakfast, lunch, and dinner. Too much stress can lower your life expectancy because of the effects it has on your body over time. Research has shown that stress can

- ✔ Increase heart rate, breathing, and blood pressure.
- ✔ Cause dry mouth.
- ✔ Cause sweating.
- ✔ Increase muscle tension.
- ✔ Change your metabolism.

Besides these physical ramifications, stress can cause accidents, absenteeism, burnout, lowered productivity, and decreased morale.

Some workers, who feel they were under too much stress, have filed legal claims against employers. Review your work policies carefully, and seek legal advice for clarification.

Symptoms of stress

Stress doesn't just sneak up on you or your employees. It builds up gradually. In fact, stress doesn't have to result from just the big things; the little things add up too. Take a long commute, for example. By itself, it can seem incidental, but day in and day out, it can become a major stressor. If you listen to your body and mind, you can realize just how stressed you are.

Feeling shaky, tired, depressed, irritable, or panicked, or constantly worried, distracted, and forgetful may be symptoms of stress. For more information on the symptoms of stress, see *Stress Management For Dummies* by Allen Elkin, Ph.D. (Hungry Minds, Inc.).

Here are some things you can do to lower the potential for stress:

- ✔ Give employees only one boss.
- ✔ Clearly define job descriptions.
- ✔ Discourage overtime or weekend work, when possible.
- ✔ Recognize your employees' accomplishments frequently.
- ✔ Empower your employees.
- ✔ Challenge your employees to grow in their careers.

If your employees are consistently putting in extra hours, beware. You may be setting them up for burnout. (See the section on burnout later in this chapter.)

Logging excessive hours may be a sign of inefficiency. Some employees take 60 hours a week to do the same job others perform successfully in only 40 — and the 40-hour staff members frequently produce higher quality work. If the workloads are indeed equal, the 60-hour employee is most likely inefficient, disorganized, or both. And what's worse, the odds are good that he's stressed. If you notice that one of your employees is always working extra hours, make sure that he's not burning himself out just to keep pace with your other workers. You may have to reevaluate his ability to perform the duties you've assigned him or send him to some time-management training.

One other thing to watch out for: Make sure that your employees are on the same page as you are if you do ask for some overtime or assign an employee a stressful project. They shouldn't think that, if they work overtime, you'll reward them with a promotion, or that they'll get a big raise if they knock themselves out polishing up that big project.

Encourage your employees to step back and see the big picture. They are sometimes so focused on getting through their lists of projects that they don't have time to put things in perspective. Encourage normal work hours, vacations, and breaks so that staff members can see both the forest and the trees.

Coping with Stress

Having at least some stress is unavoidable. How you react to that stress is what's key. The secret to controlling stress — both yours and your employees — is to better manage your reaction to it. Sometimes that means seeking a solution; sometimes that means recognizing that some things are out of your control and you need to let go. Of course, accepting that things are beyond your control is easier said than done.

Stressed employees can still be satisfied with their jobs

Even if your employees are feeling overwhelmed by stress, don't assume that they're unhappy in their jobs. The nature of the work, not the amount of job stress, most determines job satisfaction, according to research presented to the American Psychological Society by psychologists from Bowling Green (Ohio) State University. An employee can be very dissatisfied with his job — and not at all stressed. Likewise, an employee can feel a significant amount of stress and still love the job.

The moral: Motivation comes from doing something rewarding. So even if your staff members' jobs are sometimes stressful, if they feel some intrinsic value in what they're doing, they won't necessarily be unhappy in their work. But even if your employees find their jobs rewarding, you should still care whether you're increasing your employees' stress and burnout because those conditions can ultimately affect their job performance.

Most people who experience work-related pressure on a daily basis cope with it in one of the following ways:

- Hoping it goes away
- Seeking fast relief
- Taking it out on others
- Seeking assistance

You need to make sure that your employees know that they can tackle tough situations and win. Your employees may think that they have no control over the stress in their lives because they're not the boss. That's not true at all. In this section, I show you all the ways in which your employees (and you) can overcome stress.

Someone else's crisis doesn't have to be your own. Allow other people to take responsibility. Lend a helping hand, but don't empathize to the point of carrying their burdens.

Think positively

One of the first things that you and your employees should do when combating stress is to think positively. Whenever a negative thought comes to mind, try and consider the positive outcomes that could take place instead.

For example, say that you or your employees are dreading an upcoming merger with another firm in your industry. Force yourself to think about the positive possibilities that the change brings. And then convey that optimistic outlook to your employees.

Or say that you have a big lunch meeting with an important client who has a reputation for being difficult. If you go to work with the attitude that your day will be stressful because of the lunch meeting, then it *will* be stressful. Challenge yourself to change that belief.

If one of your employees has a difficult lunch meeting with a client, point out an occasion when someone got along with the client and actually persuaded him to change his mind. Talk about how that change occurred. And empower your employee by demonstrating your confidence that he can work effectively with the client.

Your mindset has a powerful effect on the employees you supervise. They look to you for leadership — to set the example. So if you appear stressed, they will become stressed.

If your employees are dwelling on the worst possible scenario, ask them to tell you the odds of it happening. Then find out what would cause it to happen. And then develop a plan to try to ensure that it doesn't happen.

If your employees are feeling stressed, try a *stress audit.* Have your employees write down what their stressors are, how they react to them, and how they can change the situation or stressor. If a large project is coming your way and it will put pressure on your staff, can any of the smaller responsibilities they place on their stress audit be reassigned, postponed, or outsourced? If not, what can you or your employees do — based on the stress audits — to help everyone get through the tough period ahead?

Here are some other techniques you can use to keep everyone upbeat:

- **Encourage your employees to think about what they've accomplished.** If they think they've accomplished nothing, they'll feel discouraged and apathetic. Remind them of their successes or create a visible chart that highlights their progress and depicts how far they've come on a particular project.

- **Help your employees break large projects into smaller pieces and develop timelines.** A multilayered assignment can seem overwhelming. Sit down with your staff and divide the work into more manageable tasks and goals. And be sure to assign each aspect a deadline. Once a goal has been reached, celebrate.

- **Let your employees go home early when they're not expecting it.** Random, happy surprises can have a great impact on employee motivation. Another option is to bring in lunch to celebrate a deadline being reached.

✔ **Maintain a favorites list.** In a central location, post a paper with the words "Favorite Book" on it. Then have employees write their favorite book. Each day, start a new list — favorite movie, favorite restaurant, and so on. Doing so helps create a lighthearted atmosphere that reduces tension.

Plan company events

When you can't reduce the amount of work, try to make the work environment more enjoyable.

One company I know of has a regularly scheduled TGIF celebration once a month — on a Friday, of course. Activities vary each month, ranging from an ice cream social to a chili cookoff to a tricycle race. Here are some other company events you can plan to help alleviate stress:

✔ **Schedule department challenges.** Why not try a culinary competition? Each department can be responsible for preparing dishes on rotating Fridays.

✔ **Start a walking club.** Employees can walk on their lunch breaks or after work to help them relax.

✔ **Arrange onsite health screenings.** You can measure fitness, body composition, or personal stress — all tests that promote taking care of yourself.

✔ **Schedule workshops or seminars.** Brownbag lunch sessions are a good way for coworkers to find out about interesting topics or events.

✔ **Start a book club.** Interested employees can meet for breakfast once a month to discuss the reading.

✔ **Place a jigsaw puzzle in the break room.** You'll be surprised at the number of people who help put the puzzle together.

One common employee worry is money

Research by the National Institute for Personal Finance Employee Education at Virginia Polytechnic Institute reveals the following:

✔ Fifty-four percent of employees worry about debt.

✔ Thirty-four percent consider their financial stress to be high or extreme.

✔ Thirty-three percent say money worries affect their job performance.

Make sure that you're paying your employees fairly (see Chapter 13). You also may consider inviting a financial planner to give a talk during an informal brownbag lunch.

Take a vacation

Have you noticed that you've stopped getting vacation requests from your staff? You've got a problem if people don't think that they have time for a vacation. By not getting time away from the office, your employees become more stressed. If your employees are continually stressed, they'll quickly burn out, which will take more than a vacation to cure. You need to make sure they take a few getaway days to recharge and refocus — and if you're feeling stressed, you should do the same.

The sign of a good manager is her ability to be out of the office for a reasonable amount of time without everything falling apart.

When your employees are on vacation, don't ask them to call the office. In fact, discourage it at all costs! When they're keeping in touch with the office, they're not truly getting away. Find people to cover for employees before they leave or delegate the responsibility (and authority) to someone else on your team.

Start with yourself

You know that your team members take their cue from you. If you're upbeat, they're upbeat. If you're willing to work in the trenches, they're willing to do whatever it takes to succeed. And if you're looking stressed out . . . they probably feel pretty stressed. So take care of yourself. Even if you're a workaholic! Remember that your team will be more effective if you know how to slow down every so often.

Following are some stress reduction tips to follow. After everyone sees how calm you've become, you may even want to consider leading your own brownbag lunch session on reducing stress.

- ✔ **Maintain a positive self-image.** Try not to take yourself too seriously and remember the good things that are part of your life.

- ✔ **Schedule time for yourself.** Even if it's only 15 minutes a day, this time can help you become less stressed.

- ✔ **Practice breathing and other relaxation techniques.** Try taking a deep breath through your nose to a count of four. Then hold your breath to a count of four, finally exhaling through your mouth to a count of eight.

- ✔ **Follow a healthy diet.** What you eat affects how you manage stress. Be sure to eat a balanced diet.

- ✔ **Get enough sleep.** If you're burning the candle at both ends, you won't be yourself. And even though you may feel like you're gaining time, you're actually losing time because everything will take you longer when you're not performing at your peak.

✔ **Take a break.** Short breaks during the day can do wonders for you and your stress levels. If you feel your staff is particularly stressed, take a collective stress break! You can do anything from walking outside to sharing a cup of coffee in the company breakroom.

✔ **Spend time with a pet.** Pets offer unconditional love and can help you relax.

✔ **Get a massage.** A massage can help you focus on the moment and feel pampered. It's also recognized as a form of preventive health for its stress-reducing effects.

✔ **Do something you enjoy.** When you do something that you enjoy, you lose track of time. If you're not sure what you really like to do, think back to your childhood. If you loved playing soccer as a kid, then consider signing up for an adult recreational league or getting a company team together. Likewise, if you love getting lost in old movies, consider renting some of your favorites one weekend.

✔ **Spend time with friends.** Having friends outside of work is important. Strong relationships help you relax and lower health risks.

✔ **Keep a journal.** Logging your thoughts from time to time can help sort out problems and provide clarity. If you want to vent, don't take it out on your staff. Write it down. You'll probably find that you feel better afterward and the problem no longer seems insurmountable.

✔ **Plan your day.** Make your to-do list the night before and always work from a written schedule. (Don't forget to "schedule" time for interruptions.) And be sure to make time for lunch. Encourage your employees to do the same.

✔ **Accept what you can't change.** As much as you'd like to, you can't control everything. That's why flexibility is important.

✔ **Become proactive.** Proactive people have less stress than reactive people. It's often a matter of control — even if it's sometimes no more than perceived control.

✔ **Be an optimist.** Expect success.

✔ **Listen to relaxation tapes or music.** There's no denying the relaxing effects of music. Consider New Age or Baroque music. These two genres are the only two proven to reduce stress and promote relaxation.

For more stress-relieving ideas, see *Stress Management For Dummies* by Allen Elkin, Ph.D. (Hungry Minds, Inc.).

Exercise

Not only can exercise help keep you and your employees healthy, but it is also calming. To gain the true benefits, experts suggest exercising for at least 20 minutes three times a week.

Consider posting some of these simple stress-reducing exercises in the break-room. The following techniques shouldn't cause too much embarrassment if employees practice them when they return to their workspaces.

- Roll your shoulders forward and back.
- Practice head rolls.
- Place your arms behind your neck and press your elbows back so that your chest pulls.
- Try arm circles.
- Spread your fingers apart as far as possible to stretch your hands.

Encourage employees to ask for help

If your employees have too much work on their plates, encourage them to ask for help. Never attach a stigma to admitting that they can't get everything done. If employees know that they can be honest with you early on in the process, you'll be able to offer them help or suggest time-management training.

When your employee comes to you for guidance, ask him the following questions:

- How can I help you reduce the stress?
- How did this situation occur?
- How can we reorganize your responsibilities or provide you with additional instruction?

If you're feeling overwhelmed, ask for help or delegate — and encourage your employees to do the same. Things don't seem as bad when you know that someone is available to back you up.

Promote realistic workload evaluations

Your employees need to be able to be honest with you. You want them to assess their workloads and other work-related situations realistically and then give you an honest opinion, even if it's one they think you may not want to hear.

For example, you ask an employee to take on an extra project. If she can't take the project on unless she gives up something else, she needs to be able to tell you so. At first, you may need to coach her by saying, "Given your current projects, will you be able to take on the Evans report and still meet all deadlines?" That way, she can respond by saying, "If I delegate the Hart project to Bill, then I should be able to do it within the timeframe." You don't want your employees to take on projects that they don't have enough time for.

If you or your employees are spread too thin, everyone will have more stress and no one will do the job particularly well.

Stand in their corner

Employees need to know that their managers support them. You need to stand up for your staff members, especially in stressful periods. If senior management or other departments are piling on problems or unnecessary projects, you may need to step in and help work things out.

Laugh

Lighten up. Don't be caught without your sense of humor. Laughter can help ease your stress and your staff's as well. According to a recent survey by Robert Half International, more than 90 percent of executives polled said they believe a good sense of humor is important in advancing to senior management.

In addition, a good sense of humor helps you build rapport and trust with your employees, which in turn facilitates open communication and a positive work environment — both important elements in reducing stress. Humor also eases tension caused by tight deadlines and other stress inducing situations.

Make lunch a priority

If you and your employees are working through lunch every day, you may be eating up your productivity. You may think that you're gaining work time, but in fact you're actually losing efficiency.

Avoiding breaks eventually becomes counterproductive. Your employees need to take time out, not only to nourish their appetites, but to feed their minds as well. Lunch breaks can help employees gain a fresh perspective on the day's activities.

Unfortunately, 19 percent of 700 working men and women surveyed by OfficeTeam reported that they worked through lunch every day, while 43 percent do so at least once a week.

As a manager, you need to encourage your staff to take a real lunch break — especially on their busiest days.

Offer professional assistance

If you truly feel that employee stress has spiraled out of control, consider encouraging your employees to see a counselor. Many companies offer an Employee Assistance Program (EAP), through which employees have access to licensed counselors who can help employees deal with all types of problems.

The Employee Assistance Professional Association says that for every $1 put into EAP, employers get a $4 to $7 return in the form of reduced accidents and reduced medical plan use. So make sure you encourage your employees to utilize this valuable service.

Conquering Burnout

Even though the word *burnout* didn't enter mainstream American vocabulary until the 1980s, everyone is talking about it today. Burnout is emotional exhaustion coupled with low job satisfaction.

Burnout occurs when people push too hard and too long. It affects your staff morale, retention, and creativity. People who are burned out lose energy, enthusiasm, and a sense that things matter. Burnout is not something that can be solved with just a vacation.

Spotting burnout

Stress and burnout are two different things. You can be stressed but not burned out. However, stress can lead to burnout. Stressed employees are often tired, while burned out ones are chronically fatigued. Employees in burnout mode often feel like they've lost control and have feelings of help-lessness and hopelessness. They may also experience exhaustion and frequent illness.

Pay particular attention to employees who regularly put in long hours and watch for signs of burnout.

Is it possible to spot the red flags of burnout before burnout grows into a full-blown problem? Ask yourself the following questions:

- ✔ Has employee output decreased, even though working hours haven't changed?

✔ Are staff members able to relax?

✔ Are they less patient?

✔ Are they more tired?

✔ Are they regularly forgetful?

✔ Are your employees often sick?

✔ Are they too serious?

✔ Are they thinking about work all the time?

✔ Are they too busy to do routine tasks?

Crying can be a sign of burnout, especially if it's an unusual response for one of your employees.

If one of your staff members is the only one who can do a certain task, and that task has become increasingly frequent, you're setting him or her up for burnout. You need to delegate the assignment and train others to do the work.

Coping with burnout

Your employee is missing deadlines. He doesn't care about his job. He lacks enthusiasm. And it's taking him longer to do the same responsibilities. You're faced with an employee who's burned out. What can you do?

Whatever you do, don't think that you can offer a quick fix, like a vacation or reduced workload. You have to spend time with your employee and come up with a long-term solution. Sit down. Listen. And then decide what to do once you determine the cause of the problem.

Here are some things you can do to try to reduce the potential for burnout in a staff member:

✔ **Encourage self-evaluation.** Ask your employee, "What makes you happy?" Ask the person to focus on those aspects of the job that are most enjoyable. After all, he or she did have a reason for accepting the job in the first place. Sometimes, simply reflecting on the positive parts of the job can work wonders.

✔ **Consider changing responsibilities.** If your employee enjoys a certain aspect of his job but hates another aspect, you may ask him to train other employees on the task he dislikes and then reassign the other tasks to someone who may enjoy it more or who wants more responsibility. Doing so helps prevent boredom, a leading cause of burnout.

✔ **Practice frequent, honest communication.** Fear and insecurity also contribute to burnout.

Chapter 21

Minimizing Office Politics

· ·

· ·

ffice politics.

If you're like most people, the mere phrase may inspire you to schedule your next vacation. Whether you like it or not, every company has office politics — those relationships within the organization that affect how things get done and how people are treated. How you and your staff navigate these waters plays a huge role in motivation and morale.

In this chapter, I show you what you can do as a manager to keep the negative aspects of office politics under control. I also give you some advice on how to encourage appropriate behavior.

Encouraging Workplace Diplomacy

Office politics refers to how things get done in the office. Do you have to know someone to get a promotion? Do you have to say the right things to get ahead? If so, then you probably have to contend with a fair amount of office politics. However, if promotions are rewarded on the basis of skills and hard work and ideas are judged on the basis of true merit, you may have less political obstacles to overcome. (See the sidebar, "Assessing your company's level of politics," to get a sense of what is really going on at your firm.)

Assessing your company's level of politics

As a manager, you need to know how political your office or workplace is, especially if you're working to ensure that your own team is free of turmoil.

To assess how political your company is, start by evaluating how people get things done. For example, do they float ideas by senior management before officially proposing a new initiative? Do you have to hold pre-meeting meetings to ensure everyone's on board with a particular agenda? If employees need to continually secure permission before offering a new idea, office politics are alive and well in your organization.

Also consider the type of work assigned — and how it's handed down. When a senior manager delegates a project, does he or she also delegate the authority necessary to see that particular assignment through to completion? What kinds of projects are delegated — and how much background information is offered? Managers and staff who are asked to achieve certain goals without a reasonable amount of autonomy or information often have to play political games to succeed.

In addition, take a look at who gets rewarded in other departments and why. Is achievement the basis for recognition and advancement? Or are promotions based on who you know? Remember that rewards reinforce the kind of behavior senior management likes to see. Are the people who get promoted solid workers who deserve more responsibility, or are they merely talented office politicians?

Even if you look around and discover that your company has a politically charged environment, your department can be different. (Of course, you'll have to play the game of office politics at meetings for managers!) If your workplace is filled with office politics — alliances, betrayals, secrets — you can still take steps to shield your team of this destructive force and lower its presence in the rest of the company. As a manager, you can spark a growth in *workplace diplomacy* — the ability to work collaboratively with others and avoid destructive game playing.

The following sections give you general guidelines that you can promote to help your team members operate effectively within your company's environment.

Encourage employees to get to know one another

Have you ever been behind a car that's going well below the speed limit on a one lane road when you're late to work? Maybe you honked a few times and tailgated the other driver, or maybe you cursed beneath your breath. Imagine that the slow car in front of you turns into the office parking lot and you realize that it's your favorite coworker. You remember that she was recently in a car accident and is a bit wary when driving now. Suddenly, you're hoping that she didn't notice you were tailgating her the past few miles. Your former foe has been given an identity and a real, complex personality, and you realize that your impatience was uncalled for.

Take this scenario into the workplace. Sure, getting frustrated with coworkers is easy when you don't understand their motives. But if you are familiar with not only their responsibilities, but their personalities too, you may not take things so personally. The same holds true of your employees.

One of the most effective ways to avoid problems in the workplace is to encourage your staff to get to know one another. When they regard one another as friends and teammates instead of unknown entities, they're more likely to be understanding and helpful.

To help employees get to know one another, give them opportunities for interaction. Ask employees to cross-train one another or assign mentors. Hold regular team meetings that cover more than merely the business at hand. You don't need to host a gossip-fest, but you should permit a bit of friendly chatter to start the session.

Promote working through the chain of command

Breaking the chain of command is a big no-no in most offices (unless the problem involves sexual harassment or unlawful discriminatory treatment, in which case your company likely has a policy in place that directs staff members to the human resources department). Whenever your employees encounter problems, you need to encourage them to turn first to you, as their manager, or to whomever you have assigned as their immediate supervisor. The manager needs to adequately respond to their requests. In some cases, this means proposing their ideas on their behalf to senior management.

You may think of a chain of command as a bit of nonsensical office protocol that inhibits freedom and creativity. But working through the chain of command decreases the potential for office politics. If employees know that you'll find a way to help them do their jobs to their full potential, they'll be less likely to try to circumvent your authority as a manager. You don't have to grant every request, but your role in the chain of command does mean that you'll objectively evaluate their needs and do everything in your power to help them acquire the tools and resources they need to succeed.

Signs of an office manipulator

Unfortunately, not all of your employees and coworkers have the best intentions in their dealings with you. Office manipulators want something, such as a promotion, less work, or whatever, and try to win you over through the game of office politics, even if they have to subtly attack their coworkers. If you fall prey to their tactics, you're encouraging other employees to behave in this manner. Here are a few warning signs that you're dealing with an office manipulator.

✔ **Speaks negatively:** Watch out for poison tongues — especially when they engage in negative talk about others in the company or about the organization in general.

✔ **Steals ideas:** Does one staff member regularly brag that all the best ideas were hers and hers alone? Beware of employees who frequently come to you with others' ideas without giving them credit.

✔ **Reneges on promises:** Address the behavior of employees who make commitments but don't tell you until the last minute that they're not going to be able to fulfill them. Sometimes this failure to follow through may be merely the result of poor planning. But in other instances, it may be a case of intentional manipulation, particularly if the staff member realizes that he or she typically maintains a favored status on your team. Hold people accountable for deliverables — the results of their promises — to discourage any game playing.

Spell out preferred protocols

Protocol is the accepted way to behave in a certain situation. When it comes to business situations, think of protocol as the unwritten rules of conduct. For example, protocol usually means that you seek your immediate supervisor's feedback on a new initiative before proceeding. And protocol may also dictate that, after you have the approval to move forward on that project, you consult with a certain individual who is recognized as your company's expert in that field.

Protocols are not necessarily documented in your procedure manual; they tend to evolve out of tradition and precedent. And that's precisely why it's important to let your staff know what they are and what they mean. Let your team members know what you expect of them when it comes to protocol issues. You may want them to lend a helping hand to a swamped coworker on occasion or refrain from disagreeing with you publicly during a team meeting. By openly communicating protocols, you leave little room for the misunderstandings and insecurities that can lead to office politics.

Mentors are a great way to help new employees learn office protocol. (See Chapter 12 for more on developing a mentoring program.)

Advise employees to communicate online with courtesy

Encourage your employees to respect one another no matter how they're communicating, even via e-mail. In other words, advise them to say only what they would say to someone's face, be discreet with sensitive information, and remember that e-mail can be easily misunderstood. Suggest face to face — or at least voice to voice — interaction as much as possible to discourage miscommunication. And remind staff to take time to cool down before automatically responding in heated situations.

Follow your own advice. Don't impulsively react at team meetings or send out terse e-mails. You're setting the example to be emulated.

Be a model of consistency

Everything you do sends a message to your staff. So if you act out of character, your action may be misconstrued. For example, say that you're browsing in your local bookstore and come across a book that you think one of your staff members would enjoy and benefit from. You buy the book and give it to that employee. That's not a problem if it's customary for you to give books or other small gifts to your staff and if you're sure the gesture won't be misinterpreted. But if you've never done this before, think about how other employees will interpret the gesture. Will they think of it as thoughtful or as proof of favoritism?

Remind employees to protect their credibility

Let your employees know that next to their job performance, nothing has more bearing on their stature or their influence within your company than their reputation for integrity and honesty. Encourage them to resist taking any action that may jeopardize their reputation. Here are some suggestions that you can make to them:

✔ **Be honest.** If they don't know the answer to a question they're asked, let employees know you'd rather they admit that they don't know and then investigate the answer.

✔ **Keep their word**. Ask your employees not to make any promises they're not sure they can keep. That way, when they say they can do something, you know they will, and you won't find yourself in a tight spot down the road.

✔ **Honor deadlines.** If they're not going to meet a deadline, ask them to let you and their coworkers know well in advance.

✔ **Admit when they're wrong.** When you make a mistake, acknowledge it and let your employees know that you expect them to do the same. When it's not your fault, though, avoid blaming others.

Request that they share the credit

As a manager, it's important that you not claim all the glory — especially since a key part of minimizing office politics is to make sure that your team always shares credit. Always mention the specific contributions made by various members of the team.

In addition, make sure that your employees don't monopolize the spotlight. For example, if a staff member is reporting the results of a project in which he was one of several people involved, encourage him to use *we* instead of *I* in both written and oral presentations.

Encourage your employees to resolve conflicts without you

If two of your employees are having a conflict, encourage them to work things out but do your best to stay out of the middle. You can't be a mom to your staff, but at the same time, you can't turn a blind eye to potential difficulties. If productivity is significantly impacted, you may need to step in and speak with each one individually. In other words, you need to treat it like the performance issue that it is. If you decide that you have no choice but to step in, have your employees focus on measurable objectives and goals, not their feelings or their interpretations of the other person's actions.

Navigating Office Etiquette

Many of the behaviors that minimize office politics center around common sense and courtesy. Unfortunately, the busier and more pressured the workplace becomes, the more likely it is that these guidelines will fall by the wayside. What follows is a list of general rules for office etiquette. As a manager, you should practice these guidelines at all times. In addition, you may want to share these tips with your employees.

- ✔ **Treat everyone from the company president to a temporary worker with respect and dignity.** Never engage in any action that may make people feel embarrassed or uncomfortable.

- ✔ **Never assume that anyone is less busy or less stressed than you.** If you have a full plate, chances are that your coworkers do too. Keep this in mind when you ask someone for a favor.

- ✔ **When employees come to you for information, give them your undivided attention.** Don't work on your computer while you're carrying on a conversation. This advice holds true for phone conversations also — it's not polite, and the clicking of keys is audible on the other side of the line.

- ✔ **Be punctual for all meetings.** If you arrive late, apologize and skip the excuses — they aren't relevant.

- ✔ **Celebrate with others.** Busy as you are, always do your best to make an appearance (even if it's very brief) at all informal get-togethers — such as a lunchtime birthday or five-year anniversary celebration for a coworker.

- ✔ **If you're good with computers and you work with people who aren't, don't be a cybersnob.** Share your expertise without making others feel inadequate.

- ✔ **Be sensitive to other people's need for privacy.** If you're in someone's cubicle and he receives a personal call, offer to excuse yourself before you're asked to leave.

- ✔ **Don't interrupt your coworkers while they're in the middle of an important project.**

- ✔ **Do your best to return every call and respond to every e-mail within 24 hours.** If you have to violate this policy, be prepared to offer an apology.

- ✔ **Whenever you're leaving a voicemail message, always mention your telephone number, the time you called, and the reason for the call.**

- ✔ **Keep your voicemail messages clear and concise.**

- ✔ **Don't make cell phone calls in public places, such as the breakroom.**

- ✔ **If a fax isn't addressed to you, don't read it.** By the same token, if you're sending a fax, be alert to the possibility that other people may read it, even though it is not addressed to them.

✔ **Try to limit any fax to no more than three or four pages.** Otherwise, it ties up the recipient's machine. If the message is going to be longer, call the person ahead of time to let him or her know it's coming.

✔ **Be careful with humor.** Never tell an offensive joke, and keep your sarcasm under wraps. It can be easily misinterpreted.

✔ **Never make changes to anyone's computer unless you've been specifically instructed to do so — even if you're just trying to help.**

✔ **Dress in accordance with your company dress code.** Even on dress-down days, never wear anything that may be considered unprofessional. Also, remember to go easy on the perfume or after-shave. Some people are allergic or are highly sensitive to cologne and other scents.

✔ **When you're making conversation, steer clear of any subject — ethnicity, sex, religion, politics — that could spark antagonism and create misunderstandings.** Stick to the basics: sports, movies, restaurants, gardening, the kids, and the precipitous slide of the Euro (just kidding).

✔ **Call people by their names, as opposed to "Hon," "Love," or "Sweetheart," which could get you into trouble under sexual harassment laws.**

✔ **If you have to attend to personal matters or personal calls, do so on your break time.**

✔ **Don't bring your personal problems to work with you.** A dark mood can quickly spread to fellow coworkers.

✔ **Don't show up for work if you have a bad cold or any other condition that may be contagious.** If you need to be in the office, let others know that they may want to keep their distance.

✔ **Don't complain about little things.** If your company no longer stocks your favorite pens, keep your disappointment to yourself. Pick your battles and realize that you can't always get everything you want (even if you are the boss).

✔ **Be a good neighbor.** If you eat lunch at your desk, avoid foods that emit a strong smell. If you borrow something, such as a directory or a stapler, return it as soon as you're finished.

✔ **When in doubt about the appropriateness of any behavior, ask yourself the following question: What would it be like to work here if everyone acted this way?**

Stopping Negative Behavior in Its Tracks

As a manager, you may not hear about workplace problems right away. After all, you're probably outside the rumor mill now. However, when poor behavior comes to your attention, it's crucial that you do something about it right away. The following sections cover some general problems you may encounter and what you can do about them.

Stopping rumors

Say that you discover an employee is gossiping about colleagues and starting rumors whenever you're not around. You may think that it's best to ignore this behavior and hope that others will ignore it. But that kind of reaction can take its toll on your staff's morale and motivation — especially the ones being discussed via the rumors! You need to meet with the lead gossip immediately, address what you've heard (be specific), and let him know the behavior will not be tolerated. If the rumor mill still flows after this verbal warning, write the employee up immediately or follow whatever disciplinary plan your company has established.

Dealing with credit thieves

Cheryl and Hal worked together on a project. But when the project was presented to the team, Cheryl acted as if she was the only one who participated. Poor Hal just sat on the sidelines, looking unhappy but not saying anything.

As a manager, you won't always be aware of this event, but when you do come across it, you need to take a stance. Hogging credit robs your team of its motivation, especially those employees who typically fill an ancillary role. Having to work with a credit hog may be just the thing to convince them they don't want to be a part of your company anymore. When you discover a credit hog, acknowledge the other players on the spot — or in a subsequent meeting, if necessary — to recognize their contributions.

If an employee complains to you that someone else stole the credit for something but you don't have any proof, ask him to document what he's doing on future projects and update you regularly. That way, you know ahead of time the accomplishments of each person on your team.

Encouraging others to pull their weight

If you've noticed that one of your employees doesn't seem to be putting much effort into his work, don't ignore this developing problem. This behavior can destroy your team's morale, especially when the person continues to get away with it.

Schedule a meeting with the underperforming staff member. Try to establish if this is a pattern of behavior or a temporary situation. Point out specific instances in which the employee's action (or lack of action) created problems for you or your team, and be prepared to discuss these incidents. Be careful, however, how you describe the details. Focus on the event — what happened and what the consequences were — as opposed to what motivations may have led to the behavior. Avoid any statement that calls into question the coworker's intelligence, competence, or commitment.

Part VIII
The Part of Tens

In this part . . .

Are you ready for some fun? No book *For Dummies* is complete without The Part of Tens, which gives you quick ideas and tips in a lighthearted, whimsical way. This part identifies a number of great companies that are doing everything. I also offer you insights into ten different employee personalities and how you can motivate them, plus ten ways to get employees to motivate one another. And if you like surfing the Internet, you'll love the two chapters that list Web sites focusing on motivating and rewarding your employees. It's a fun section — and it's not short on information!

Chapter 22

Ten-Times-Ten Motivating Ideas from Seven Great Companies

In This Chapter
▶ Motivating ideas by the dozen
▶ Including some far-out stuff

*N*ot every motivational technique, management practice, or benefit works for every company. In other words, no one-size-fits-all approach to motivation exists. You have to consider your firm's goals and objectives as well as your employees' needs, and then create your own recipe for success. To spark your creativity, this chapter presents several companies that have developed their own unique formulas for motivational excellence.

Keeping Employees Satisfied at The Container Store

For the top executives at The Container Store, the nation's leading retailer of storage and organization products, having contented employees is a fundamental corporate objective, ranking right up there with profitability and customer service. The hard work of Kip Tindell, president and CEO, and Garrett Boone, chairman, has landed their company in the top spot on *Fortune* magazine's "100 Best Companies to Work For" list for two consecutive years.

No single magic trick is used to motivate employees at The Container Store. Rather, the combination of commonsense policies, customized training programs, and progressive benefits is what keeps the firm's turnover at a low 24 percent annually in an industry where the yearly average is 73.6 percent.

Kip and Garrett — as they're known to all their employees — can often be found dusting shelves or carrying customers' packages at one of the store sites. Their zeal for the work and for helping the customer affects the company's hiring process, which is designed to recruit people who share the cofounders' passion for customer service.

After being hired, new full-time employees at The Container Store are given 235 hours of training their first year. (The average amount of training in the retail industry is seven hours.) Training continues for all workers, with the content customized to the specific job and the individual. To help staff become more knowledgeable, trainers work full-time at each of The Container Store's 22 sites to demonstrate the features and benefits of each item the company sells. Employees are also taught the keys to great customer service, such as being Gumby — that is, being as flexible as possible in helping customers find products that solve their storage problems.

Open communication is a priority. All employees know daily sales information and other financial data. At the firm's distribution center, employees receive performance reviews every six months, allowing regular feedback and discussion.

Salaries and benefits are generous. Wages are considerably above the industry average, according to *Fortune* magazine. Flexible "mom" and "dad" shifts are offered to those who need them. Workers receive a 40 percent discount on merchandise. After ten years, employees are eligible for a sabbatical.

The result? Employees responded to a questionnaire by the Great Places to Work Institute with comments such as "TCS is my family" and "I will never leave."

Synovus Financial Supports the Whole Employee

For three years straight, Synovus Financial has made the top ten on *Fortune* magazine's annual list of the 100 best companies to work for. In 2000, the payment services and bank holding company also made *Working Mother* magazine's listing of the 100 best companies for working mothers. A glance at how the company handles professional development and assists employees with work/life balance reveals the reasons for these accolades.

Synovus invests significant effort and expense in team members' professional growth and development. Through the Personally Developing EveryONE (PDE) program, Synovus trains its more than 11,000 team members to work together in a team-based environment. Service — to customers and team members — is emphasized. To further empower team members, Synovus uses a decentralized approach to management, in which teams at each affiliate bank formulate the policies most appropriate for the customers in their communities.

Each team member participates in RIGHT STEPS, a three-phase program for measuring performance. In Step 1, the supervisor and employee set expectations and decide how to measure the individual's progress. Step 2 involves two-way communication about progress and updates. Step 3 is a review of the employee's success at meeting performance expectations. RIGHT STEPS is designed to connect what each team member does with what she wants to do and the company's goals. So job responsibilities connect with career goals, which connect with corporate goals.

Synovus has made promoting from within one of its guiding policies, as evidenced in The Leadership Institute at Synovus and the Foundations of Leadership program. Employees with managerial potential are trained to be "servant leaders" at the Leadership Institute. The curriculum teaches trainees how to turn the company's vision into techniques that motivate and empower team members.

The four-day-long Foundations of Leadership program shows team leaders how to bring the company's leadership expectations — which include "live the values," "manage the business," "make others successful," and "share the vision" — to the day-to-day work experience.

The leadership programs are also used to advance the company's family-friendly policies. In The Leadership Institute, for example, managers spend at least a week learning how to implement flextime, job-sharing, telecommuting, and compressed and part-time scheduling.

In addition to nontraditional scheduling, Synovus also supports working parents through paid leave for new parents and 20 hours of paid family education leave per year for parents or grandparents to participate in their children's or grandchildren's school activities.

Women are also well represented in the workforce. They make up 60 percent of Synovus's employees.

Taking Flight at Southwest Airlines

Southwest Airlines is known for its offbeat corporate culture that features wisecracking, fun-loving employees. The Dallas-based carrier is also widely respected for its financial success. The company has generated profits every year since its founding in 1971, and its stock has appreciated significantly.

A causal connection exists between these facts. And it can be traced to cofounder Herb Kelleher's daring reformulation of conventional business wisdom — namely, that the *employee* comes first.

According to Kevin and Jackie Freiberg's book, *Nuts! Southwest Airlines' Crazy Recipe for Business and Personal Success* (Broadway Books), the company's culture rests on such key philosophies as:

- Employees are number one.
- The way you treat your employees is the way they will treat customers.
- Always practice the Golden Rule (Do unto others as you would have them do unto you).
- Irreverence is okay.
- Southwest is a customer service organization that happens to be in the airline industry.
- It's difficult to change someone's attitude, so hire for attitude and train for skill.
- Have fun at work.

But these feel-good phrases aren't just words posted on a bulletin board in the employee break room. Through a number of innovative practices, Southwest regularly puts its principles into action.

Feedback from employees is actively sought. A culture committee, made up of 127 representatives from all areas of the company, meets annually with Southwest's executive vice president to discuss employee concerns and identify priority issues. Smaller teams of employees then tackle such challenges as employee burnout and the training of newly hired staff.

Employees are also invited to write directly to Kelleher when they have questions, suggestions, or complaints. Management responds to every letter.

Fostering professional growth is another high priority. The company assigns mentors to new employees and runs a comprehensive training program. Workshops and classes are available for employees who seek advancement.

Compensation and benefits are yet another way Southwest makes employees feel they're number one. In addition to profit sharing and generous stock options, the airline offers full medical benefits, attendance incentives, and free air travel for employees and their families.

In the words of an employee who responded to a survey by the Great Places to Work Institute, "They treat you with respect, pay you well, and empower you."

"Rules of the Garage" Still Central at Hewlett-Packard

Any discussion of progressive benefits and unusual perks eventually comes around to Hewlett-Packard. The company practically invented the concept of corporate culture. The now-famous HP Way, which delineated the vision and values of founders Bill Hewlett and Dave Packard, is still the cornerstone of the firm's policies.

Hewlett-Packard recently updated the rules to reflect the impact of changes in technology and the marketplace. The new Rules of the Garage include such inspiring ideas as: "Believe you can change the world" and "Radical ideas are not bad ideas." Employees are also encouraged to "Share tools and ideas. Trust your colleagues" and "Invent different ways of working." They are reminded that "The customer defines a job well-done" and to "Believe that together we can do anything."

The company translates these and other lofty ideals into practical and tangible benefits and perks for its employees. The Total Rewards program compensates employees in a variety of ways for their hard work and loyalty. In addition to earning competitive base pay, employees can earn company performance bonuses of up to 15 percent, pay-for-results bonuses, and sales incentive bonuses. Employees can buy common stock at a 15 percent discount, and top performers get options to buy shares.

The company retirement plan provides benefits to employees based on their final pay, as well as their length of service with HP. These benefits are funded by the company and require no employee contribution.

In addition, the Tax Saving Capital Accumulation Plan (TAXCAP) provides a company match of $1 for every $1 of employee contribution on pay up to 3 percent, then $0.50 per $1 of employee contribution on the next 2 percent of pay.

Hewlett-Packard's approach to vacation and leave is also innovative. All employees accrue FTO (Flexible Time Off), beginning with their first day of work. This paid time can be used for vacations, sick leave, family leaves, and other personal needs. Employees can take time off by the hour, day, or week.

Supporting and Celebrating Employees' Professional Growth

Great Plains Software, Inc., a manufacturer of business management software based in Fargo, North Dakota, has developed a comprehensive set of programs to foster and recognize the continuous professional development of its employees.

The company offers tuition reimbursement for continuing higher education or professional and technical certification. In addition, employees can take advantage of online courses, workshops, and classroom training opportunities. Subjects include technical training, leadership development, time and project management, global cultures training, and presentation skills. The company uses a Lotus Notes electronic system to track the hours of training each employee receives.

To ensure that team members are versed in the corporate culture and practices, a three-month orientation exists for new hires.

The company's investment in employee development is complemented by programs that are designed to recognize outstanding performance and achievement. Daily comment cards (with messages like "We can't spell s ccess without U") provide an informal means for team leaders and members to give each other praise and feedback. Individuals and teams are formally honored at quarterly ceremonies and at the annual Pioneer Days, when employees nominate coworkers for Excellence Awards. Awards include the Heritage Award (for customer service), the Harvest Award (for commitment to quality), the Frontier Award (for continuous learning), the Pathfinder Award (for outstanding supervision), the Zezula Award (from the Native American for *one who helps*), and the Jesse James Award (for fresh ideas and daring innovation).

Rewards take other forms as well. Employees who work at least 20 hours per week are eligible for stock options. Compensation ranges for all positions are reviewed frequently and may be adjusted based on the most current data about market rates and salary levels at comparable high-tech firms.

Also, employees are eligible for a four-week paid sabbatical every seven years.

Little Things Mean a Lot

Although standard benefits such as medical plans and 401(k)s are important to working professionals, often the small, relatively inexpensive touches are what earn a company the reputation for caring about, and taking care of, its employees.

CDW, a computer distributor, has fine-tuned the art of the little thing. Through a generous assortment of unique perks, the company has brought the comforts of home to the workplace.

All employees at the headquarters of the Illinois-based company enjoy subsidized meals at the onsite cafeteria, while those who work the second shift get a complimentary dinner. Every Tuesday and Thursday, CDW offers free bagels, fruit, and other breakfast items. Full-service coffee bars feature free coffee, tea, and hot chocolate every day. In the summer months, workers can cool off with free ice cream.

To assist staff with work/life balance, CDW has onsite daycare and fitness centers. Busy employees can even drop off and pick up their dry cleaning without ever leaving the grounds.

An annual summer picnic and yearly holiday party foster community and connection among employees. The name of the human resources department was changed to Coworker Services, suggesting a uniquely employee-centered philosophy.

When the firm became the leading computer reseller in the world, workers were rewarded with free, three-day trips for two to any destination in the continental United States. More routine rewards include holiday cash bonuses and quarterly bonuses to recognize employees' hard work and achievements.

Silicon Valley–style Perks in Minnesota

BORN, a technology and e-business consulting firm based in Minnesota's Twin Cities, goes to creative lengths to recruit, reward, and retain its employees.

Convincing employees that the company is a great place to work starts during the hiring process. Candidates undergo as many as five interviews with various company representatives. The emphasis is on finding people who not only bring valuable skills to the company immediately, but who also will stay for the long term. The rigorous hiring process can take up to ten weeks. Current employees receive a $750 bonus if their referral results in a hire.

Once hired, new employees receive a $250 clothing allowance, 1,000 stock options, and a new laptop. And that's just for starters. All employees are allowed access to any of BORN's dozen vacation cabins located around the country. Workers planning a family vacation or weekend getaway can check the company intranet for vacancies.

Other benefits include a $2,000 adoption assistance and an annual, expense-paid, three-day family weekend at a Brainerd resort for Twin Cities workers (employees at other sites get comparable weekend vacations). In addition, working parents can participate in a daycare pager program. The company also offers its employees tickets for sporting events and concerts.

The rewards don't end there. Each year, one employee at each BORN location is recognized for exceptional performance through the Spirit of Success program. Those employees who are selected choose $1,000 worth of premium catalog merchandise.

To celebrate BORN's 10th anniversary, all 1,200 employees (and their families) were treated to a lavish two-day party at the lakeside estate of the firm's founder and CEO, Rick Born. The gala, two-day event included fireworks, a petting zoo for kids, free food, performances by '70s rock stars, pony rides, and free access to Camp Snoopy at the Mall of America.

It's not all fun and games, however. BORN has invested heavily in employee development and training. At an onsite learning center (BORN University), employees can take a single technology class or earn a mini-MBA through the University of St. Thomas. In addition, the company runs a mentoring program that allows employees to hone their skills by working on specific projects with senior staff members.

The efforts and expense pay off — in an industry where annual employee turnover can be as high as 60 percent, BORN's original tactics have kept its turnover rate at less than one-third of that figure.

Chapter 23

Almost Ten Web Sites to Help You Motivate

● ●

In This Chapter

▶ Connecting fast and free to lots of useful material

▶ Exploring professional connections that you may want to make

● ●

*I*f this book hasn't given you your fill of motivational advice, don't worry. You can find much more material on the Internet. In this chapter, I give you ten (okay, eight) Web sites to help you with your motivational efforts. Enjoy!

The Economics Press

www.epinc.com

The Economics Press is a company dedicated to providing motivational services. At the Web site, you can access all the training and motivational materials you need. You also have the option to sign up for free e-mail lists, including:

✔ "Bits & Pieces," which consists of inspirational quotes

✔ "Sites & Insights," which recommends featured Web sites and offers motivational tips

✔ "Success Online," which sends you motivational messages every Monday and Thursday

Fast Company

www.fastcompany.com

The Fast Company Web site is stocked full of material you'll find interesting. At the site, you have access to the current issue of the magazine *Fast Company* and you can even take advantage of a free trial offer. In addition, the site offers you interactive tools, expert opinions, and advice on topics such as leading your team and introducing change to your staff.

Incentive Marketing Association

www.incentivemarketing.org

Believe it or not, an organization exists to promote the use of incentives in the workplace. The Incentive Marketing Association (IMA) is made up of incentive suppliers such as advertising agencies, consultants, distributors, and trade presses. In addition, IMA helps educate businesses so that they can effectively use incentive programs as a motivation tool.

At the IMA site, you can read tips on developing an incentive program and also find information on how the Internal Revenue Services taxes incentive awards.

Society for Human Resource Management

www.shrm.org

At the Society for Human Resource Management Web site, shown in Figure 23-1, you can find out everything you need to know about human resource techniques. You can view late-breaking HR news and browse the information center and library. You can even access *HR Magazine* at www.shrm.org/hrmagazine.

Figure 23-1:
Everything
HR-related
is at your
fingertips at
this Web
site.

National Association for Employee Recognition

www.recognition.org

If you're looking for the official word on recognition at work, then check out the Web page of the National Association for Employee Recognition (NAER), shown in Figure 23-2. This nonprofit organization was created with the sole goal of advancing recognition in the workplace.

At the Web site, you can find articles relating to recognition strategies, as well as information on becoming a member. A calendar of events that pertain to recognition is also available on the site.

You can contact the NAER at 1805 N. Mill St., Suite A, Naperville, IL 60563; by phone at (630) 369-7783; or by e-mail at NAER@recognition.org.

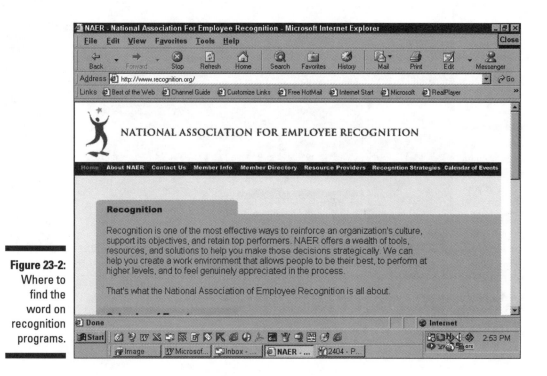

Figure 23-2:
Where to
find the
word on
recognition
programs.

Workforce

www.workforce.com

A handy resource site, the online magazine version of *Workforce* offers you a virtual cornucopia of information (see Figure 23-3). Not only can you find out about motivational topics, but you can read about other work-related subjects, such as compensation, staffing, trends, and benefits. You can even use Workforce Online's research center to access all articles on a particular subject. It's like having your very own library on your computer!

If you sign up for its free newsletter, *Workforce* will even notify you weekly of new articles. Do you want to find out more about the article described in the newsletter? Just click the link, and you're whisked back to the *Workforce* Web site.

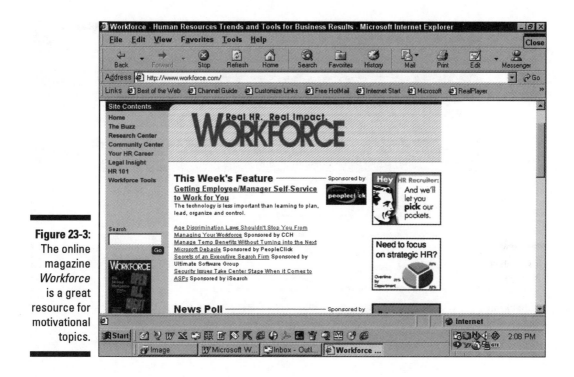

Figure 23-3:
The online magazine *Workforce* is a great resource for motivational topics.

Workplaceissues.com

www.workplaceissues.com

At this Web site, you can find out about . . . well, the title says it all! Not only can you learn how to better motivate your employees, but you can also get tips on how to recognize them. You can even sign up for free weekly motivation tips to be e-mailed to you so that you won't have to return to the Web site weekly — although you may want to! (See Figure 23-4 for a motivation tip.) How's that for motivation?

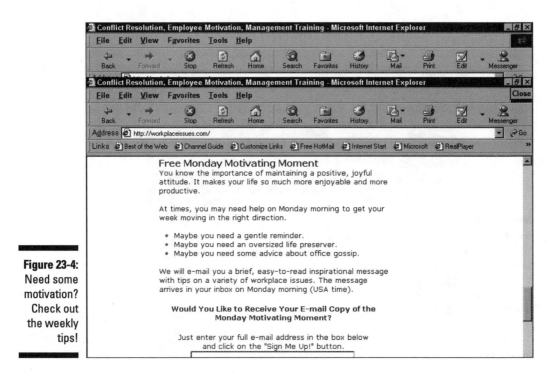

Figure 23-4:
Need some
motivation?
Check out
the weekly
tips!

Goalmanager.com

www.goalmanager.com

Need some ideas on how to motivate employees in your particular line of
work? Interested in case studies of how other companies create winning
teams or implement incentive programs? Then check out this site. You can
also find information about motivation-related events in your area, get ideas
for incentives, and read advice on important topics such as improving sales
goals and increasing production.

Chapter 24

Ten Different Employee Personalities — and How to Motivate Them

In This Chapter

▶ Motivating everyone from the office gossip to the office know-it-all

*Y*ou understand that each employee brings different skills, talents, knowledge, and experience to the job. Each employee also brings a unique personality to the job with unique motivational issues. Although I can't offer you a complete list in this chapter of all the personalities you encounter as a manager, I do cover some of the more common ones.

The Social Butterfly

You're probably familiar with the social butterfly; almost every office has one. He shows up for work on time but isn't at his desk until much later. Instead, he's at the coffee machine grabbing donuts and chatting with colleagues. The rest of the workday is no different. He's constantly in coworkers' offices, half an hour at a time, for what should be a five-minute conversation. You think he socializes more than he works. And, with all this chatting, he may very well be the root of your department grapevine.

So how do you deal with the Social Butterfly? One of the first things you should do is set higher goals for that individual. If you give the Social Butterfly an extra project or two, maybe he won't have so much time for visiting!

If the extra work doesn't curtail the social scene, then perhaps you need to take him aside and discuss the matter personally. Mention that you've noticed a lot of extra visiting going on, and, while you don't mind friendly chatting, you do want to ensure that everyone can be productive. Point out that his socializing is limiting his potential to take on additional responsibilities and, therefore, advance his career.

The Underachiever

The typical Underachiever arrives at work at the last minute, never volunteers to stay late so that the team can meet occasional, important deadlines, and always completes work with minimal effort. She doesn't go above or beyond; she just gets her work done. But occasionally, on certain projects or in particular situations, you see her shine. She outdoes herself, and you wonder why you don't see that level of performance more often.

How do you motivate someone who is doing an acceptable job but who could be doing so much more? To start with, you need to find out the source of the problem. If Shirley demonstrates her talent and dedication only once in a great while, then maybe she's not feeling challenged by her routine responsibilities. You may want to set higher expectations, which will encourage higher performance. Or you may notice that specific projects spark her creativity and commitment, which means she may be in need of a shift in job responsibilities. Can she supervise on a regular basis those pet projects that truly engage her? Would a lateral move benefit her — and ultimately your company? Find out why someone like Shirley is only getting by, and then be sure to play to her strengths.

The Office Know-It-All

The Office Know-It-All has been with the company a number of years. She has been there and done that, and won't hesitate to tell you so. Sure, you can come up with different ways to get the job done, but she'll look at you with disdain in her eyes because she knows, deep down in her heart, that her way *is* the best way. In team meetings, she has an answer for everything, and she doesn't hesitate to show her contempt for innovative approaches or solutions.

Not all Office Know-It-Alls are this blatant. But how you handle them, whether they're subtle or egregious, requires the same basic strategy. You need to recognize these individuals as having an abundance of knowledge while encouraging them to be team players. Tell them what they do well and let them know you'd like their expertise in finding new ways to resolve recurring issues or in brainstorming new opportunities.

Find out if they're interested in attending seminars or courses to further develop a particular skill area. As they develop, suggest they share their knowledge through formal training sessions or in team meetings. That way, you let them engage in their preferred behavior while making sure that the rest of the team benefits. Another idea: Ask them to be mentors to new staff members.

The Why-Can't-I-Be-Promoted-Now Employee

Some employees look around and see others getting promoted and think that a promotion is owed to them, whether or not they have the necessary skills and experience.

When you're dealing with a person who thinks he deserves a promotion *now,* schedule a meeting with him. Ask him what position he'd like to have and then ask him to research the position's major responsibilities. Then meet again and discuss those responsibilities. How do the person's current skills mesh with the position? Chances are, you'll be able to point out some necessary skill development that has to precede a promotion, and you'll prompt him to focus more on what he can do to *earn* a promotion. (For more on career planning for employees, see Chapter 11.)

The Glass-Is-Half-Empty Employee

Every day is a bad day for this employee, whether it's the traffic congestion, the empty coffee machine, or the too-long staff meeting. A coveted project is just more work. A new employee is just someone else to spend time training. An end-of-year bonus just isn't enough. Nothing seems to qualify as good news.

So how do you deal with Glass-Is-Half-Empty employees? You guessed it — meet with them to discuss their behavior. Give them examples of how their actions sabotage the team's morale. Discuss how their views may be more negative than realistic, and acknowledge their veracity when they're offering an accurate assessment of a challenging situation. Above all, be an example. Your attitude can and will influence their attitude.

The Constant Competitor

For some employees, every project is a contest. Every mistake is a reason to blame someone else. Everything said is a slam against them. Even more, inactivity brings out the worst in them.

So how do you motivate the Constant Competitor who easily gets upset and angered at imagined slights or perceived defeats? Keep the Constant Competitor busy with work. The more he has to do, the less time he has to think about the game. You may also channel all that competitive spirit into a sales role. You want his competitive streak to be focused on the competition, not other employees.

The Leisurely Worker

This is the kind of worker who you might almost describe as lethargic. Even though she owns a watch, she never wears it because she isn't interested in the time. She moves slowly through her work, shows up late to meetings, and is basically in her own world. Type A she isn't!

So how do you motivate Leisurely Workers? Stress the importance of promptness. Tell her why you're giving her a deadline and how it affects the bottom line. When she turns in a project late, explain to her how it affects the team.

The Natural Born Leader

Carla acts like she's the team manager, but she isn't. She's one of those people who always spoke up in class, always led her group at school, and is constantly taking charge.

So how do you deal with someone like Carla? Don't regard the Natural Born Leader's leadership skills as a challenge. Rather, take advantage of them. Encourage Natural Born Leaders to be active participants in team meetings (although they probably already are!) and give them leadership roles, perhaps through mentoring.

The Insecure Employee

This employee doesn't feel like he can do anything right. He's constantly in your office, asking whether handling something a certain way is okay, even though you meet with him every week for hour-long training sessions when he can ask whatever he'd like. He's so afraid of making a mistake, or that upper management or another coworker doesn't like him, that he's immobilized by his fear and insecurities.

So how do you deal with an Insecure Employee? You're probably already giving him lots of feedback, so continue to do so. But instead of telling him what to do, nudge him to make his own decisions without you. Praise him lavishly when things work out; when they don't, help him learn from his mistakes. Never blame him. When you encourage an atmosphere of risk taking without retaliation, you can help this type of employee to overcome fears.

The Innovative and Impulsive Employee

Olivia is the typical Innovative and Impulsive Employee. She makes on-the-spot decisions without thinking things through. She doesn't like to do administrative tasks and can successfully juggle multiple projects. She easily gets bored and loves the excitement of a crazy day in the office.

To motivate this type of individual, embrace her enthusiasm while reminding her of the importance of careful reasoning. Ask her to tell you why she made her decisions and whether she would have done something differently if she had waited a few hours. Let her know that you appreciate her trying to make deadlines, but that you would rather she think things through a little bit before taking action, if she has the time to do so.

In addition, give her plenty of variety in her jobs. You may even be able to give some of your team's high-stress projects to this type of individual, who usually thrives on deadlines.

Try to avoid saying no too often, which doesn't inspire her best performance.

Chapter 25

Ten Ways to Get Employees to Motivate One Another

*O*ne person can make a difference — especially if that one person is the boss. Acting alone, you can play a significant role in your staff's morale. Amplify the positive effect you can have times ten or twenty to picture a team where everyone helps motivate everyone else. If your entire team is involved, rooting for each other, you've produced a truly dynamic workplace.

The more you encourage your employees to motivate one another, the easier it is to maintain everyone's commitment and energy over the long term. You strengthen the group through collaboration. In this chapter, I show you ways to inspire your team to join you in your motivational efforts.

Create a Sense of Community

For employees to motivate one another, they need to *want* to do so. If staff members feel overly competitive and envious of a teammate's success, they're not likely to generously encourage that individual. One of the first steps you can take to unite your team is creating a sense of community. Go to lunch together occasionally. Advocate caring and compassion. Encourage employees to say thank you to each other. Help them appreciate one another and the job that each person does. Find little ways to foster the "all for one, and one for all" approach to day-to-day operations.

Share the Big Picture

If your employees know the company's overall objectives, the department's role in achieving those objectives, and how their jobs fit into the big picture, they're more likely to feel motivated and to motivate others. They understand the expectations — for themselves as well as their coworkers, which means they can readily reprioritize and assist as needed. Their jobs become less about what one person has to do and more about what the team needs to accomplish. See Chapter 2 for more on sharing the big picture.

Communicate Often and Openly

You should share not only the big picture, but the details as well. Take time to answer questions from your staff. And, when appropriate, suggest that they turn to each other for ideas and information. Also, be sure to address concerns and celebrate accomplishments as soon as possible; don't wait for a better time. When an employee expresses doubts about a particular goal, find a way to resolve the matter quickly. If you do so, you can likely prevent any demotivation from spreading through your team.

 If someone receives a promotion, send out an e-mail announcement right away. Coworkers are more likely to congratulate a teammate on his or her success when everyone feels like they're sharing in the news of the moment.

Hold Team Meetings

Team meetings serve many purposes, but the main purpose is to facilitate communication. Regularly scheduled meetings not only allow you to impart crucial information — such as policy changes that affect everyone's jobs — but they also provide an opportunity for team members to find out what each person is working on. Teammates get to know each other, personally and professionally. You can address questions that may apply to the group, problem-solve together, and discuss challenges that may have been encountered during the past week. And the more that employees feel like part of a team, the more they'll lift each other up when necessary.

Promote Sharing of Information

If someone does something well, why not encourage that person to share her skills with the team? Ask top performers to offer their knowledge about key projects or skills during staff meetings. Encourage team members to send e-mails when they discover something from which the whole team can benefit. By promoting an open exchange of information, you limit the potential for competition and support effective teamwork.

Lead by Example

Your behavior can make or break your team. Staff members emulate what you do. So if you want employees to encourage each other, then you should do the same — with your colleagues in management. Even though your staff may not officially know of your efforts, word will eventually get around. And team members will ultimately see that you practice what you preach. In addition, you'll be more knowledgeable in the best practices of motivating coworkers because you'll be discovering new methods on your own. So, offer to assist a manager in another department who is a bit overloaded. Send e-mails to your colleagues with useful information. Set the example you want others to follow.

Praise, Praise, Praise

Recognition plays a key role in any motivational plan. If you like what your employees are doing, tell them. Use team meetings as one tool to publicly reinforce behavior you like and want emulated. When employees see that coworkers are recognized for encouraging other members of the team, they'll take the hint and start doing the same. For more on recognition, see Chapter 14.

Brainstorm

Schedule occasional brainstorming sessions to help solve challenges facing your department. By doing so, you tell your team that you're all in this together and that one person isn't responsible for solving all of the problems. The goal is for your formal brainstorming sessions to foster informal, creative get-togethers throughout the department.

Provide Mentors

By pairing veteran employees with new hires, you accomplish three things. First, you send the message to new employees that you care enough about their future with the company to take steps to ensure career success. At the same time, you also recognize current employees for things they do well. The result is an environment where people take pride in helping others — and everyone feels free to rely on one another's assistance. And, of course, mentoring partners not only share knowledge, but they motivate each other as well. For more on mentoring, see Chapter 12.

Index

Notes

Notes

Notes

Notes

Notes

Notes

YOUR ONLINE RESOURCE

WWW.DUMMIES.COM

Discover Dummies Online!

The Dummies Web Site is your fun and friendly online resource for the latest information about *For Dummies* books and your favorite topics. The Web site is the place to communicate with us, exchange ideas with other *For Dummies* readers, chat with authors, and have fun!

Ten Fun and Useful Things You Can Do at www.dummies.com

1. Win free *For Dummies* books and more!
2. Register your book and be entered in a prize drawing.
3. Meet your favorite authors through the Hungry Minds Author Chat Series.
4. Exchange helpful information with other *For Dummies* readers.
5. Discover other great *For Dummies* books you must have!
6. Purchase Dummieswear exclusively from our Web site.
7. Buy *For Dummies* books online.
8. Talk to us. Make comments, ask questions, get answers!
9. Download free software.
10. Find additional useful resources from authors.

Link directly to these ten fun and useful things at **www.dummies.com/10useful**

For other titles from Hungry Minds, go to **www.hungryminds.com**

Not on the Web yet? It's easy to get started with *Dummies 101: The Internet For Windows 98* or *The Internet For Dummies* at local retailers everywhere.

Find other *For Dummies* books on these topics:
Business • Career • Databases • Food & Beverage • Games • Gardening
Graphics • Hardware • Health & Fitness • Internet and the World Wide Web
Networking • Office Suites • Operating Systems • Personal Finance • Pets
Programming • Recreation • Sports • Spreadsheets • Teacher Resources
Test Prep • Word Processing

FOR DUMMIES
BOOK REGISTRATION

Register This Book and Win!

We want to hear from you!

Visit **dummies.com** to register this book and tell us how you liked it!

- ✔ Get entered in our monthly prize giveaway.

- ✔ Give us feedback about this book — tell us what you like best, what you like least, or maybe what you'd like to ask the author and us to change!

- ✔ Let us know any other *For Dummies* topics that interest you.

Your feedback helps us determine what books to publish, tells us what coverage to add as we revise our books, and lets us know whether we're meeting your needs as a *For Dummies* reader. You're our most valuable resource, and what you have to say is important to us!

Not on the Web yet? It's easy to get started with *Dummies 101: The Internet For Windows 98* or *The Internet For Dummies* at local retailers everywhere.

Or let us know what you think by sending us a letter at the following address:

For Dummies Book Registration
Dummies Press
10475 Crosspoint Blvd.
Indianapolis, IN 46256

...FOR DUMMIES™

BESTSELLING BOOK SERIES